Leadership
When the
Heat's On

Leadership When the Heat's On

By **Danny Cox**

With **John Hoover**

McGraw-Hill, Inc.

New York   San Francisco   Washington, D.C.   Auckland   Bogotá
Caracas   Lisbon   London   Madrid   Mexico City   Milan
Montreal   New Delhi   San Juan   Singapore
Sydney   Tokyo   Toronto

Library of Congress Cataloging-in-Publication Data

Cox, Danny.
    Leadership when the heat's on / Danny Cox with John Hoover.
        p.   cm.
    Includes index.
    ISBN 0-07-013267-4   —ISBN 0-07-013312-3(pbk.)
    1. Leadership.   I. Hoover, John.   II. Title.
HD57.7.C69   1992
658.4'092—dc20
                                       92-7806
                                         CIP

First McGraw-Hill paperback edition, 1994

8 9 0   DOC/DOC 9 8 7

ISBN   0-07-013267-4 (HC)
ISBN   0-07-013312-3 (PBK)

2 3 4 5 6 7 8 9 0 DOC/DOC 9 8 7 6 5

The sponsoring editor for this book was James H. Bessent, Jr., and the production supervisor was Pamela Pelton. It was composed in Baskerville by North Market Street Graphics.

Printed and bound by R. R. Donnelley & Sons Company.

I've had some mentors who taught me great things, but no one has taught me more or greater things than my wife. Through her loving example, I've learned how to be stronger, more patient, more understanding, more giving, and a better listener. She is a great leader.

I proudly dedicate this book to my friend and wife, Theo Cox.

P.S.:   I'm making progress, but still working on the "listening" lesson.

Contents

Chapter Three. The 1st Step—Team Building When the Heat's On

Chapter Four. The 2d Step—Goal Setting When the Heat's On

Contents

Chapter Five. The 3d Step—Time Planning for Higher Productivity

Chapter Nine. The 7th Step—Managing Change When the Heat's On   180

Chapter Ten. Meeting Tomorrow's Leadership Challenges Today   190

Foreword

As a young man, I had the good fortune to have close, personal friendships and, in some cases, business relationships with Thomas Edison, Henry Ford, Harvey Firestone, and Charles Lindbergh. My insights into and memories of those great leaders and shapers of the twentieth century are documented in my book *Uncommon Friends*.

Here, in the 1990s, the twenty-first-century Fords and Edisons are in the developmental process, discovering what does and does not work. *Leadership When the Heat's On* provides a unique and invaluable "technology" for these emerging leaders and brings the tremendous personal experiences and acquired knowledge of Danny Cox to bear on the increasingly vital subject of leadership.

James Newton

Preface

The natives called it *cave of the tall people.*

One of my jobs while working my way through college was exploring and mapping caves for the geology department. Several years later, while on temporary assignment in the South Pacific with the Royal Australian Air Force, I was intrigued by the mountains on the island of Samar and figured there must be some good caves to explore. With the assistance of a Filipino, I found my way to the legendary cave and crawled inside through a narrow passageway.

I was fascinated by the name, "cave of the *tall* people." My enthusiastic spelunking that day led me to a coral-walled room where I discovered a pile of human bones. I could barely contain my excitement as I reported my find.

An Ohio State University professor later estimated the bones to be between 35,000 and 40,000 years old. The bones also indicated the tribal people buried there were significantly taller than contemporary Filipinos.

It's exciting to discover something which contributes to the expansion of scholarly knowledge. My brush with the "ancients" set me to thinking about my *own* life. The most salient and haunting question of all was, "What will *I* leave behind after *my* death?" The more I pondered my life, the more troubled I became.

It was almost as though the tall people who had gone to that cave to die or, at least, were placed there after their death, were trying to tell me something. What was it? Perhaps they were urging me not to wind up as only a pile of bones. Although the bones are an archeological curiosity, they tell us little about what significance those lives had on their world. So what was I going to do that would leave more to future generations than a pile of bones? The question became a challenge.

Over the ensuing years, development of human potential became my trade. My focus is on the living. My goal is to help people make a positive difference in their own lives and a positive impact on the lives of those around them. More importantly, the legacy I leave behind will not lie hidden in a remote cave until some spelunker happens upon it. The impact I have on the world will never die as long as some people apply the knowledge I've acquired to their personal and professional lives.

Leadership is about making a positive difference in people's lives. *Leadership When the Heat's On* is about being the best you can be in an atmosphere of change and uncertainty. Leadership in fair weather is hard enough. Leadership in the midst of economic and business turmoil requires everything you've got, focused through the lens of enlightened methods and techniques. This book is the manual for achieving a place of importance in people's lives that will outlive you.

Danny Cox
17381 Bonner Drive, Suite 101
Tustin, CA 92680
(714) 838-3030

Acknowledgments

I want to express my appreciation to the many leaders who served as my mentors after my boss told me he was looking for my replacement. They helped pull me out of the fire then and continue to be an inspiration to me.

The business books and periodicals that have been so instrumental in my development also receive a king-size portion of thanks. No other country in the world has so many "behind the scenes" secrets available through the printed word for increasing productivity.

John Hoover, my collaborator on this project, has earned my undying appreciation for his commitment and talent for taking mainly my spoken words and getting them "nailed down" on paper. It was not an easy task but he rose to the occasion.

Our sponsoring editor throughout this process has been Jim Bessent. John and I thank him for his enthusiastic support and unique contribution to *Leadership When the Heat's On*.

Danny Cox

Leadership
When the
Heat's On

Chapter One

The Leader on the Hot Seat

Good Old Ticky

As I was growing up in a small coal mining town in Southern Illinois, there was a rather odd fellow about town whose nickname was "Ticky." Now old Ticky wasn't the brightest citizen in those parts. We all liked him, mind you, but he was what you might call a few bricks short of a load. We were never sure if he had both oars in the water. We used to joke about his elevator not making it all the way to the top. As we used to say, his grits weren't in the center of the plate.

One day Ticky wandered into Orie Hifle's blacksmith shop. Orie had just pulled a horseshoe out of the fire a few moments earlier and it was lying on his anvil. It wasn't glowing, but it was close.

Sure enough, Ticky reached down and picked up that horseshoe with his bare hand. Instantly realizing the error of his ways, Ticky let out a scream and threw it down.

"Oh, did you burn yourself, Ticky?" Orie asked.

"No," Ticky shot back. "It just don't take me long to look at a horseshoe!"

There is a lesson for all of us in Ticky's misadventure. He never picked up a horseshoe again, hot or cold, as far as anyone could remember. It was the eloquent management genius, Peter F. Drucker, who said, "A crisis must never be experienced a second time." Ticky and Peter are on the same wavelength.

As we explore the dynamics of leadership throughout this book, it would be wise to remember Ticky. For one thing, he didn't realize that the horseshoe was hot. All too often, we find ourselves on the hot seat without a clue as to how we got there. There is no shame in discovering we're sitting on a hot stove, *unless* we've been there before.

We should learn quickly and resolve not to repeat the behaviors that result in heated situations. I talk to business people all over the country who regularly find themselves picking up *that same darn horseshoe*. The secret to

1

leadership when the heat's on is to develop a personal early-warning system in addition to techniques for swift and skillful resolution of difficulties. I would even go so far as to say that the skillful and effective leader is the person who has a long and well-integrated memory, constantly open to new input.

The Heat

A manager who starts smelling smoke is experiencing friction. When movement meets resistance, the resulting friction produces heat. It's really pretty simple. Put this book down and rub your hands together briskly right now. See? Remember rubbing two sticks together as a young scout trying to start a camp fire? Have you ever rubbed your arms or legs to stay warm?

Interestingly, most dictionaries will also list "conflict of opinions" or "differences in temperament" as definitions of friction. As an individual who is concerned about leadership, you are probably already forming images in your mind of *heated* situations. As you do, imaginary beads of sweat might be forming on your brow. Madison Avenue tells us the mark of success and confidence is the ability to appear *cool* in a *hot* situation. And they're quick to recommend the right deodorant to help stop the perspiration.

It follows that, if you are the person feeling the heat, you must be at or near the point of conflict or friction. In the 1990s, business people have more things "rubbing together" than ever before. The most prominent pressure point is found where the *down pressure* of the organization's demands meets the *up pressure* from employees and your own personal needs.

Everyone, from the individual entrepreneur to the head of a multinational concern, feels the innate pressures of the business world regardless of whether the market is up or down. Pressures from the outside can come from customer demands, banking and financial issues, regulations, taxes, competition, or any number of sources. Pressures from within can come from employee demands, new technology and knowledge integration, organizational growth pains, and productivity problems, just to name a few.

Heat is created at the point at which the manager finds himself or herself squeezed in the vise. The two sides of the vise might be the outside pressure versus inside pressure or top side pressure from the organization (down pressure) versus bottom side pressure from the organization (up pressure). *All four forces* might be in opposition with the manager caught in the middle. When the manager feels the heat, this experience is the pinch between opposing forces.

The *down pressure* is predominantly a result of the increased urgency to do more with less. The business manager is being asked to increase production while decreasing expenditures and to achieve larger goals with smaller staffs. I'm not sure which is worse: the expression on the face of an employee whose job has been "downsized" or the business banker's expression while tightening the screws on your credit line.

The *up pressure* comes from the "new employee" we hear so much about. They're not new in the sense of just hired. The newness refers to the different expectations and characteristics of the nineties work force. Staff members are becoming increasingly independent and demanding. This new autonomy on the part of employees is the other side of the vise that managers find themselves in. Good people are no longer satisfied with merely accepting anything and everything that tumbles down the organization chart and into their laps. Nor should they be. Valuing people is at the top of my list and I'll spend more time on that in following chapters.

Whether it is pressure from above versus pressure from below, or pressure from the right versus pressure from the left, or pressure from everywhere, when *you* are the one in the vise, you can feel the temperature rising. Although we are often insensitive to others and their pressure, I have yet to meet anyone who doesn't know when he or she is on the hot seat.

A Working Definition of Leadership

It's important to understand exactly how leadership is defined in the context of this book. After all, it's kind of hard to do well at something if you're not sure what it is you're supposed to be doing. Leadership is a term that is often used inappropriately. Some of the many active definitions of leadership include:

1. To go ahead of
2. To show the way
3. To guide
4. To cause progress
5. To create a path
6. To control actions
7. To direct
8. To influence
9. To command
10. To be first
11. To be chief
12. To begin

Any and all of these active terms can be a metaphor for the act of leading. You can probably come up with a couple dozen more that might fit your particular leadership challenge. No matter what your precise definition is, the title of leader is an honorary degree that is bestowed by those who are led. In this book, I only refer to leaders who have earned that title through a successful relationship with their people. For this reason, I will refer at times to managers instead of leaders.

Managers are people who have been given the assignment to lead others but lack the skills or motivation to do so. Any effort to become a leader, such as studying materials like this book, moves you one step farther away from a management role and closer to a true leadership role. However, top management can't appoint leaders any more than leaders can appoint themselves. In the end, it will be those who subscribe to your leadership that grant you the honor. Otherwise, you will simply be managing. People *can* manage well without ever breaking through to the ranks of effective leadership. It's those people who aspire to become leaders who will want to ingest all that this book offers. Those who have been granted the honor of leadership by their people and feel unprepared to fully accept the responsibility can get that information here as well.

What looms above any other quality of leadership, no matter who makes up the list of qualities or how long the list goes, is *responsibility*. Above all else, a leader is responsible for getting a job done. Regardless of how many people are involved with accomplishing the task, the leader is ultimately responsible. It doesn't matter if you're a new leader who is responsible for very little or a higher up in an organization with other leaders reporting to you. Your leadership is defined largely by the responsibility you have accepted.

It's important to understand that we are where we are because of the *choices* we have made. Philosophy is not my game, but I've got to hang that one on you right out of the chute. Otherwise, you might think that I'm talking about things *somebody else* should be doing or things that *somebody else* should be responsible for. The same people who grant you the title of leader will expect you to be the model of responsibility.

The bottom line is that leadership is a challenge to be accepted and we are never in leadership positions without accepting the challenge. In other words, *accepting a leadership role is our own choice*. We are individually responsible. I'm not setting you up for some kind of guilt trip here. On the contrary, giving way to full acceptance of our individual responsibility is extremely liberating. Ask any effective leaders and they will invariably claim full responsibility for their actions. It's just part of being effective.

Figure 1-1 contains some more "self-talk" to help you indelibly etch this notion of responsibility on the inside of your forehead. I call it my "Declaration of Personal Responsibility."

Declaration of Personal Responsibility

"I currently possess everything I've truly wanted and deserved. This is based on what I have handed out to date. My possessions, my savings, and my lifestyle are an exact mirror of me, my efforts, and my contribution to society. What I give, I get. If I am unhappy with what I have received, it is because, as of yet, I have not paid the required price. I have lingered too long in the *quibbling stage*.

I fully understand that time becomes a burden to me only when it is empty. The past is mine and at this very moment I am purchasing another twenty-four hours of it. The future quickly becomes the past at a control point called the present moment. I not only truly live at that point, but I have full responsibility for the highest and best use of the irreplaceable *now*.

I accept full responsibility for both the successes and failures in my life. If I am not what I desire to be at this point, what I am is my *compromise*. I no longer choose to compromise with my undeveloped potential.

I am the sum total of the choices I have made and I continue to choose daily. What I now put under close scrutiny is the value of each upcoming choice. Therein lies the quality of my lifestyle.

"Will my future belong to the *old me* or the *new me*?" The answer depends upon my attitude toward personal growth at this very moment. What time is left is all that counts and I am personally responsible for how my time is filled. With newfound maturity I accept full responsibility for how good I can become at what is most important to me.

With personal growth comes a fear of the unknown and new problems. Those problems are nothing more than the lengthening shadow of my personal growth. I now turn my very real fear, with God's help, into a very real adventure.

My life now expands to meet my newfound destiny. *Old me*, meet the *new me!*"

Figure 1-1.

Now that you and I realize that we are personally responsible for being in a position of leadership as well as personally responsible for our actions, we're ready to become more effective leaders. Our effectiveness as leaders is directly proportionate to our effectiveness as human beings. Sure, there are exceptions to everything. Some people win the lottery. Some people lip-sync to songs that others record and make millions. But I'm talking about the long haul. I'm talking about *real* people like you and like me.

Some people can be fooled temporarily, but lasting leadership requires a full-blown commitment to the challenge of living effectively. To be effective leaders, we must fully accept the challenge and our "declaration of personal responsibility."

Leading Is an Art

Science requires hard evidence. Facts are incontestable and empirically provable. It might be argued that the *results* of leadership are empirically provable. However, just what exactly caused the results is always debatable. Suffice it to say that there is much less debate over who is responsible for poor results than good results. The argument tends to flow up or down the organization ladder, depending on how favorable the results are and whether folks want to claim them or deny them.

Since leadership involves people, whether we are acting alone or in concert with others, we must expect a certain measure of inconsistency and unpredictability. Human nature just isn't scientific. There is too much margin for interpretation. We are emotional creatures. The particular emotional composition of any one of us is ultimately a mystery to everyone but God Himself. Remember though, no matter what bolt of cloth we were originally cut from, we can always weave new and colorful threads into our individual and unique fabric.

As much as some accomplishment-minded people would like to see mechanization of human functions, I have to believe that the complexity of the human being exceeds any possible synthesizing, at least in this century. So we've got to keep our options and minds open. Knowing how to tap dance in tight spots is a terrific and sometimes lifesaving, nonscientific talent. The great leaders are *artists*, not scientists. William Shakespeare could have been writing about the challenge of leadership when he said, "All the world is a stage and we are but players." Effective leaders resemble vaudevillians more than scientists.

How well we play our role becomes the issue. What kind of picture we paint with our particular palette of colors and selection of brushes is what makes us unique—as individuals and as leaders. Our effectiveness is a reflection of or, better yet, a measure of who we are.

The Myth of the
Natural-Born Leader

In sharing with you a part of my history, I hope to illustrate just how these leadership concepts became integrated into my personal and professional philosophies. I wasn't born with a knowledge and awareness of what makes a good leader. Neither were you. Leaders are not born, despite the popular maxim, "She's a natural-born leader." A doctor in the delivery room doesn't hold up a newborn infant and exclaim, "Well, looky here. We've got ourselves a natural-born leader." The local paper doesn't report the birth of a seven-pound, six-ounce leader yesterday at 2:30 in the afternoon. The skills of leadership can only be learned through experience. As the son of a coal miner, I'm here to tell you that sometimes the greatest lessons are learned through mistakes and getting your hands dirty.

A 79,000-Horsepower Mistake

I started out as a "sonic boom" salesperson. It was the early 1960s and the new supersonic jet aircraft the Air Force was testing kept "breaking" the sound barrier, much to the displeasure of residents in communities surrounding military facilities. Some folks thought the world was coming to an end; others thought our "booms" would stunt the growth of their children and garden vegetables.

Since I was one of the Air Force test pilots who was up there breaking the sound barrier, I was asked to explain the phenomenon to the curious, and mostly annoyed, civilian population. Later, in my civilian life, I would rocket from new salesperson to first vice president of one of America's largest firms in three and one-half years, ultimately helping to increase sales for the company by over 800 percent.

One could get pretty heady about such accomplishments if it weren't for the fact that my eventual success was made possible by a series of enormous mistakes and miscalculations along the way. As Paul Harvey would say, here's the "*rest* of the story."

During the ten years that I flew supersonic fighters as a test pilot and air show pilot, I made many wonderful suggestions to the United States Air Force on how they could improve their organization. After ten years, I began to realize that my list of sensational suggestions was being summarily ignored.

Almost anyone, in any organization, has many wonderful suggestions on how the organization can be improved, at least early in his or her career, before the optimism of youth wears thin. As for me, I looked for opportunities to increase my recognition factor as the years passed. And then one day, bingo!

I received a call from the Thunderbirds, the crack Air Force aerobatics team, who asked if I would join their elite group. You see, I had been flying the most powerful fighter in the air in those days. 79,000 horsepower is more horsepower than all the cars in a running of the Indianapolis 500 combined *and multiplied by three*. Every time I shoved my throttles forward, I held the power of 263 Porsche 911s in my hand. It's no wonder we kept "breaking" the sound barrier.

The Thunderbirds were impressed with my credentials and their call was a dream come true for me. After I had passed a grueling, six-hour interview and the team leader walked over to me, extended his hand, and said, "Congratulations, you've made the team!" I knew I had arrived. My dream had come true. Nothing could stop me now. Nothing, that is, except the Air Force.

You see, I was in the *all-weather* fighter command and the Thunderbirds were in the *day* fighter group. The bureaucratic snag came when my request for transfer was denied. All-weather pilots had extra training and the Air Force didn't have a surplus of them at the time. You can imagine at that point where I felt they could put all of their "extra training." I was not a happy fighter pilot.

Driven with the enthusiasm and confidence of a man who had just been selected to join the elitist of the elite, I executed Plan B. I sent in my resignation, certain that, once they realized the full measure of my conviction and the error of their ways, they would dispense with all further bureaucratic nonsense. When they signed my resignation, I was a civilian overnight, wondering what on earth I was going to do with the rest of my life. I had no money saved up and no retirement pay coming in. What I *did* have was a wife and three daughters with a very expensive habit of eating. So I did what many people were doing in those days. I packed my family in the car and headed for California. My plan was to fly with the airlines. After all, I had some pretty impressive credentials.

Wrong again. There was nothing wrong with my credentials as a pilot, mind you. The airlines were extremely impressed with my 2400 hours of high performance fighter experience without an accident, etcetera, etcetera. It was just that their minimum height requirement of five feet eight inches for pilots was a goal that I had yet to achieve in my life. I could fly the plane just fine, but they had an image problem with passengers thinking that a short little fella was going to fly their great big airplane.

The Sonic Boom Salesperson

A desperate inventory of my life accomplishments revealed that I didn't have much in the way of employable skills on the open market. However, I figured that if I could convince a hostile crowd of unnerved citizens that sonic booms were sufferable in the cause of national defense, I could adapt to a civilian occupation.

For once I was right. In my first year working in sales, I earned more money than in any given year of my Air Force career, and I didn't have to risk death every day on the job. Things were looking up. In fact, I was doing so well that the company came to me and asked if I would manage one of their offices after only one year of selling! Getting a little heady once again, I remember thinking that it obviously didn't take this company long to recognize talent. At this point, I was feeling like a natural-born leader. My promotion was to be effective immediately. Their only request was that I give them enough time to drive over to the office and fire my predecessor.

My entire management training course consisted of being told to turn in my advertisements on Tuesdays and Thursdays and not to mess the office up any more than it already was. Seriously. That was about it. Nothing about leadership. Fortunately, there were only four people in that office and they received Social Security checks every month. In my first 12 months of managing, I managed not to mess up that office any more than it was when I arrived. I considered myself a leader.

Strike Two

At the end of that year, the same executives came to me and asked if I would consider managing the number one office out of their 36-office chain. It was one head trip after another. I was convinced by now that leadership was an innate ability. My excitement was multiplied by the fact that the number one office was where I had been the rookie salesperson just one year before. After all, now I had appointed myself a leader.

You can imagine how happy the salespeople were to see the former rookie salesperson returning a year later as their boss. They hated me with a passion. I arrogantly urged them to think of me not as the boss, but rather as a friend who is always right. My goal was to turn everyone who worked for me into a carbon copy of *me*. It was logical. After all, I was red hot.

Transforming the sales office to my own image seemed to be what the company wanted me to do. Or so I thought. After all, if they hadn't been impressed with my style, why would they have made me the boss? Furthermore, if I could get them to do the job like I had done the job, they wouldn't bring me any problems I hadn't already survived. Therefore, I would no doubt continue to be promoted up through that big company. It made perfect sense to me.

Thanks to my "natural" leadership abilities, the number one sales office was soon Number 36 out of 36. Even the four pensioners in my old office were beating us. I hadn't the foggiest notion what the problem was. Little did I know that I wasn't going to be given the opportunity to find out.

The Turning Point

One day my boss paid me a visit and his usual smiling demeanor had been replaced with a scowl. He delivered the following terse message through clenched teeth and tight lips. "Cox," he began, "I can see it was a mistake making you manager of this office and I feel that it's only fair to inform you that I've already begun looking for your replacement."

Let me tell you, that was not only the shortest, but the most effective motivational seminar I ever attended. I searched the room with my eyes as if I was going to spot an appropriate reply for my boss. All I could think to say was, "I've got to learn how to do this."

Without missing a hitch, he shot back with, "You haven't got much time." As he disappeared through my doorway, I called after him, "You don't know how *motivated* I am." Everyone in the office now knew that the proverbial shoe was on the other foot. The clone-maker just got his plug pulled. Nobody rushed to order flowers or plan a bon voyage party. I think they wanted me to die a quiet death.

I wondered how I could have distanced myself from the very people I depended upon for the success of our office. Why did they all dislike me so much? Why didn't they just conform to what I had envisioned them to be? The more I pondered my dilemma, the clearer it became that I really didn't need answers as much as I needed to begin asking the *right* questions.

Before long, it came to me. It wasn't a clap of thunder. The heavens didn't open up and drop a stone tablet at my feet. But as soon as the thought hit, I knew it was profound. I needed to work on *me*, not *them!* My focus had been all wrong. My eyes had been fixed on the bottom line, to the exclusion of anything or anyone else. I was focused on whipping them into shape with no regard to what kind of shape I was in.

Almost instantly, the truth began setting me free. Despite my predicament, I felt a sense of liberation. The realization swept over me that *employees can only get better after the manager does*. It's unreasonable to expect students to be ahead of their teachers or for children to behave more appropriately than their parents. The big difference in my old thinking and this new information was that I shouldn't expect anybody to be me.

I had established a track record of expecting people to respond to me and my agenda without much, if any, regard for theirs. In the end, I got back what I gave out, which was not much empathy, tolerance, or understanding. The clone-maker had duplicated himself all right. All of the intolerance and lack of genuine concern I had demonstrated for my staff, they ended up demonstrating for me. I was about to exit this office as unceremoniously as I had allowed many of my top salespeople to do during my "reign of terror."

If you think I'm making a case against management by threats and intimidation, you're correct. I *am* a walking, talking case example against basing any form of human relationship on threats and intimidation. Impatience, intolerance, and rigidity have never inspired anyone; scared them maybe, but never inspired them to reach for higher goals.

Ken Blanchard calls this style of managing "sea gull management." He describes the sea gull manager as someone who storms in, flaps his or her wings noisily, flies around squawking and making messes on everybody's head, and then flies out again. The proud tradition of "Mr. Dithers" (Dagwood Bumstead's impatient and punitive boss from the "Blondie" cartoon strip) or drill sergeant managers grew out of the post-World War II military, hierarchical organizational chart. *News flash! This is the nineties!* The "new employee" is burning that type of intimidation, win-lose leadership at the stake. It's not that the new employee won't work. An employee will work as hard and ethically as the manager. The heat's on the manager.

I Went to Work on Me

As it turned out, I didn't lose my job. Now that I think about it, I doubt that they could have found any sane person willing to take over that office after what I had done to it. More importantly, though, I jumped in with both feet, rolled up my sleeves, and resolved that I would be the best manager I could possibly be, which was an invitation, through more effective and genuine relationships, for all of my people to be the best that they could be. To my amazement, everyone in the organization responded and responded quickly. We began to give the appearance of and function like a team. I stopped demanding that they be me and began helping them be themselves.

Four short months later, we were number one again. Together, we climbed right back through that field of 36 offices to the top spot. All these people wanted was to be supported, encouraged, and respected for their individual and unique talents and abilities. Once I began giving them what they needed, as opposed to what I wanted, their production skyrocketed. I conduct seminars for all types of companies year in and year out and have yet to see an organization that doesn't see immediate and positive results from this change in focus.

As we continue through the balance of this book, bear in mind that all of the skills, methods, and techniques I will describe are intended to sharpen you as a leader who values your number one asset: your people. They will get better after you do. By reading this book, you have already gone to work on *you*. As people start getting better, they turn the heat down on you by easing off on the "up" pressure. Likewise, when productivity goes up, "down" pressure from those above you will relax as well.

Leadership Is Not Manipulation

Genuine regard for your people, and I include everyone you deal with, is not something that can be faked. People can not only sense your true sincerity, but they can only be fooled by insincere words for so long before your actions will expose you. That's why confidence artists have to keep moving while old, slow-talking Joe can stay in business on the same corner for over thirty years.

Manipulation means causing others to act against their will and, possibly, to their detriment, while providing a *perceived* benefit, though temporary, to the manipulator. The ultimate cost of manipulative tactics is an eventual decline in morale and productivity. Good leadership is made up of carefully and strategically thought-out growth-producing techniques that motivate team members to achieve new heights of quality in current tasks in addition to encouraging new and innovative actions.

Good leadership results in development of potential and achievement of team goals. There is no question that morale soars in an environment of good leadership. In other words, only when the leader's vision includes the goals and ambitions of his or her people can the experience of success be sweet for everyone. More importantly, success that is enjoyed by all is more likely to be repeated.

Blowing the Lid Off

Effective leadership not only produces the results that relieve *down pressure* from superiors, stock holders, and/or customers, as well as *up pressure* through improved employee relations, but also expands your personal horizons. Once my office got back into the number one spot in the organization, I learned a new and exciting lesson about personal limitations. I wish I had thought to use the experience of breaking through personal limitations as a metaphor for sonic booms during my Air Force public relation soirees, but I just hadn't learned the lesson yet.

After reaching the number one position again, our office's production curve leveled off. Once we returned to our previous level of performance, we unknowingly reached our own *self-imposed* barrier and went no further. Notice that I emphasized the word *self*. The barriers I'm referring to are not *company-imposed* or *customer-imposed*, they are *self-imposed*. There is a world of difference and leaders who understand that can make a difference in the world.

Remember that once leadership improves, organizations and individuals within organizations improve. Once leaders learn to *push the limits of their envelope,* others will follow. Pilots talk about the envelope that rests between minimum acceptable performance and maximum performance. For example, there are minimum safe air speeds for various aircraft and weather conditions as well as maximum air speeds, sometimes referred to as "never exceed" speeds. Structural stress tolerance and other safety factors all fall within their respective envelopes as well. The range between the minimum and maximum is considered the safety "envelope."

I've flown supersonic fighters outside of the envelope and lived to tell about it. That's kind of what being a test pilot is all about. An airline pilot would and should lose his or her job for operating outside of safety specifications. Similarly, as leaders, we are responsible for the safe conduct of our operations.

However, to be effective and progressive leaders, we all need to have a little test pilot in us. Otherwise, we will constantly be halted at our self-imposed barriers. If there were no test pilots or leaders "pushing the envelope," there would be precious little innovation and progress anywhere.

I define self-imposed barriers not as walls around our lives, but as the margins of our lives where nothing has been written yet. The key word is *yet*. Imagine what our world would be like if explorers and conquerors throughout history had believed that if you hadn't been somewhere before, you couldn't go.

Our production slope leveled off even though there was no tangible barrier. Furthermore, I soon learned that it wasn't an organizational barrier we had reached, but rather the collective individual self-imposed barriers of the team, working in concert with each other, that halted our growth.

My people were not slouches by any means. We were so successful in our field that our office received numerous awards for one broken record after another. We were the subject of numerous articles in business publications. When your name appears in print, preceded by a glowing account of your achievements, it's easy to be seduced into thinking you have soared about as high as you can soar.

Don't let success become a barrier. The great Walt Disney is remembered to this day throughout the Disney organization for enjoining his staff not to rest on their laurels. If any group deserved to get fat on success, the Disney team did. Many generations of young and old alike are thankful that they continued pushing the envelope.

Good versus Best

Another great executive once told me, "Good is the enemy of best and best is the enemy of better." When some people get to be good, they think, "What's the point of struggling to be best?" When many people get to be best, the tendency is to stop improving. I prefer to think of best not in terms of how our performance compares to the performance of others, but rather of how it compares to our personal capabilities. In that light, we are never really at our best. And that's O.K., as long as we keep trying.

An Envelope for Everyone

As I mentioned earlier, my people were top performers. They proved that time and again. As our efforts received increasing acclamation, I was frequently asked where these great people came from. Some thought I had stolen them away from other top companies. Others thought I recruited at the top business schools. It became obvious that these curious folks were missing the point. Let me profile several of these industry leading professionals, complete with their self-imposed barriers.

One of my people in that record-setting office was a woman who had tired of making $20,000 per year as a secretary and entered the sales field to redraw her horizons. She had been selling full-time for four years when I met her and, in each of those four years, her commissions totaled almost $20,000 to the penny. The lid had been taken off of her jar, but she hadn't given herself permission to jump any higher.

Fortunately, she was a quick study. All I had to do was point out what was occurring in her life and she instantly broke through her self-imposed barrier. At last report, she had a net worth of over $2 million as a result of her successful sales career. I don't believe a leader can receive a higher honor or a more rewarding feeling than to applaud the success of someone who has been influenced by his or her leadership.

I also had a couple of cowboy character actors who were getting a little too old to fall off horses in "B" westerns. They had no sales training at all. I handed them our sales training manual and said, "Gentlemen, here is your script. Study it hard because the customers already know *their* lines." A glow of familiarity came to their faces. They didn't go out on sales presentations; they went out on sales "auditions." They did very well. Once again, I was proud of their accomplishments.

Making More than Dad

There was another fellow in the office who darn near drove me crazy. This man earned $2,000 per month in commissions. Month in and month out, it was incredible how close he could get to $2,000 by the end of the month. He became a basket case in front of our eyes if he somehow earned his $2,000 early in the month. I swear to you if someone had walked in the door and insisted on buying from him after he had reached his $2,000 lid, he probably would have directed them to another salesperson.

Determined to get this guy through his barrier, I "big brothered" him for an entire month. I did everything but move in with him. He couldn't go to the men's room without me standing guard at the door. I never let him out of my sight. As you might expect, I nearly burst with pride when, at the end of the month, he had earned $4,000 in commissions.

The following month he earned $0. The month after that he earned $2,000, and the month after that the same. Unlike good old Ticky who learned from his mistake, I had picked up the same horseshoe and burned my hand *again*. I had tried to clone myself. This fellow proved to me once more that successful growth, if there was to be any, had to be on *his* terms, not mine.

I knew right away he had put square wheels on my wagon. I asked him in to my office for a chat. Before long, he revealed that he had never had any more money in the bank than his father had as he was growing up. His self-imposed barrier was situated where he would be assured of never outdoing his father. It's important from time to time to reflect on who we have chosen as models for our own definition of success.

I took a stab in the dark and asked, "Is that the role model you intend to set for your own children? Do you want them to be forever limited by your barriers?" He shot out of his chair and I sunk into mine thinking he was about to take exception to my comment by leaping over my desk. Fortunately, he was simply energized by the instant clarity of the analogy.

What came out of his mouth next sounded rehearsed. He said, "My God, that's exactly what I've been doing. I've been setting a role model for my kids to never achieve any more than I have achieved. I'm not going to keep doing things that don't work." He went out and blew the lid off of his self-imposed barrier and was still pushing his envelope when I moved on.

The Fork in the Road

As managers, we experience a great deal of heat that is generated by unnecessary friction. When we, or people on our staff, continue to repeat nonproductive behavior, we increase the urgency of making measurable progress. In other words, if we remove nonproductive tasks from our agendas, we will ease the pressure to accomplish our goals by expanding available time.

Take a piece of paper and, to the best of your ability, write down everything you do in a day. Then review your list, identifying what works and what doesn't in terms of achieving your goals. Then stop doing those things you know aren't helping. This sounds incredibly simple and almost trite at first blush, but it's one of the most powerful leadership techniques I have ever encountered. It qualifies as what Tom Peters calls "a blinding flash of the obvious." None of us can take an inventory of our ongoing behavior and honestly claim that none of our time is being wasted on old, familiar, and comfortable habits that crowd out more productive activities.

How do we recognize what doesn't work for us? Usually it is something we've been doing for a long time. It sounds funny, but it's our tendency to repeat nonproductive behavior that eventually exposes the fallacy in our conduct. If you ask yourself or people who work for you why something is currently being done in a particular way, you will likely be told, "It's always been done that way," instead of being given a rational and operative explanation.

Each day, sometimes moment by moment, every one of us stands at a fork in the road (see Figure 1-2). One road leads to personal and professional growth which we've already established as an antecedent of effective leadership. The other road represents the repetition of what has been done before.

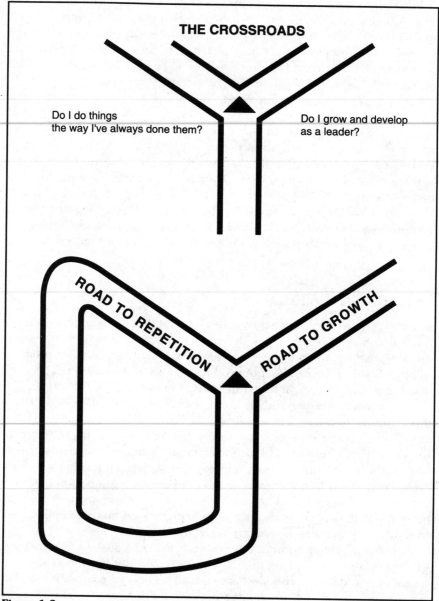

Figure 1-2.

Why do we so often choose the road to repetition? Because it always brings us back *safely* to the same familiar fork in the road. Familiar ground always feels more comfortable, even if it's nonproductive. Many organizations find themselves stuck in the mud and call it tradition. To me, these people drive into the future with their eyes fixed on the rearview mirror. They somehow manage to be unhampered by progress.

Let's look at what lies ahead on these two roads:

THE ROAD TO REPETITION	THE ROAD TO GROWTH
No goals	New goals
Familiarity	Excitement
Stagnation	Higher productivity
Another yesterday	A new tomorrow
Something to live on	Something to live for
Burn out	Quality
Amusement	Enjoyment
Problems	Problems

The Problem with Problems

Anywhere we go, there are bound to be problems. The difference between the effective leader and ineffective manager is not who has more or larger problems than the other, but how effectively each one responds to his or her problems. The ineffective manager *reacts* to problems. The effective leader *responds* to problems and learns.

Many people stand at the fork in their road and think, *I'll follow the road towards growth just as soon as I resolve the problems I'm currently facing.* It will never happen. People often wait their lives away in search of the precise moment when all of their problems clear up. The terms "old" and "bitter" are frequently used to describe someone who realizes too late there is no magical moment when all of life's problems disappear, making it safe to take the other road to opportunity and success. Waiting until all of your problems are behind you before moving is like sitting in a parking lot at one end of town and saying to yourself, "I'll drive across town just as soon as every traffic light turns green." You'll never leave the parking lot.

Earlier, I mentioned how different the world would be if somebody didn't push the envelope from time to time. The same thing applies to not allowing problems to hold us back. Let me introduce you to some people who had what many would consider good reasons not to succeed. I'm thankful these people didn't wait until all the traffic lights had turned green before they started down the road toward growth.

1. He was labeled unsociable and mentally slow and didn't begin talking until he was four years old. His own father said that he was not normal and would never amount to anything. He was even expelled from school.

2. The next man entered the conflict a Captain and was busted down to a Private. He left the service and became a farm laborer. This person's progression of rank and career growth were stuck in reverse.

3. The next person's childhood music teacher said that he had no voice at all.

4. The next man's employers told him that he didn't have enough sense to wait on customers. He was relegated to stocking shelves and the like at the dry goods store where he worked at the age of 21.

5. His editor at the newspaper described him as being "void of creativity" and fired him for lack of good ideas.

6. Consistently at the bottom of his class, his teachers said that he was too stupid to learn anything and he was finally educated at the knee of his patient mother.

7. Her parents received a letter from the acting school where she was enrolled explaining that the teachers felt she had no talent and recommended that they waste no more money on her theatrical training. She failed at auditions and struggled to overcome a crippling disease. She didn't walk for two years. Finally, at age 40, she landed her first noteworthy role as an actress.

8. She was born to a 12-year-old as the result of a rape. When she was five years old she was running errands for prostitutes and pimps.

Who are these people? 1. Albert Einstein. 2. Abraham Lincoln. 3. Enrico Caruso. 4. F. W. Woolworth. 5. Walt Disney. 6. Thomas A. Edison. 7. Lucille Ball. 8. Ethel Waters. Rags-to-riches stories abound, yet I never tire of hearing how success can all but erase old problems and set the tone for managing future ones. Dr. Norman Vincent Peale once said, "You're only as big as the problem that stops you." I, for one, am thankful to these and many other men and women who were bigger than the problems that would have stopped so many others. The world is better because *they* got better.

You Don't Know Me . . .

None of these great people were available to me in person or accessible during the dark hours when my boss was looking for my replacement. However, I started looking for articles about successful contemporary people in newspapers and magazines. I telephoned those who were local and said, "You don't know me, but my name is Danny Cox and I've just destroyed the number one office in my company by taking it from first place to thirty-sixth in three months time. Can I have lunch with you?"

These people not only took my calls, they agreed to have lunch with me. Some sensed the urgency in my voice and others simply wanted to meet someone who could wreak as much havoc as I had wreaked. The commonality of these successful people was their entrepreneurial spirit. They all saw me as a challenge. I *listened* to what these people had to say and applied what I learned. Regardless of what measure of success I can now apply to myself, I continue to passionately seek out effective leaders and I hang on their every word.

Making Definitions Relevant

Now that we've journeyed through a part of my history and explored some generalized leadership issues, let's look at active definitions of leadership to see how it takes shape and how its principles will take the heat off of you.

1. *To go ahead of* defines a spiritual, not a literal, relationship with the people you have agreed to lead. People will share the heat with you in difficult situations if they feel you are willing to do the same for them. If your commitment to supporting your people through thick and thin is genuine, they will know it and reciprocate. Your willingness to jump into the fire alongside your people will be the core of their loyalty to you and what you stand for.

2. *To show the way* means defining for your people what the broad goals and intentions are for the greater good of the organization. Showing the way is *not* leading by the hand and doing the thinking for them. How tasks are accomplished and how ideas are developed and thought through should always be a reflection of the unique and innovative versatility of your people.

3. *To guide* is necessary when the individual performers within your organization are contradicting each other. If possible, guiding should involve no more than introducing people to alternative methods and directions. However, it might be necessary to close certain doors and block certain avenues when you determine that continued movement in those directions is counterproductive. Guidance is not the removal of personal responsibility, but rather the process of "shaping" performance.

4. *To cause progress* means to set in motion those people and activities that will result in progress. Effective leaders understand that good people in the correct context will create results. It's not a matter of forcing things

forward. Progress is the natural tendency when the proper environment and stimulus are provided. When progress is lacking, examine how fertile the environment is and work to meet your people's needs. When the environment is positively energized, progress is inevitable.

5. *To create a path* is the process of opening selected doors while closing others. Some might picture a person hacking a path through the jungle with a machete. However, given the complex nature of business in the 1990s, as well as the range of opportunities and choices, the "path" is more a reflection of the leader's values and visions than a narrow corridor to restrict lateral movement.

6. *To control action* is the shadow side of creating a path. When lateral movement and tangential behavior begin to dilute the effectiveness of the work being done or impede progress, the effective leader will move to exercise a measure of corrective control. The key to effective control is to gently yet persuasively reaffirm the values and visions which define the direction of the organization. It is always preferable to focus on intentions rather than to dwell on what should be avoided.

7. *To direct* is to interpret. Even when goals are clear and people are comfortable exercising their unique talents in achieving those goals, a functional vision must be maintained which synchronizes movement. Directing is in many ways synonymous with leading. Again, the most effective leader does not direct by pushing, but by drawing the best out of his or her people, en route to goal achievement. No two people or groups of people will produce an identical composition of talents and abilities. Each group must be interpreted and directed accordingly.

8. *To influence* is most often simply a matter of being genuine. Influence is important because people need to believe that something is worth doing. If the fingerprint of values and visions is to be found upon an individual or team of individuals, the leader will first need to be genuinely invested. People can detect the genuineness of the leader's commitment to them and to the organization's goals and will be influenced proportionately.

9. *To command* means to exert authority. In the context of effective leadership, authority is a quality that instills confidence in the team. Authority should not mean intimidation. If authority needs to be used to threaten and otherwise force compliance, then the proper environment has not been established, including the appropriate staff. People appreciate being in step with power. But always remember that power is given by those who agree to respect it.

10. *To be first* doesn't mean that you need to get there ahead of your staff, literally or rhetorically. You don't have to be first to unlock the office in the morning or first to discover the big idea. It's far more important for

the leader to graciously relinquish the concept of first and honor others for their willingness to come to work early, for discovering the big idea or for producing the most results. The leader's de facto seat of honor is the substance of his or her building up of others. A leader should be "the first" to congratulate worthwhile effort.

11. *To be chief* places the leader in a seat of judgment. Ultimately responsible, the leader must evaluate the merits or liabilities of what happens. Judging is, by nature, a hazardous practice. The leader can damage his or her own effectiveness by behaving punitively or condescendingly. However, a chief is the bearer of ultimate responsibility and, as such, fulfills a sacrificial role for the entire group.

12. *To begin* means to set into motion. Without motion there can be no growth or progress. Beginning something can refer to the original movement or the stimulus that perpetuates movement. "Let's begin" means "let's accomplish our goals." When the focus and intention turn from establishing goals to realizing them, something has begun. The effective leader knows the emotional as well as the practical importance of beginnings. Every beginning is an opportunity for a brighter future. An opportunity is a beginning when someone accepts leadership and declares the task under way. Declaring a beginning is one of the most important and valuable functions of leadership.

Chapter One Closure

Good old Ticky learned from his experience. Hopefully, the rest of us will learn from his experience as well. When you're on the hot seat, your *number one* priority is to put out the fire and to make sure you never get burned again. In order to do that, we must cherish our mistakes and misfortunes. The leader who has never suffered is living in a fool's paradise. If you haven't experienced enough suffering of your own, learn from someone else who has.

If you thought I was going to tell you that leadership under pressure could be navigated without wrinkling your clothes, you were mistaken. It's far more important to learn that wrinkled clothes and dirty fingernails never killed anyone. Your survival and ultimate effectiveness as a leader, new or veteran, depends largely upon your willingness to work on *you*.

First and foremost, this is a personal improvement manual. The methods, techniques, and principles throughout this book are meant to be woven into *your* fabric. Any improvements in the leader will eventually be reflected in those who are led. You can think of it this way: somebody, somewhere is going to be better because *you* read this book!

Chapter Two

The Emerging Leader Process

"You'd better take somebody to lunch before somebody else eats yours." —THE AUTHOR

When my boss's search for my replacement launched me into a learning frenzy, the heat was on, and I was going down in flames! I met with successful people as often as I could and I studied everything about them. I was starving for knowledge. Not just head stuff, but meaningful ideas I could transform into meaningful action. To this day I continue to study great people.

To paraphrase the great twentieth century philosopher, Yogi Berra, "We're bound to see something if we watch long enough." So I keep watching and I keep seeing new and exciting things. I'm no spring chicken either. Age is irrelevant when it comes to acquiring and refining leadership skills. It doesn't matter if you're new at the game or if you've been working hard at it for most of your life.

The quality of leadership is not determined by the urgency or size of the task to be accomplished. Some of the greatest leaders I've ever observed or read about spent most of their time dealing with common details. What *made* these people great was the uncommon way they dealt with everything in their lives, whether it was an ordinary detail or a major challenge.

After studying many great leaders over the years, I've narrowed their most salient qualities into my top ten characteristics of an effective leader:

22

Leadership Characteristic 1: Cultivating a High Standard of Personal Ethics

A high standard of personal ethics is at the top of my list because it seems to be the most important quality. Don't be misled by anyone who tells you that your personal standard of ethics can be different from your professional ethics. Unless you're comfortable living a double standard, your professional ethics must match your private ethics. Honest Abe Lincoln, who walked miles to return a customer's change, is a classic example of how personal ethics are reflected in professional conduct. At the core of any high standard of personal ethics is the declaration of personal responsibility I talked about in Chapter One. A person who refuses to accept responsibility lacks the ethical armor to stand against temptation.

You could also look at it in terms of *staying power.* It is not uncommon in the business world to see people take off like a rocket. We're all initially impressed with their spectacular accomplishments. The press and publishing communities invariably chronicle their glory and we spend the big bucks to listen to them address major conferences and seminars. Unfortunately, it is all too common for great success stories to fade into oblivion within a couple of years, if they don't crash and burn sooner. I'm sure everyone can recall more than a few recent *riches-to-rags* scenarios where folks didn't have the high standard of personal ethics to effectively fight the fire when it flamed up.

What brought these and so many other successful people down? They had a rupture in their standard of personal ethics or never established a standard to begin with. I'm not trying to say that *all* successful people are corrupt or don't deserve what they accomplish. In fact, I studied many extremely successful people who were known for their high standards of personal ethics.

How many people could have been saved tremendous damage and/or pain if only they could have known which people in trusted positions were charlatans or would turn their backs on the accomplishments that elevated them into positions of power in the first place? One of the advantages of living in a small town is that strangers have to prove themselves and, if someone proves him or herself untrustworthy, it's a long and difficult road back into the public trust.

Where I came from, we used to describe an untrustworthy person by saying that we couldn't trust him or her any further than you could throw a soggy mattress up a spiral staircase. If your neighbor told you that about somebody, would you buy from them? The *Wall Street Journal* should publish a *soggy mattress list* every month just to snip off the fringes of the financial investment industry.

Ethics can be an entire book in itself. There are many great books on the topic of personal and professional ethics. More than anything else, ethics is a study in right and wrong. In virtually everything we do and say, there is a distinction between what is best for the greatest number of people in consideration of their long-term quality of life.

Ethics and ethical considerations need to be viewed as multidimensional issues. In every decision, there will usually be a vertical consideration of the immediate rightness or wrongness in addition to the horizontal perspective of the decision's positive or negative impact over time. Every decision rests somewhere within the envelope of the best for the most over the longest period and the worst for the most over the longest period.

Before you write me off as an evangelist waving a moral flag in your face, consider that ethics in business is the cornerstone of success. Without a commitment to right conduct, any enterprise is ultimately doomed. I'm talking dollars and cents.

One of the strongest indicators of ethical orientation is the willingness to help someone else, even when there's nothing tangible to expect in return.

My wife, Theo, and I traveled to Holland a couple of years ago to begin a journey that would take us on a cruise up the Rhine river to Switzerland. We arrived in Amsterdam and caught a taxi down to the dock our boat was supposed to depart from that evening. When we arrived, there was no boat.

The cab driver drove us around in search of our missing boat. He eventually decided we had paid enough fare and turned off his meter. I told him it was OK to keep charging us, but he waved me off and finally took us to a nice restaurant near the dock where the boat was supposed to be.

It was Sunday evening and the local cruise office was closed. Once inside the restaurant, the bartender sympathized with our plight and handed us off to a very friendly and helpful waiter who sat us down for dinner and promptly got the restaurant owner, Jaap Mous, involved.

Before long, the bartender summoned me for a phone call. It was the folks at the cruise line. Word of our dilemma had reached them and they were sending a limousine to pick us up.

The departure city had been changed at the last minute from Amsterdam to Rotterdam and we had already begun our trip before they could get word to us in the United States. As we waited for the limo, Jaap and his staff served us a wonderful meal and provided good company.

The limo driver got us to Rotterdam in record time, but although we could see the boat in the distance, he couldn't find the right streets to get us there. He finally flagged down yet another cab driver who led us through the maze of streets until we finally reached the right dock with the correct cruise ship.

As I trotted toward the lead cab driver, peeling off bills to compensate him for rescuing us, he waved me off, just as the first cab driver did, and drove away without accepting anything for his efforts. A high standard of personal ethics ran right through each person we encountered in Holland.

Each one of us is responsible for our own conduct and, as leaders, we have additional responsibility for the conduct of our people as it relates to our professional relationships. No organization can force us to compromise our standard of personal ethics. Heroes and heroines from the beginning of time have been identified by how much they were willing to sacrifice to uphold their standard of personal ethics. We're never too old to begin building or repairing our ethical spine. More than any other quality, each of us is known by our standard of personal ethics.

Leadership Characteristic 2: High Energy

High energy also became evident in my study of great leaders. Great leaders are simply not worn out by dealing with petty issues. These people not only know right from wrong, but also know the difference between *interesting* and *important*. There is a world of difference between the two. An effective leader must develop a sense of discretion and be able to draw clear distinctions between what is truly important to the organization and what is merely interesting.

Much of this discriminatory ability is the result of experience. Take it from Ticky. There is no better teacher than experience, especially *hands-on* experience. However, even the emerging leader, who might lack experience, has a valuable tool at his or her disposal: *common sense.* Regardless of how much your common sense might have been maligned by a critical parent, everyone has got some. Our biggest problem with common sense is not whether we have enough to come in out of the rain, but rather whether we *trust* our own common sense enough to allow it to help guide our judgment.

People often refer to great leaders as people who can "see the big picture" or "stay cool under pressure." In either case, what these leaders are really getting credit for is the level of trust they have in their own judgment. While others are running around like headless chickens, the effective leader is calling upon his or her sense of judgment to remedy the situation. There are times when even the experienced leader is facing a new and unique crisis, in which case the playing field becomes level. At such times, the experienced leader and the inexperienced leader must call upon their individual common sense for guidance.

Companies are all but destroyed by pettiness. I'm sure you experience pettiness in one form or another almost every day. I've seen entire offices get bent out of shape over what brand of office supplies to buy. Should an effective leader sweat over whether or not to supply the office with Eagle Brand #2 lead pencils? Believe it or not, things like that can be the subject of memos. What is even more amazing is that employees sometimes spend inordinate amounts of time *discussing* memos concerning pencils. They even band together to have lunch and discuss the pencil crisis.

How about the office that ceased providing postage to commissioned sales people. The place nearly came apart at the seams. You would think that lives and careers had been shattered. At the obligatory lunch conference following the announcement, one of the ring leaders in the pending revolt was reported to have said, "If this company thinks I'm going to put out the price of a stamp in order to earn a $500 commission, they'd better think again!"

Effective leaders have to be bigger than that. Remember that your people won't get better until you do. By the same token, they won't get *bigger* until you show them *how.* Go with what's important and dispatch what's not. Any company, from an individual proprietorship to a multinational, can get bogged down and practically grind to a halt under the burden of petty considerations.

Petty issues are small and go undetected easily. Yet they accumulate like dirt in your air filter, eventually choking off your supply of oxygen. Policies, rules, and regulations are often painstakingly drafted and enforced to smooth out the smallest wrinkles. Tremendous energies are frequently applied to handle miniscule problems. Sledgehammers were not designed to kill fleas. In fact, it's the wrong tool for the job.

The larger an organization grows, the greater the tendency to *over*regulate. Of all the companies I've ever observed, I have yet to see one operate perfectly. Never once has the factor of human error been eliminated. To the contrary, in organizations where the human factor is acknowledged and accepted, there seems to be much higher productivity and much, much higher morale than in highly regulated organizations.

When relieved of the burdens that petty concerns and endless regulations impose, people have a natural tendency to focus more enthusiastically on the task at hand. Customers get better service, and jobs, in general, are handled more efficiently. I swear, some companies have a challenge displayed in the conference room that reads, "How difficult can we make it for customers to buy from us?" Surely nobody *intends* to promote such a dreadful thought. Yet it is unwittingly true of many organizations with an inward focus on petty issues instead of an outward focus on people and what they need.

In the Air Force we used to say it like this:

> Some die by shrapnel.
> Some go down in flames.
> Most die inch by inch
> playing at little games.

The big question that you and I need to ask ourselves each night is: *did I play at big games or little games today and at what will I play tomorrow?*

Leadership Characteristic 3: Working Priorities

Effective leaders are also good at *working priorities.* Setting priorities is important. However, the distance between setting and working priorities is often enormous. Most lists of priorities end up in the landfill of life, having never been realized. The difference between merely setting priorities and working priorities is not unlike the difference between a dreamer and a doer. It's important to dream and to plan, but all the dreaming and planning in the world doesn't accomplish a thing. It's the doer that makes things happen. When the heat's on, I will trade you 1,000 people who ponder the possibilities for one person who will make things happen. As we used to say back home, it's O.K. to grab a tiger by the tail if you know what to do *next!*

Working priorities are essential for *stability under pressure.* Why? Because stability under pressure is the antecedent of sound problem solving skills. Many people can solve problems when given enough time and an amicable atmosphere in which to work.

However, when financial demands from above are coupled with production and personnel pressures from below, the friction produces heat. The heat, in turn, frightens off the less confident and leaves those with true mettle to face the problems. Leaders invariably have the ultimate responsibility for problem solving, and their mettle is proven time and again by their stability under pressure.

The great leaders that I've studied work their priority lists from the top down. All too often, we set our priorities and then jump in somewhere in the middle. Not the great ones. They go after that *number one* priority with all they've got. That number one priority gets *number one attention.* Ignoring that big item at the top of the list won't make it go away. Jumping into the middle of the list instead of starting at the top is kind of like tearing off a Band-Aid slowly. You didn't pause to savor every drop of that awful cough syrup your mom used to feed you with a spoon when you were a kid. You gulped it quickly. The shorter the painful experience the better. Back home in Southern Illinois, we used to say it like this:

If you've got a frog to swallow, don't look at it too long. If you've got more than one to swallow, swallow the biggest one first!

If you've been swallowing your frogs in order all day long, then you shouldn't be taking any of them home for dinner with you at night. Frogs that don't get swallowed grow bigger and multiply! The best way to be an effective leader and avoid becoming a frog farmer is to take care of those guys, biggest to smallest, *in order, every day.* The effective leader will finish with the number one priority and then go on to the *new* number one priority. That's right. When the number one priority on the list is dispatched, the next item on the list is not treated like the number two priority. It becomes the new number one priority. What was once the second most important item becomes *the* most important. There is a different intensity with which we approach priorities, depending upon where they fall on our lists. When number two becomes the new number one, we bring the same intensity to it that is reserved for the number one priority.

If we work on our number three, four, and five priorities as if they are third, fourth, and fifth in importance, there is a corresponding drop off in quality throughout the day. Everything seems exciting and energized in the morning when energy is being invested in the number one priority, but, by the end of the day, there is a feeling of disappointment and letdown.

The secret to energy at the end of the day is to be working on a number one priority at the end of the day. You've witnessed it many times when there was a deadline to be met and the whole office struggled frantically to beat the overnight courier. Energy stays high. Do the same with everything. It's a matter of working priorities as if each consecutive priority is number one. Indeed, each one *is* number one, in its turn.

The effective leader works the list of priorities and doesn't back off or compromise just because of where some activity was originally placed. The great ones get to the point where everything has been crossed off for the day except "pick up the laundry on the way home." Guess what? They pick up their laundry better than anyone else. It's simply a matter of finesse and style. Great leaders pump gas at the self-serve station better than anybody else pumps gas.

Leadership Characteristic 4: Having Courage

Courage. The cowardly lion in the *Wizard of Oz* realized that being a safe plodder was not the way to succeed in life. The great leaders I studied were courageous people. I'm not recommending that anyone act irresponsibly. It's simply a difference in the way that the courageous person and the timid person approach life. The courageous one is willing to walk near the edge and do things slightly off balance when necessary—not for the sake of living dangerously, but rather for the sake of getting the job done. The willingness to take risks and accept responsibility for their outcomes are consistent qualities among effective leaders.

The safe and timid plodder is cautiously tiptoeing through life, hoping to make it safely to death. That is substance abuse. It is like eating the banana peel and throwing the banana away. I've heard the abuse of life's substance measured by the amount of life in our years as opposed to the number of years in our lives. It seems like some people are in a hurry to get to the end so that nothing bad will happen to them.

The safe and timid plodder is the one you will find waiting in that parking lot at one end of town for all the traffic lights to turn green before starting out. Not only is the guy I described in Chapter One still waiting in the lot, he probably will be for the rest of his life. Do you want to spend your time in life's parking lot? If you do, perhaps I can offer you some assurance. I believe that, if you're cautious enough, nothing really bad *or good* will ever happen to you.

The safe and timid plodder is the person who turns pale or balks entirely when you say, "Let's give it a go!" To put it another way, you've got to do what you fear or fear will be in charge. There is no middle ground. Either you or your fears are in charge of everything you do.

Leadership Characteristic 5: Working Hard with Commitment and Dedication

Are you a *committed and dedicated hard worker?* What do you think people are saving all of their energy for? Think about that for a moment. Where is that reservoir full of energy that they've saved by not pushing themselves too hard? Typically when we observe a dedicated and hard worker, we compliment them on how hard they seem to work. Yet, when we point out how hard they appear to be working, they invariably reply that it doesn't seem like hard work because they love what they are doing.

Nobody ever worked themselves to death in a job they loved. People work themselves to death in jobs that they hate. Working in a job you hate will produce ulcers, a form of cannibalism that begins to eat up the person you're not happy with. I'll bet you any doctor will agree that not many happy people come to them complaining of ulcers.

The ones who love their jobs constantly think about how they can do the job better. It's not uncommon for them to get a great idea at 4:00 in the morning and scramble to write it down so they can get to the office early and try it. Remember, it's the risk takers who are always anxious to give it a go.

You'll also notice that committed and dedicated hard workers don't tend to be depressed people. They don't have the time to waste being depressed. It's when their fellow employees get their hands on them that they slow down. In fact, that's exactly the advice they get from their peers. "You better slow down or you're going to ruin your health. One of these days you're going to drop dead from a heart attack."

I don't think anybody truly believes the solemn advice giver is really concerned for the high performer's health. When I talk about committed and dedicated hard workers, I'm not talking about workaholics who use their jobs to shield them from personal or family problems. I'm referring to people who have the support and encouragement of their friends and family.

I'm talking about achievers whose priorities are in the right place and have supportive families that are proud of their professional accomplishments.

When the heat is on and you need to be highly effective and efficient, you want to surround yourself with committed and dedicated hard workers. If you possess those qualities as their leader, there is no limit to what you can accomplish with a team of people who love what they do. On the contrary, it's a miserable scenario either when a group of people who love what they do are led by someone who doesn't share their enthusiasm or when an enthusiastic leader doesn't have a committed and dedicated staff. However, dedicated and committed hard workers eventually develop dedicated and hard working organizations, regardless of who you start with.

In the best of all possible worlds, each of us would be employed in activities that we would enjoy doing even if we weren't getting paid. Most of the successful leaders I've encountered don't give much conscious consideration to what they are paid. They do what they love and the money comes with it. The big question that stops most people I present it to is, "What would you be doing if money was not a primary consideration?" The great leaders will always say, "I would do exactly what I'm doing." If you don't give that same answer, perhaps you should consider a change. If a change seems too scary or uncertain, perhaps you should reread Leadership Characteristic 4.

Leadership Characteristic 6: Going with the Urge to Create

Effective leaders in any field are a bit *unconventional with an urge to create*. If the truth were known, they are also a bit mischievous. These people bore easily. They are not likely to stay for very long with something that's not working. If you need something monitored for a long period of time that's not likely to produce much in the way of results, it's better to give that assignment to one of those folks who is worried about saving his or her energy. Those careful plodders make good kettle watchers. The effective, enthusiastic ones won't have the patience to wait for a phone to ring before acting.

The effective leader is an innovator. You might have heard them described as people who would rather ask forgiveness than permission. I'm not talking about irresponsible loose cannons. Recall important characteristics such as sound judgment, common sense, and personal responsibility, and you'll begin to see how these great qualities of leadership complement one another.

I had a few of these folks working for me and they would come into my office from time to time and say, "Danny, I just tried this or that unorthodox thing." I would turn pale before asking, "You did *what*? What happened?," not really wanting to hear the answer. "They gave us a big order."

"Congratulations!" I would spout with all the confidence in the world. "Good work." (I told you tap dancing was a handy trick for effective leaders.)

By the same token, my people would learn when something didn't work and not beat a dead horse. Experience can't be beat. In Tom Peters's popular best seller, *In Search of Excellence,* he talks about "perfect failures." I think that's a terrific way to put the educational value of a failed attempt into perspective. Every organization should have its share of perfect failures. Ticky had one when he picked up that horseshoe. It's O.K. to have new perfect failures, but they shouldn't be reruns. Learning eliminates reruns.

In my Air Force days, I used to fly a supersonic fighter in air shows, in front of 75,000 people, at 25 feet off the ground. Not many people did that. When you see a tree shoot past your wing tip at 700 miles per hour, you know you're living in the fast lane.

It was always important to remember that, when flying at 25 feet off the ground, one should gain a little altitude before rolling into a turn. The penalty for forgetting one measly time would have been a 700 mile per hour cartwheel. It might have been a spectacular sight for the crowd, but not very cost-effective for the Air Force or good for my career. I wouldn't be coming in to work tomorrow, if you know what I mean.

After my big teardrop-shaped turn, I would make another pass over that runway, 100 miles per hour slower, at 600 miles per hour . . . upside down. Hanging in the cockpit by my shoulder straps, I had to also remember that, while flying upside down, the control system is *reversed*. Thank God I never had a lapse of memory. The one word I never wanted to hear myself use during an air show was "oops."

My point is that the gray hair I sport these days didn't come from flying upside down at 600 miles per hour. My gray hair came from the unorthodox people who worked for me and were constantly inventing new and unique ways to do business. I'm proud of my gray hair, and I'm proud of those people who taught me so much about innovation.

Leadership Characteristic 7: Getting Goal Oriented

Great leaders I have studied also possessed the *goal orientation* needed to face tough decisions. Tough decisions don't have to be big ones either. How about making a few simple changes in your life, like turning off the tube at night and having someone over for dinner that you can learn from? How about reading or taking some quiet time to be creative? These might seem like insignificant things, but they can represent some of the subtle differences between the life of an immensely successful person and someone who can't figure out why she or he can't seem to get ahead.

At other times, tough decisions might involve cutting some people out of your life. If friendships do not include mutual regard and *reciprocal* support and encouragement, the chances are that you are becoming the battery charger for someone else's inoperative alternator. I'm not saying to turn your back on people in need. I'm saying you need to associate with people who are taking the same career and lifestyle bus that you are. Like likes like. As the Good Book says, iron sharpens iron. Choosing your associations intelligently is more than being picky about friends. It is *shaping your community*.

All of these issues require a sense of where you intend to go or goal orientation. Selecting appropriate people to spend your time with is an example of knowing the difference between those who take responsibility for what they can become and those who cry because they haven't got there yet. When someone takes responsibility, breakthroughs begin to happen.

When people on your staff become a contradiction to the goals you have established in the best interests of the organization and its people, it's time to part company. I'll talk more specifically about the art of firing nonproductive people in my next chapter on team building. Keeping a nonproducer in a job where she or he is not contributing is not doing your organization or that individual any favors. We are not placed in jobs to keep them the same; we're put in jobs to make them better.

A goal oriented fellow I know once told me he never works hard to pay bills; he works hard to have fun with the money. Otherwise, you won't have enough to do either one. I hasten to add that you ought to love what you do, even if you don't get paid, as discussed earlier.

I did a program once with former heavyweight champion George Foreman. Even though he is the *former* champion, I still called him Champ. If I'm not tall enough to fly with the airlines, I'm certainly not big enough to survive annoying George Foreman to his face. As we had lunch together that day, I observed his nose from across the table. Let me tell you, a heavyweight boxer's nose is a work of art.

George Foreman's nose is a monument to goal orientation. It has been sculpted by some of the strongest, meanest punchers ever to step into a ring. I can personally attest to the pain one feels when you take one right on the nose. It gets your attention right quick!

I was on the varsity wrestling team at Southern Illinois University. Moving around the mat one day, I was looking for an opportunity to take down my opponent, the Missouri State Champion. I was feeling confident. For some reason I really felt like that day was going to be special. I was right. Not for the reasons I thought, but I was definitely right. That day was going to be an experience like no other.

I took a look at his feet and decided to launch into the old flying-tackle type takedown, going for his feet and taking him by surprise. I launched and dived for his feet. For future reference, if you ever do that, you will want to make sure your opponent is not about to do the same thing to you at the same time. My opponent did.

My coach had taught me to keep my face up so I could see were I was going. "Watch for your opponent's mistakes," he would always say. He was right. I kept my head up and saw that my opponent had made a mistake. In midair, I determined that my opponent wasn't as well coached as I. He had lowered his head and was completely unaware that my nose was about to do great damage to the top of his approaching skull.

POW! The only way I can describe the pain would be to have you imagine an atom bomb going off inside your nostrils. Skyrockets went off inside my head. I saw Roman candles. White hot flames shot up behind my eyeballs. Don't tell me they weren't there. I saw them! Even my feet itched. You know you are experiencing ultimate pain when your feet itch. I shiver when I even think about it.

My wrestling experience made me admire George Foreman's nose all the more. I looked at that thing and wondered how he could have ever endured the incredible pain of so many powerful heavyweight boxers popping him on the nose. So I asked him exactly that. George replied calmly, "If I see what I want real good in my mind, I don't notice any pain in gettin' it." Perhaps that philosophy is what brought him back for a chance at the heavyweight championship at age 43!

That's sound philosophy for a professional boxer or for anyone else. Our kids could do with a dose of sacrifice to attain something worth having. But remember that we need to lead by example. Some people come to me and say, "Danny, you don't understand how sensitive to pain I am." When that happens, I ask them if they've ever been working around the house or garden, cut themselves, and not noticed right away. I know I have. I've gazed more than once at an awful looking wound and wondered how and when I sustained the injury. The point is our minds can only concentrate fully on one thing at a time and the mind will shut out even a painful cut when we're fully committed to a task. If you picked up a knife and said, "I think that I'll cut my finger now," the pain would be instant, wouldn't it? Goal orientation produces a drive and energy that shields us from the pain and weariness of accomplishment.

Leadership Characteristic 8:
Maintaining a Constant
Enthusiasm

The great leaders I've studied have an *inspired enthusiasm*. They're like a pilot light on the burner. I'm sure you have friends like that or work with people who can light up a room when they walk in. Their genuine enthusiasm is contagious. As a leader, your people look to *you* for enthusiasm. Not that they need to borrow yours, it's just that it seems inappropriate somehow to have more enthusiasm than the boss. They need permission from you to let it loose. Enthusiasm comes from witnessing the accomplishment of your daily goals which are part of a larger plan.

Actually, some people simply have too much enthusiasm to be held back. One woman who worked for me several years ago had everything going against her. She came from a very poor background. Her family worked in the tomato fields of California and she worked right alongside them as she grew up. Because of the demands of life in an agricultural labor family, she never made it past the eighth grade and speaks with a heavy Hispanic accent.

To put it simply, she was not an Ivy League M.B.A. Nevertheless, she worked her way to the top of her field and broke every record our company's top salesman ever set. This woman outsold an entire office of 20 people. When I asked her how she did it, she twinkled and said, "God didn't make me with an *off* switch." Life would be so much simpler for many of us if we didn't have an "off" switch that keeps getting bumped.

I was the one in the leadership position, but she was the one who inspired all of us in that organization. My most responsible leadership maneuver was to pave the way for her to keep doing what she was so excited about doing. I was not about to allow anything I felt or any unreasonable company policy pour cold water on her pilot light.

I hope this next thought will pop your eyes open like a good whiff of ammonia. I mentioned earlier that inspired enthusiasm is contagious. If you don't have contagious inspired enthusiasm, then *whatever you do have is also contagious.* Now that's a scary thought! It's also true. If you are hoping that the people who work with you won't get what you've got, rest assured that they have.

Growth and improvement as a leader, especially a leader under pressure, requires genuine inspired enthusiasm. If you're confused about how people can have such enthusiasm about what they do, reread the previous seven leadership characteristics. Again, I say there is a distinct, interactive relationship between these qualities.

If someone is portraying phony enthusiasm as a compensation for some other inadequacy, anyone working with that person will detect it quickly. People with phony enthusiasm change jobs and locations frequently. They hop from job to job, always coming in the door, impressing everyone with their enthusiasm. However, if it's not genuine, it will fade in short order.

As leaders, each of us needs to examine our own enthusiasm to determine if it truly emanates from our love of what we do. At the same time, we need to be sensitive to what drives the enthusiasm of our people. If there is any doubt in either regard, then we once again find ourselves standing at that fork in the road. Which road you will follow should be determined by whether or not your enthusiasm and the enthusiasm of your people are driven by the accomplishment of or progress toward goals. Accomplishment is the appetizer of enthusiasm, followed closely by sound relationships that build character.

Leadership Characteristic 9: Staying Level-Headed

Effective leaders are *level-headed* people. They grasp the facts in a hurry. They have the ability to organize chaotic situations. They see things as they really are as opposed to how they wish they were. Effective leaders don't *react* to problems, they *respond* to them. Reacting is like a reflex knee-jerk which will invariably produce the same type of behavior that helped generate the heat in the first place. Responding means invoking the type of common sense judgments that take the organization down a new and better road. When internal pressures combine with external pressures to produce a storm of uncertainty and disruption, the realistic leader can bring order and set corrective measures into motion. This is a leadership quality for tough, heated moments.

These people prefer to fix problems rather than talk about them. I'm sure you know the different types. Some people come to you constantly with worried expressions, reporting problems that seem unsolvable. These same people will discuss the problems at length with anyone who will listen. Interestingly, long after the problems are solved or no longer relevant, these people are *still* talking about them.

Not those who approach life realistically. They act without being told to because they understand that, in the real world, problems aren't stopping places; they are *decision points*. Problems are not to be feared. Problems are to be expected. The level-headed leader doesn't go into a state of shock when he or she is on the hot seat, but calmly and confidently deals with the situation. To panic is to be unrealistic.

I learned about being realistic as a test pilot. I know what it's like to be flying a supersonic jet fighter, all alone, with 79,000 horsepower, at 60,000 feet, 1200 miles per hour, 20 miles per minute, upside down . . . on fire. There I was, with every red light on the control panel flashing in my face. At least I *think* they were flashing in my face. There was too much smoke in the cockpit to really tell.

Not having read Peter Drucker at that point in my life and forgetting what I should have learned from old Ticky back in the Ozark hill country where I grew up, I wound up in the precarious position just described more than once. At any rate, I did my best to *be realistic* in the face of disaster. It started with self talk. "Be realistic, Danny," I would think to myself. "You are a test pilot with the right stuff. You're used to living on the edge. This is

America up here. The nation is depending on you. The whole world is listening in on the emergency frequency. Remember that *before* you touch that microphone button."

Sufficiently under control, I would reach over to shut down whatever I thought was causing the fire with one gloved hand and simultaneously press the microphone button on the control stick with the other. In the most macho voice I could muster, I hit the button and called control center. "May-Day, May-Day, May-Day. I'm at 60,000 feet, upside down, and on fire. Request landing instructions."

As I recalled, each word of my transmission was clear, calm, and distinct. A Hollywood actor in a simulator couldn't have been more composed. As far as I could tell, I couldn't have been calmer ordering ham and eggs at the chow hall. Of course, after I managed to get down safely (don't tell me God doesn't answer prayers), the controllers would play back the tape of my emergency transmission for me to hear. For some reason, that calm, composed, macho voice ended up sounding like an amphetamine-crazed chipmunk to the controllers in the tower.

My mythical sense of realism in the heat of the moment gave way to the adrenalin coursing though my body at such intensity I didn't even recognize my own voice later. It never failed to give the controllers a chuckle or two. My high-pitched babbling was so fast that sometimes they recorded my prayer that was supposed to follow my transmission. I didn't get my thumb off the button quickly enough and I usually broadcast my negotiations with God. Test pilots' prayers are, by necessity, *brief.* Most of them sound something like: "God, get this thing back on the ground and I'll taxi it in for you." There has been a time or two in my civilian life when I've thrown up similar prayers. A good example was the time my boss came in and told me he was looking for my replacement!

The people with the information we need to develop the leadership qualities I'm listing for you are all around us. Remember, leaders are not born, they simply drink from Elbert Hubbard's "ocean of knowledge." Nothing promotes a level-headed sense of realism as much as knowledge. Likewise, ignorance, prejudice, and narrow-thinking result from lack of knowledge.

Leadership Characteristic 10: Helping Others to Grow

Every great leader I studied had a *desire to help others grow.* That desire is at the core of Dale Carnegie's success. He made millions by helping and encouraging others to make millions. True leaders not only want their people to succeed, but also to grow and develop. When an organization functions in a nurturing environment where pettiness is eliminated and ideas are openly exchanged, the result is synergy.

With synergy, the organization *and* the individuals within the organization will become more than the sum of their parts. Every once in awhile, a sports team of some sort will rise above its potential, or so the sports analysts will say, and win the big game or championship or even the gold medal against all odds and predictions, defeating higher-rated teams in the process. Whenever this happens, we are witnessing individuals and their organization achieving synergy. However, as my sales staff once proved, you don't have to be rated as a preseason champion to succeed.

We should *never* pour cold water on anyone's dreams. Being unenthusiastic, down-in-the-mouth, and generally nonsupportive is the fastest and most effective way to choke any hope of synergy and growth out of your people. Believe me, if you are like soggy cereal at the company breakfast, you ought to reconnoiter and then reconsider leadership and you.

Developing good people depends upon your willingness to support and encourage them, no matter how farfetched their ambitions seem to be. When I was flying fighters out of Tucson, Arizona, I met Hal Needham. In those days, Hal was a stunt man in the westerns they were shooting around there, falling off of horses for $500 a trip. We were buddies. We both lived life a little differently than the average citizen.

If Hal would have told me back then he intended to become Hollywood's top stunt man, I might have said, "Hal, there's no way you're going to do that. You've already got 43 major bone breaks, not including fingers and toes. You're not going to *live* that long." If he would have said, "Danny, I intend to write a movie someday that will rank in the top ten movies of all time, sharing box office honors with *Gone With The Wind, The Sound of Music* and *Star Wars,*" I would have said, "Hal, you're an ex-tree trimmer with a ninth grade education. Are you planning to write that script with a crayon clutched in your fist?"

If he would have said he also intended to team up with another friend of his, who is a butcher by trade with a *hobby* of engineering, and build a supersonic car, I probably would have said, "Stop right there, Hal. You're talking to one of the world's foremost authorities on supersonic machinery and I'm telling you there is no way an automobile will ever go supersonic. The rubber wouldn't even stay on the wheels at those speeds."

He might have said to me that he and his butcher buddy had already anticipated that problem and elected to have all-metal wheels on their supersonic car. At that point, I would have probably said sympathetically, "Hal, old buddy, I think you've fallen off one horse too many. Let me drive you back to the hotel. You need your rest." Fortunately, Hal didn't describe his many dreams to me until I had learned not to pour cold water on people's ambitions.

Sure enough, a while back, Hal called me and said it had been some time since we had seen each other and we should get together for dinner. As we sat there in Malibu, watching the waves roll in, he told me how he had become the top stunt man in Hollywood. He told me how he had written *Smokey and the Bandit,* which, at that time, was tied with *The Sound of Music* for fourth place in all time box office sales. I never imagined I would ever hear *The Sound of Music* and *Smokey and the Bandit* in the same sentence, but at that time they shared that distinction in motion picture history.

He went on to say, "Danny, next week I'm doing something I want you to be a part of." "What's that, Hal?" I asked. He said, "I've got this friend who is a butcher by trade and his hobby is engineering. The two of us have built a car and we're going to punch it through the sound barrier. I want you to be there." I said, "That must be quite a car!" He said, "It's eighteen inches wide and forty feet long. It has a rocket-powered engine and even has metal wheels."

"Of course," I said in stunned amazement. "Rubber would probably come off the wheels at those speeds." This former tree trimmer with a ninth grade education was blowing me away. He went on to say that they were going to run the car on the dry lake bed at Edwards Air Force Base. So there I stood, one week later, on the same lake bed where the space shuttles land, my wife on one side of me and Chuck Yeager on the other. Chuck had been the first man to *fly* through the sound barrier and he was now watching Stan Barrett squeeze himself into that tiny cockpit.

It took Stan 20 minutes to maneuver his body into a car that was only 18 inches wide. As he twisted and turned, inch by inch, it occurred to me that he *wanted* to get in. I couldn't imagine how long it would have taken to get me into that car, not because I'm wider than Stan Barrett, but because my kicking and screaming might have slowed me up. Once Stan was inside, they *bolted down the canopy!* That simply means you're in there until somebody comes and unbolts you. I don't think I have enough of the right stuff for that.

The speed of sound varies with temperature and other atmospheric factors, but *that* day the sound barrier was at 730 miles per hour. That's about 500 miles an hour faster than A.J. Foyt and the boys come down the straightaway at the Indianapolis 500. The countdown commenced and the rocket engine ignited. Even with our ear protection, the noise was deafening. A rocket engine delivers total thrust instantly. As Stan later described it, "It's a whole lotta gone in a hurry."

They told Stan it would take three runs to punch through the sound barrier when he agreed to drive. My wife and I were observing ignition number 16. The rocket car raced out of sight over the horizon although we could still see the fifty-foot rooster tail of dust and smoke. When they unbolted Stan, he still hadn't reached the sound barrier.

He described each time how he felt he just couldn't drive any faster. Yet, again and again he squeezed inside to give it a go. The following week, Stan tried again. Seventeen seconds after ignition, he was traveling nine miles an hour faster than the speed of sound. Stan later gave me a picture of the event and pointed out that his rear wheels were a foot off the ground while he was supersonic.

"Were you aware that you were only on your nose wheel?" I asked. He replied, "It's hard to know anything when you've got your eyes closed and your fingers in your ears." I should include a *confident sense of humor* as my 11th characteristic of great leadership. They all seem to have it, from presidents who have just been shot to test pilots who are out of control.

After the successful run, Chuck Yeager strolled over to the car, pointed up to the American flag on the tailfin and said, "Where else but in America could a tree trimmer from St. Louis with a ninth grade education finance a $2,000,000 car and run it 17 times at an average cost of $75,000 per run, built by a butcher who only had a *hobby* of engineering and driven by a man whose school teacher had lifted him out of his seat by his cheek as a youngster saying that he would never amount to anything?"

Chapter Two Closure

Don't ever pour cold water on somebody's dream. And, for heaven's sake, never pour cold water on your own. *An organization will never rise above the quality of its leadership.* Once again, the 10 most prominent characteristics of the great leaders I've studied:

1. A High Standard of Personal Ethics

2. High Energy

3. Good at Working Priorities

4. Courageous

5. A Committed and Dedicated Hard Worker

6. Unorthodox and Creative

7. Goal Orientation

8. Inspired and Contagious Enthusiasm

9. Staying Level-Headed

10. A Desire to Help Others Grow and Succeed

A final question: On a scale of 1 to 10, how do you stack up on each of the characteristics and what's your total score? Would your employees give you the same score? If not, consider the possibility *you* might be contributing to the friction in your organization. Subscribing to these 10 qualities of effective leadership will not only make you a better leader when the heat's on, you will also become a calming agent for your staff by never picking up a hot horseshoe for the second time.

Chapter Three

The 1st Step– Team Building When the Heat's On

"Gettin' good players is easy. Gettin' 'em to play together is the hard part." —CASEY STENGEL

Rising above the Pettiness

Are you afraid to hire someone who is better than you? Many managers are. Yet the greatest leaders go out of their way to recruit premier talent. It's logical. The organization won't get better any faster than the leader does, and one of the signs of good health in leadership is the willingness to applaud the accomplishments of others. If others are never allowed to soar any higher than the manager does, then there will always be a lid screwed tightly over the organization's potential and the potential of every individual in the organization.

In any organization where the manager refuses to hire anyone better than she or he is or to allow anyone to receive higher acclaim, there will surely be the odor of pettiness. Effective leaders are big enough to permit others to be bigger than the leader. I'm not recommending you abandon your charter as the head of the organization and attempt to displace the responsibilities that are rightfully yours. Instead, I am stating that any leader who has the qualities you just read about in Chapter Two will be eager to hire the best and to get the best out of everyone she or he hires. Many people assumed I must have recruited top talent by raiding other companies in order to achieve the tremendous success my number one sales office achieved. You've already heard their stories. Do your people have any less potential?

This chapter on team building is one of the most important in the book because building the best team possible is the very foundation of effective leadership. There are many aspects of team building to be covered. In addition to building a good team, there are the tasks of establishing effective communications, focusing the organization, and laying the foundation for motivation. The down pressure you feel from above can be relieved in large measure by getting a quality team firing on all cylinders; likewise, the up pressure from below can be reduced or practically eliminated by a well-functioning staff, free of disruption and friction.

View from the Shoulder

The victories belong to *everyone* in the organization. How often have you seen a football team charge over to their bench after winning the big game, hoist their coach onto their shoulders, and parade around the field? It's a ritual after a particularly meaningful victory. But look closer. A bunch of players, sweaty, battered, and bruised after sixty grueling minutes of punishing competition, run over and hoist up a person who hasn't carried the ball one time or made one tackle in the entire game.

What's wrong with this picture? The way many managers think, if they were to allow their team to go out and perform tasks they themselves are not capable of, the team would charge his or her office following a victory and demand to be carried on the boss's shoulders. But that's not how it works. The team still comes to the leader and lifts him or her up to celebrate the victory.

Damage occurs and hostilities erupt when the manager expects or, worse yet, demands that the team honor him or her for something *they* have accomplished. You never see the football coach demanding to be lifted onto the players' shoulders. Can you imagine the coach at the postgame interview taking all the credit for the victory? How would that make the players feel? Would they play nearly as hard for that coach ever again? I doubt it. Nevertheless, organizations frequently *heat up* as a result of friction between those who deserve praise and applause and those who attempt to steal the spotlight.

Fostering a Genuine and Generous Exchange of Regard

It's an up pressure issue as well as a down pressure issue and one of the most complex tasks facing any leader. People don't care how smart or talented you are. They really don't. What people care most about is your attitude toward *them*. Only after you have established credibility, based on genuine regard for others, will others extend the same regard for you as a leader. Humility and equal regard are the ingredients for quality leadership. A fire extinguisher to battle the flames of jealousy and suspicion would be better filled with the genuine ability to build other people up.

A leader cannot effectively clone him or herself. The ultimate result of a "make everyone just like me" approach is disaster. Cloning effectively eliminates most of your available human resources by reducing a broad range of talent and enthusiasm into a narrow universe of paranoia-engendered people who would think to attempt such a thing as cloning in the first place. It's simply a waste of terrific people. I ought to know. I did it!

How Not To Fan the Up Pressure Flames

There are many ways to create friction in the workplace. Some you have control over and some you don't. Demands from above for increased performance at reduced costs always tend to raise the temperature. These edicts from on-high are very much like being told to run the engine hard, but not being given the money to buy oil.

Share this experience with your team. It's vital to let them know that *you* know the demands are difficult, if not impossible, but you'll be right there along side of them to confront the challenge and experience the victory, no matter how great or small, while the entire organization pushes the envelope together. It's exciting when individuals and organizations break through self-imposed barriers. Major directives from above are really nothing more than challenges to your organization's self-imposed barriers.

Remember whatever the leader has is contagious. If the leader has a case of panic-scramble-for-survival, then everyone else is going to be infected. Some of the many ways leaders typically exacerbate up pressure while reacting to down pressure include:

1. Attempting to force square pegs through round holes

2. Rubbing people's faces in perfect failures

3. Abandoning ship while the crew fights the fire

4. Criticizing honest effort that comes up short

5. Questioning the loyalty of the team

6. Threatening the team with loss of jobs

7. Playing one person against another

8. Allowing favorite people to goof off

9. Taking credit away from those who deserve it

10. Not listening to input from the team

11. Not publicly accepting responsibility

   This list could go on and on. Anyone with any experience working in an organization, large or small, and in either a leadership or a support role, has surely experienced these and other transgressions a thousand times. I know I have. Sadly, I must admit that, on too many occasions, I was guilty of pouring gas on the fire with my conduct.

Turning Down the Down Pressure Heat

As leaders, we can turn up the heat above us as well as below us, making things uncomfortable for everybody. By the time my boss came to me with smoke coming out of his ears to say that he was looking for my replacement, my staff had been severely burned already. Let's look at how to turn down the heat.

10 Sleepless-Night Questions

Getting better so your people can get better is an ongoing process. The following list of ten questions will help you focus on how the dynamic between leader and staff is actualized. Try to push back the limitations of self-imposed barriers as you honestly answer these questions.

1. Either I'm in charge of my organization or outside influences are. Which one is it?

2. If my people would be as good at their jobs as I am at being their leader, how good would they be?

3. I know my employees will improve as they see me improve as their leader. How much improvement have they seen in me in the past twelve months? The past six months? The past month?

4. If one of my people would ask me to describe my own personal plan for growth as a leader, what would I say?

5. On an individual basis, how does each of my people feel after a conversation with me?

6. As a whole, my people get as much out of their time as I do as their leader. How are we doing?

7. The people in my organization have their future with me planned as well as I have mine planned with them. How far into the future is that?

8. My people are committed as much to the success of my organization as I am committed to the success of *each* individual. How much is that?

9. My people take as much pride in working with me as I take in having them work with me. How proud are we?

10. When an organization succeeds, the leader stands in the midst of the group and says, "They did it!" But, if the same group *fails*, the leader must stand out front and say, "I am responsible." Am I willing to accept that responsibility?

Contrasting Definitions of Leadership

Many people prefer to talk in terms of *management*. I prefer to reduce management to its more basic component of leadership. Management, of course, must include some amount of leadership. The pattern seems to be that the less effective one is as a leader, the more one immerses oneself in "managing." As I previously mentioned, you aren't truly leading until those people under your leadership award you that rank. Until then, you're merely managing. I formerly subscribed to a very traditional definition of management that went like this:

Management Is Getting the Job Done through People

This definition places a higher value on getting the job done than on the success of the people involved. A fiery, Type A-personality boss would find no fault in that. To managers like him or her, employees like Dagwood are as replaceable as spark plugs. Employees are like tools to be selected for whichever job is appropriate. The job is supreme. The employee exists to serve the job. If the job suffers, the employee suffers more. You've heard the tales of searching out the innocent and punishing those who were not involved.

Not any more. Times have truly changed in that regard. The *new* news that really *isn't* new news at all is, when the people aren't led properly, the job suffers. It's always been that way. Management was simply not in the mood to accept responsibility. The new employee we hear so much about needs to trust the people he or she is going to work with as well as the organization itself. Employees are much too valuable to treat like interchangeable parts. When they soar, so does productivity. The pivotal point between people soaring and people being shot down is the quality of leadership they receive.

Think for a moment about how differently the concept of trust positions the leader and the individuals in the organization. Successful employment for each individual depends in large measure upon the trustworthiness of the leader, which is trustworthiness as a person. Most managers are used to asking if an employee is trustworthy. What a switch it is for the shoe to be on the other foot. Yet that is where the responsibility belonged all along.

I confess that Danny Cox was one of those managers who was using people as a tool. I would pull them out of the tool box to get a job done and then toss them back into the tool box until I needed them again. It's not hard to see why I was taking my office down the tubes. I systematically deprived my people of their humanity by devaluing their individual and unique identities and talents.

Shortly after my boss told me he was looking for my replacement, I coined a word I use to this day: *humanagement.*

Humanagement

Humanagement is quite simply the ability to use the job to develop the person while having fun in the process. Instantly, my entire emphasis changed and I stopped *managing* my people like a bunch of livestock and began *leading* them as people. It occurred to me I could help each individual unlock the talent he or she had inside, as well as to:

1. Set more meaningful goals
2. Better understand and plan *their* time
3. Use more of *their* creativity
4. Better handle *their* stress
5. Feel safe pushing *their* envelope

If I had an office full of happy, growing people, I thought, there's no telling what we could accomplish. Sure enough, when they began taking a new and enriched mind home at night, instead of a sore, tired, and aggravated one, our entire universe expanded beyond anything we would have previously thought possible.

Don't forget the ". . . while having fun in the process" part of my revised definition. By that, I don't mean you open the office with a joke every morning. My experience has proven time and time again that people who grow and develop to the point where they can handle problems they would not have been big enough to handle in the past are happier people. They are happier because they are more fulfilled and actualized as human beings. When an office full of people becomes more fulfilled and actualized, morale goes up. I've never seen it fail.

With high morale comes low staff turnover. With low morale comes high staff turnover. With low staff turnover comes more bonding and team spirit. With high turnover comes suspicion and a lack of personal investment in the job. It's difficult to settle and get comfortable if your probability for losing your job is high.

There are the managers who swear their organization has a terrific atmosphere, but people leave because the money is not competitive. On the other hand, there are those bureaucracies where people stay forever even though they are miserable. The latter organizations are so corrupt and inefficient, they couldn't stay in business without some type of monopoly on the business they do. People tend to murder each other in inefficient and corrupt businesses.

In both cases, nobody is having any fun. People are leaving the first organization because they're not happy, not because they can make more money elsewhere. I know there are exceptions to everything and a significant difference in money is more likely to make the difference. However, the Hawthorn Experiment, along with subsequent employee surveys, indicates working environment and intraorganizational relationships are valued more highly than wages.

You'll recall that, in the Hawthorn Experiment, management was testing various light levels in the production facility to determine if productivity could be enhanced. The unexpected finding was that management coming out into the production facility to interact with the staff there had the impact of enhancing productivity.

I encounter situation after situation where people will actually work for less in an organization that provides them with a place where they enjoy working. The antiquated notion that all employees ever want is more money simply doesn't hold. The value of having fun on the job ranks above money. The ability to enjoy the work and the working environment is a stronger hold on people than higher wages in an unpleasant job and environment.

Is the Manager Happy?

You might not enjoy your job as manager. Many people who accept management positions actually long for the good old days when they loved what they were doing. The tragedy is that they inadvertently allowed themselves to be promoted away from the rewarding activity they used to enjoy. This very practice of promoting people beyond their "comfort zone" produces a crust of unhappy and somewhat resentful managers setting a new, downbeat tone for those who are still enjoying what they do.

Those managers who recognize they've been caught in this trap can remedy their situation in a couple of ways. First, they can acknowledge what has happened and attempt a return to that which made them happier in earlier positions; or second, they can engage in learning new and effective leadership skills that will bring new vitality to their management position. They should *never* simply accept the leadership role and then grumble about it. Nor should they attempt to do their old job from the manager's office, thus pulling the rug out from under others in the organization.

All Eyes Are on You

All of this ties in with what was discussed earlier about your attitude as a leader being contagious. I really believe that nobody in your organization is going to enjoy their job more than you do as their leader. They will try. You often see renegade bands of merrymakers attempting to liven the place up. But if the experience of truly enjoying the workplace and all of its relationships doesn't emanate from you, the leader, it will eventually rain on everyone's parade.

As your people watch you for clues and cues, a new level of self-correcting staff supervision begins to develop. The old Golden Rule comes into play just as naturally as falling off a log. People begin to give *themselves and each other* the same type of attention and support you give them. What does this mean to you? *It means that the up pressure is eased off!*

The Horizontal Advantage

Believe it. Your people can become virtually self-regulating. They will solve problems among themselves they formerly brought to you. Wouldn't it be nice to hear your people talk in solutions instead of problems? They will even go so far as to police one another if the team has reached a high level of cohesion. Those who build each other up and support one another can and will hold each other to higher standards of ethical conduct and productivity, without you having to be the cop.

People who have never seen an organization function like a well-oiled machine might write such scenarios off as fairy tales. But, take it from me, horizontal organization produces higher productivity than vertical organization in almost every business environment. Of course, *you* are responsible for protecting against the possibility of cliquish elitism, where the stronger people band together to exploit the weaker folks. However, there is little chance of that type of thing happening in a well-balanced organization.

For now, be aware when you see a bunch of happy folks burning up the track, with the leader at the wheel and the staff hitting on all cylinders, odds are you're looking at a well-balanced and self-regulating organization. A super-successful organization is one that has surely blown through self-imposed barriers. It's a cinch the leader isn't sitting on everybody's lids.

Three Characteristics
of an Effective Organization

Creativity

These days, many businesspeople hear the word "creativity" and automatically think of finances in the same way that "stretching" used to be something you did during exercise. That's not what I'm talking about. The creativity at the top of the list of organizational characteristics refers to the originality of thought and execution which are becoming increasingly necessary in today's business arena.

When the heat's on, chances are the same old way of handling situations just won't cut it any more. In fact, it's often the same old routines that got us into trouble in the first place. Down pressures are changing in nature and intensity. Up pressures are coming from the rapidly changing dynamics of a workforce with a new identity. If we lack originality in our thinking and behavior as leaders, we're obviously oblivious to the vise slowly closing on us.

Creativity in thought and action is necessary to stay at the head of the game as well as to avoid being overtaken by problems. Creativity is the steam that powers the locomotion of progress. Mark Twain used to tell the story about the train that was so slow they moved the cow-catcher from the front and mounted it on the caboose. You see, the train moved so slowly there was little chance they would overtake any cows. However, there wasn't anything to keep a cow or two from climbing aboard from the rear. Creativity will keep you and your organization moving along.

Energy

Any effective organization has a certain energy you can sense as soon as you enter its office. Even if there is only one person sitting in the office at the time, you will still be able to feel it. The thought might even pop into your head that this might be a fun place to work.

By the same token, when you walk into the other kind of office, the one with low or no energy, you feel that too. It's almost like walking into a big refrigeration unit. The chill almost makes you feel like shivering. Even if there is only one person sitting there at the time, the sensation is there. Some offices might as well have a sign on the wall that says, "Fun is forbidden. Anyone caught enjoying what they're doing will be punished." Where there is no fun, there is no energy.

Change

Change is what happens when you mix creativity and energy. An effective organization is a changing organization. I don't say that the other way around because it is possible for management to change the look, the staff, the location, and a thousand other things about an organization in an attempt to artificially produce effectiveness.

The problem is change which does not emerge from a healthy combination of creativity and energy will look, feel, and taste synthetic. I've never heard of the chef getting a compliment on rubber chicken. Creativity combined with energy produces change from *within* the organization. Changes imposed from the fringes of the organization feel like impositions. Changes from within are self-regulatory and attentive to the realities of the day. Impositions are irritating.

Building Blocks of an Effective Organization

There are four basic components that need to be present in the foundation of any effective organization. Each of the four needs to be present in order for the foundation to be strong enough to support the organization's future growth. The four basic components of an effective organization are:

1. A sense of urgency
2. A commitment to excellence
3. A healthy discontent for the way things are
4. An appreciation for the awesome responsibilities of leadership

A Sense of Urgency

Right now, I'm extending my arm four to six years into the future and plucking something out to give you. Here it is: the Yellow Pages from the future. For some people, it's the stock exchange index or Dunn and Bradstreet directory. For many, it's the company organization chart. The question is, are you listed? In what capacity? Are you surprised at what you see?

If you have a sense of urgency about growth and effectiveness as a leader, you and your organization should be in a prominent position. If you don't, chances are good you might crash and burn by then and there won't be a trace of you left. Your attitude, shaped by your sense of urgency, will be largely responsible for producing the results you're looking for.

A Commitment to Excellence

We live in the age of the consumer. The greatest businesspeople throughout time have been consumer-oriented. However, the consumer's power today is so great that any business which fails to be responsive will surely perish. Thanks in large part to the media, the heat on business is turned up a few degrees by the fact consumers are increasingly *aware* of their power.

Our society assumes the consumer is entitled to fair value for his or her money. As consumers ourselves, we strongly defend this notion. Yet, in this climate where business is guilty until proven innocent, the pressure is on leaders to avoid living a double standard or requiring their people to compromise their ethics. It shouldn't be the threat of exposure that motivates us to service our customers' needs.

A pervasive desire to do the right thing, beginning with ourselves and permeating every personal and professional relationship we have, marks our commitment to excellence. Remember the ethical model where the best choice benefited the greatest number of people for the longest period of time? That makes excellence a goal we never fully achieve and, hopefully, never stop pursuing. I think everybody's grandmother said at one time or another, "If it's worth doing, it's worth doing right." That's good leadership advice, Grandma!

A Healthy Discontent
for the Way Things Are

A healthy discontent is like a little burr under the saddle making it slightly uncomfortable to sit back and stop leaning forward. When Walt Disney told his people not to rest on their laurels, it was because he was a leader who understood the consequences of complacency. Constantly looking for new directions and ways to improve what we're doing doesn't need to spoil the pride and sense of accomplishment we deserve to feel after a job well done. But we must continue to grow in new directions.

Walt Disney illustrated the need to constantly scan the horizon for growth opportunities when he resisted his advisers' urging to produce a sequel to the enormously successful *Three Little Pigs*. They pressured him and he reluctantly agreed. After the sequel turned out to be a box office bust, Disney called his advisers together and announced a new law that is heard around the Disney organization to this very day. He simply told them, "You can't top pigs with pigs."

An Appreciation for the Awesome
Responsibilities of Leadership

When someone comes to work for you, he or she is essentially laying his or her life on your desk and saying, "I trust you and I trust this organization to do right by me and my family." That, my friend, is a heavy responsibility. For example, if that person wastes a year or two of his or her life, that's time that will never be recovered. It's gone.

People's lives should be enhanced and opportunities should abound for them and their children because they had the good sense to come to work for you. Working successfully with you can mean a college education for the kids or simply an overall quality of life they might not enjoy in other circumstances. Your effectiveness as a leader has a long reach into people's lives. You must never forget that.

A Challenge for You

If I were to say that, for the next five years, you would not be allowed to hire any new people, would you rethink how you lead the people you have? If no new blood was allowed to enter your organization, could you continue to grow and prosper? You bet you could! If you truly faced a moratorium on hiring, I have no doubt you would begin discovering some diamonds in the rough.

Your new discovery does not indicate the diamonds weren't there all along. It indicates that you, the leader, haven't been sufficiently motivated to uncover them. You will be amazed at the untapped potential in your people if you look at them through different eyes and fully own the long reach you have into their lives. All of us have room to grow.

Three Steps to Growing As a Leader

Learn and Clearly Visualize How Successful Leaders Think and Act

This is the reading and studying I've been harping on. The difference is you shouldn't wait until your boss comes in and tells you she is looking for your replacement. If I had known then what I know now, my boss never would have had occasion to come in and set my pants on fire.

The way in which others successfully handle pressure can be an education for you that helps to insure you'll never have to experience similar situations. When we observe someone who never seems to be on the hot seat, it might well be that, while we were scrambling around with our nose to the grindstone, that person's head was up where he could look around and learn a thing or two from other people's experiences.

A head that's up and looking around means:

1. Reading books, magazines, and newspapers

2. Attending seminars

3. Gobbling up audio and video training tapes

4. Taking to lunch people from whom you can learn

5. Monitoring your own people for things you can learn

When I was having such difficulty in my sales office, it came as no big surprise that none of my people wanted to come to my sales meetings. However, I heard there was a car dealer down the street who had terrific sales meetings. People came out of his gatherings full of enthusiasm and excited about their jobs and each other. I had lunch with that car dealer.

Begin to Do What Successful People Do

It's not enough to merely study. True learning is the *application* of knowledge. Putting successful techniques into practice is when things get exciting for everybody. Keeping all of your great new knowledge in your head won't do a thing but make you an educated failure.

I speak three to five times every week, all over America, and I don't think I have ever been in front of an audience that didn't have at least a few educated failures. Some of them possess enormous amounts of information about the latest leadership methods, yet they're still failing. They sometimes ask me with a certain cynical smirk on their faces, "What's the point of all this leadership babble anyway, Cox? I've been coming to these seminars for years and I read all the new books. But nothing ever changes in my organization."

When I ask them how many of the new techniques and strategies they have incorporated into their organization's daily routines, it's like a light bulb switches on in their head. Isn't that true of most all of us? Isn't there a gap between how we do our jobs and the way we know how to do our jobs? I can't tell you the number of times that thought has popped into my head. You know, the one that says, "I know I can do this job better than this."

My advice to educated failures is to "use it or lose it." It's no use cluttering their minds with information they don't intend to use. It's better to focus on applying the most basic of the concepts they know. If they do, energy and creativity will take care of the rest. The content of our intentions will determine the content of our results. We must do what we know in order to know what we're doing.

Develop Leadership Characteristics

The following list of characteristics is a report card on your effectiveness as a leader. I established this list in the last chapter. It appears here as a tool for grading your effectiveness. Grade yourself 1 through 10, with 10 being highest, in the first column and, when you're finished, I'll tell you what to do in the second column.

1. A high standard of personal ethics   _____   _____
2. A high energy level   _____   _____
3. Good at working priorities   _____   _____
4. Courageous (willingness to take risks)   _____   _____
5. Committed and dedicated to hard work   _____   _____
6. Unorthodox and creative   _____   _____
7. Goal oriented   _____   _____
8. Inspired and contagious enthusiasm   _____   _____
9. Realistic and level-headed   _____   _____
10. A desire to help others grow and succeed   _____   _____

TOTAL LEADERSHIP SCORE   _____   _____

Now that you have scored yourself, go back and score yourself again the way your people would rate you as a leader. If you're gutsy, you might want one or more of your people who has read the last chapter to do the rating. Whether the two scores match or not, the score your people give you is the real one. That's right. We're only as effective as our people's perception of us.

Fortunately, I didn't have such a report card to circulate at the time my boss was looking for my replacement. If I had, my personal self-rating would have been substantially different from the rating my staff would have given me. They might have coined the phrase "less than zero" long before it ever became a movie. In retrospect, I must admit theirs' would have been the accurate rating. The rating the staff gives their leader is always the most accurate measure of effectiveness.

Who to Hire

Mavericks. Hire as many strong people who make things happen as you can. The people I'm talking about are sometimes referred to as "hard to work with" or "hard to control." I'm not saying to create chaos. You already have a good system to guide your leadership process. With the ten leadership characteristics as your guiding pillar of fire, you can lead some pretty wild folks successfully through challenging times.

When building a new team, the selection process is guided to some degree by what jobs you need handled. That is the easy part. Deciding who is the best to handle the job and/or who is going to contribute the most to the team's effort is more difficult. To determine someone's compatibility with you as a leader and the balance of the staff you will select, I suggest you use the 10-step report card you just used for your personal evaluation. You might wish to rewrite your own version of what constitutes a great leader, but the point is your criteria need to be consistent for *everyone*.

Whether you are assembling a new team or adapting an existing group to a new leader or a new assignment, consistency in your announced values is critical. In short, I'm suggesting is that you look for the same qualities in new people you expect from yourself as their leader. Are you cloning yourself? No. You're simply setting forth what you believe constitutes the highest ideals in business conduct and using those ideals as a *standard* measure.

If you're not afraid to hire people who might be better than yourself and you're big enough to encourage all of them to realize their full potential, you're on your way to building the most effective team possible. If you use a different report card for your staff than you do for yourself, you've created a double standard. The closer people come to realizing their full potential, the lower the up pressure on you and the greater the morale among your people.

Hiring, like most things, is largely a judgment call. More often than not, people tend to repeat patterns of behavior. For example, if a person has moved from job to job without much stability, it's likely he or she has yet to learn or put into practice some of the characteristics we've been discussing that would reduce that kind of inconsistency.

When interviewing new prospective team members or getting to know existing staff a little better, it's important to discuss specific issues relating to the 10 leadership characteristics. It's important to check references and get an accurate picture of a person's previous patterns. Then discuss that information with the new person and let him or her know you don't intend to judge them on past performance as much as how they intend to handle similar situations in the future.

You can learn a lot by how someone tells you they intend to behave. Someone who never intends to make another mistake is pretty naive or not realistic. I might suspect right away this could be a safe plodder and not the creative and unorthodox type I'm looking for. Suppose an interviewee told me, "Danny, when I get going, I'm likely to make a mistake now and then. But I would rather keep pushing hard than just kind of crawl along. I always try to learn from mistakes and rarely repeat them." I would probably hire that person and put him or her in the office next to mine so some of that enthusiasm might rub off on me.

The ideal team would score itself and each individual member, including their leader, high on the 10 leadership characteristics. There would probably be characteristics for each person that rate higher than the same characteristic for the leader. I would hope that to be the case in any organization I was leading. The synergy would be tremendous.

A Laundry List of Strengths

I've given you my *top* 10 leadership characteristics. Now you can browse through my laundry list of strengths I look for in people. The more of these strengths a person has, the more valuable I predict that person will be to the organization. I'm presenting it in checklist form so that, for hiring or assessment situations, you can have a record of any given individual's best qualities (see pages 60–61).

Recruiting Made Easy

When you've got a team that's really functioning well together, if they're hitting on all cylinders, your people don't want you to dump sugar in the gas tank or toss a wrench in the gears. They want things to run as smoothly and effectively as you do. Hiring is as important to the people on your team as it is to you as a leader.

Because of their relationship to you, as leader, and to each other on the team, your people become your best recruiters. Good people want to work with good people. Not only will your people encourage you to hire quality talent, they'll go out and find it whenever possible. Your people will actually talk you and the organization up through their own personal testimonials.

Lean on Me

That might make a good song title, but it's a lousy way to relate to your people. A good leader is not a person to lean on. A good leader makes leaning unnecessary. You should not lean on your people, nor should they lean on you. The latter is frequently the case when a manager only feels important when someone needs him or her. You know the type. They carry pagers everywhere, 24 hours a day, seven days a week. They thrive on solving their people's problems for them.

More bad news about managers who like leaners is that they tend to *hire* people who *will* lean on them. They encourage people to lean on them. The net result is these managers surround themselves with people who depend on them. What an important citizen that makes them! However, it makes the manager ineffective. In reality, the biggest problem is not the staff needing the manager as much as the manager needing the staff to need him or her. Situations like this deteriorate quickly into pettiness and the playing of little games.

Motivating the Team

Motivation is the by-product of desire. Desire and motivation can't be separated. To best understand how desire increases, and motivation along with it, I must point out there are three levels to motivation. The lowest level is *compliance.* Compliance is essentially doing something because you were told to do it. There isn't much motivation or personal desire in that. Character is not built at the compliance level. The second level is *identification with the goal.* Identification gives the individual some measure of investment in the goal and produces increased desire and motivation. The highest level of motivation is *internalization.* There is no greater commitment than when someone feels the goal is truly theirs.

LEVEL THREE → INTERNALIZATION → GREATEST MOTIVATION

LEVEL TWO → GOAL IDENTIFICATION → MORE MOTIVATION

LEVEL ONE → COMPLIANCE → LEAST MOTIVATION

There is no trick to getting people on level one. Simply order them around as if they can't think or reason for themselves and have no special ability or investment in getting the job done other than not getting fired. To help people reach level two, you must include them in why the job needs to be done and how it is in their best interest to do it well. When there is something to gain, people invest more. To reach level three, a person needs to understand why he or she is uniquely suited for the task. Not only will he or she feel there is a benefit for a job well done but, more importantly, he or she brings a part of himself or herself to the job.

Nobody in your organization will be able to sustain a level of motivation higher than you have as their leader. If a person rises above the leader's level of motivation and wants to stay there, he or she has to leave you and go somewhere else. Therefore, it behooves you to internalize the goals of your organization and build everyone else up to that level. I've heard it described as "organizing the energies around a goal." What a responsibility! What a challenge!

Techniques for Internalization

There are several things you can do as a leader to help your people internalize the goals of the organization:

1. Be an outstanding example as a leader
2. Give each person individual attention
3. Recognize and highlight individual growth

The Fence Technique

When my boss came in and announced that the search for my replacement was on, I did what any sane and logical manager would have done. I went to the beach. I went out to be alone with my thoughts and the waves and the sand. It was there, with sand between my toes, that it dawned on me. There was a barrier or fence in my organization. My people were on one side of the fence and I was on the other. With this revelation came my first major team-building technique.

There was only one uniting factor in all of the people on the other side of the fence. They all hated me. It wasn't a healthy bond, although it was a strong one. My challenge was clearly to reunite with my people and put an end to our segregation. I could have invoked the power of my position, such as it was, and *ordered* my people to join me on my side of the fence. However, that option immediately seemed hopelessly impractical. Experience had already taught me that yelling at people simply didn't produce cooperation.

Another option available to me was to crawl over to their side of the fence and try to recreate the wonderful camaraderie we had when I first came on board as the new sales guy and they took me under their wing. The most obvious problem with that approach was there wouldn't be a leader anymore. That seemed unacceptable. Being in their clique wasn't the answer. In fact, from a leadership standpoint, it was a bad idea all around. Then it came to me.

It occurred to me I was not going to reunite with all of my people at one time. At best, I was only going to earn their trust on an individual by individual basis. However, who to start with seemed like an important decision with implications down the line. My first thought was to go after the highest producer in the office. But something told me my intentions would be more subtle and less threatening if I were to begin with a solid, middle producer. A good, salt-of-the-earth-type person who would deal straight with me. More importantly, my solid, steady people in the middle wouldn't feel excluded by the attention I would pay to the superstar.

Finally, it dawned on me that the most influential member of the team was the person whom the others respected the most. It was a good, better, and best situation. The third choice ultimately made the most sense. Not the superstar. Not the middle producer. But rather, the person most respected by his or her peers. Generally, the most respected person is the one who has demonstrated dependability and consistency over time.

Using this new criteria, I rated my team members from the most respected to the least respected. Already, I was incorporating the values of my people into my thinking. The ratings I was using were really *their* ratings, not mine. So I went to work on the number one person on my list. Before long, that person was actually saying some fairly decent things about me. Why? Because that person was beginning to truly feel as if I was open and receptive to the team's way of thinking.

As I continued to execute my strategy, number two on my list softened, then numbers three, and four, and so on. Once the two or three most respected people take a more amicable attitude toward you, it becomes less important exactly who numbers five, six, and seven are. The attitude of the organization begins a natural transformation and, because it is the people in the organization who make the decisions based upon their own values, it is a healthy foundation for a transformed working environment.

When the process starts, the fire is raging and you're boiling in the kettle. If you've truly tuned in to the values of your people, they will come up one by one and begin to extinguish the fire. However, if you have merely tricked your people through some sort of manipulative ploy, you can bet that the fire will be rekindled, hotter than ever.

Your people vote every day to decide which side of the fence to be on. This is true even if you've been managing the same group of people for many years. They will get better just as soon as you do. The first ballot is private and the second is public. In other words, each person decides secretly on which side of the fence he or she feels most comfortable. It's a personal decision. Then, when the staff is working together, they poll each other and the group makes a corporate decision. Initial decisions are not permanent. People who decide to join you can drift away again. Your efforts to involve them *must* be genuine.

How to Focus on Strengths if You're Used to Focusing on Weaknesses

For each person in my organization, I made a list of what I perceived to be his or her weaknesses. You see, weaknesses in my people were the easiest for me to get in touch with because I had spent so much time concentrating on them. As human beings, we all tend to spot weaknesses first. It might be because we hear those things pointed out to us constantly from our earliest childhood.

When it came time to write down the strengths I saw in each person, I got stuck. Whatever had made me a weakness finder had all but blinded me to strengths in others. I figured there must be *something* good in each person.

So I took it as a personal challenge to identify strengths. It wasn't easy at first, because the harder I thought, the more my thoughts would return to weaknesses. Before long though, I got one.

It might have been mathematical ability, loyalty to the company, a good sense of humor, an appreciation for the finer things in life, and so on. Things I wouldn't have necessarily associated with strengths on the job began to add up. I began to realize the things which added strength to a person as a whole were strengths he or she could apply to his or her job. My focus began to shift. The old dog was learning a new trick. Once I realized how many strengths a particular employee had that weren't being recognized or put to use in our organization, I was bursting at the seams with enthusiasm the next time I talked to her. Don't think that she didn't notice I was enthusiastic about *her!*

Another person ceased to hate me with a passion. Why? Because I reflected back to that person the things that were important and valuable to him. What he thought and felt became my priority in place of ramming my priorities down his throat. When have you ever heard anyone say they hate someone because they feel understood and respected? As I touched upon earlier, it's a natural human tendency to like someone who shows an interest in you. Your interest in that person might be the only thing the two of you have in common. But there is no stronger common bond.

We can transplant hearts and other vital organs from one person to another, but we can't transplant strengths. Each individual has to develop his or her own. If each of us had a gauge that showed how much potential we have available versus how much has been developed, I'm convinced we would have a new lease on life. There would be hope and enthusiasm everywhere.

We must be *aware* of the weaknesses. That's why it is important to make lists. Furthermore, you'll keep adding to your lists over time. The same is true of strengths. As more and more strengths develop and become apparent, your list will grow. A word of caution: *The responsible leader does not leave these lists lying around the office.* Use your head. This is an exercise for you and you alone. Keep your lists at home.

However, don't just make these lists; *use them.* Learn to do the most important thing you can ever do with people—communicate with their strengths.

Communicating with Their Strengths!

My greatest and almost fatal failure early in my professional life was to communicate with people's weaknesses. It wasn't uncommon for me to be heard saying, "If I were you . . ." Of course, nobody ever heard the end of

A Laundry List of Strengths

____ Active	____ Hard-Working
____ Aggressive	____ Health-Oriented
____ Ambitious	____ Helpful
____ Analytical	____ Honest
____ Anticipates	____ Humor
____ Appearance	
____ Appreciative	____ Imaginative
____ Articulate	____ Impressive
____ Attentive to Detail	____ Independent
____ Aware	____ Industrious
	____ Influential
____ Believable	____ Innovative
____ Bilingual	____ Inspirational
	____ Intelligent
____ Capable	____ Interested
____ Character	____ Interesting
____ Cheerful	
____ Civic-Minded	____ Judgment
____ Communication	
____ Confident	____ Kind
____ Conscientious	____ Knowledgeable
____ Consistent	
____ Cooperative	____ Likable
____ Courageous	____ Likes People
____ Courteous	____ Listener
____ Creative	____ Logical
____ Customer-Oriented	____ Loving
	____ Mannerism
____ Dedicated	____ Mature
____ Dependable	____ Motivated
____ Determined	
____ Dynamic	____ Open-Minded
	____ Optimistic
____ Eager	____ Organized
____ Educated	
____ Efficient	____ Patient
____ Ego Drive	____ People-Oriented
____ Empathy	____ Perceptive
____ Energy	____ Perseverance
____ Enthusiastic	____ Planner
____ Ethical	____ Poise
____ Experienced	____ Polite
____ Extroverted	____ Positive Thinker

A Laundry List of Strengths

____ Precise	____ Spirited
____ Professional	____ Stable
____ Punctual	____ Successful
____ Qualified	____ Tactful
____ Quick-Thinking	____ Tenacious
____ Reliable	____ Thoughtful
____ Resilient	____ Time Management
____ Resourceful	____ Tolerant
____ Reputable	____ Trustworthy
____ Responsible	____ Understanding
____ Sales-Oriented	____ Upbeat
____ Scrupulous	
____ Self-Assured	____ Versatile
____ Self-Discipline	____ Vitality
____ Self-Starter	
____ Sensitive	____ Willing
____ Service-Minded	____ Witty
____ Sincere	____ Youthful

that statement. Why? Because I was not them and they were not me. Therefore, the comment is irrelevant, no matter how well intended. When I began opening up my comments by saying, "With your strengths . . . ," suddenly people listened and listened close. It worked. It was exciting to see production absolutely turn around.

If you feel as though the thrill is long gone out of your leadership position, I *guarantee* if you will commit yourself to identifying and developing the strengths in your people, you will experience a resurgence of excitement in your career. I have found nothing more professionally stimulating than encouraging growth and development in my people.

The only time you get to work on your people's weaknesses is *when they want you to.* Any attempt on your part to work on their weaknesses before they're ready is wasted time, both yours and theirs. Rest assured, though, they will come to you for assistance with their weaknesses after you have done a good job communicating with their strengths.

A Case in Point: Dinner with Bugs Bunny

One of the best illustrations of hidden strengths I ever heard came out of the most unlikely situation. The late maestro of character voices, Mel Blanc, was having dinner at my home a few years before his death.

Mel is known for his four hundred or so voices, including Bugs Bunny, Daffy Duck, Elmer Fudd, Foghorn Leghorn, and so many others. On this particular evening, the conversation ran toward an automobile accident which had nearly cost Mel his life a few years earlier.

Following the accident, Mel was brought to the hospital unconscious and remained that way for several weeks. Doctors repeatedly attempted to get a response from him by asking if he would lift a finger, squint his eyes, or in some other way acknowledge he heard them trying to communicate. He never responded. The doctor's hopes were fading, when one day, a physician on his rounds visited Mel's bedside and began reading his chart. Not really expecting a response from Mel after all this time, the doctor mumbled, "Let's see how Bugs Bunny is doing today."

To the doctor's amazement, Bugs Bunny answered him. The line couldn't have been more classic. "What's up, Doc?" came the rabbit's familiar voice. True story. I got it straight from the rabbit's mouth. According to Mel's account, the rejoicing doctor said, "Say it again, Mel. You're back." There was no response. After several more attempts to communicate with Mel, the doctor got a hunch that it wasn't Mel who had responded to him earlier. So he said, "Bugs, how's Mel?" Sure enough, the voice of Bugs Bunny came out and said, "He ain't so good, Doc."

Before the evening with Mel Blanc was over, I had shared with him the substance of this team-building concept. He agreed his experience was relevant in that the doctors kept trying to communicate with Mel Blanc, who was almost killed in the car accident. Bugs Bunny didn't get a scratch. Mel pointed out there were over four hundred strengths inside of him just waiting for somebody to talk to them. When someone did . . . Bingo!

Try this Exercise

Everyone in your organization has strengths inside, just waiting for you to talk to them. There is no telling how helpful they can and will be to you once you become aware of them and talk to them. Peter Drucker pointed out that strong people will always have strong weaknesses. When you think about it, that's only logical. Show me a successful person and I'll show you someone with a few chinks in his or her armor. Drucker then went on to stress that *focusing on strengths makes demands on performance*.

In other words, don't try to force a square peg through a round hole. Force only makes things worse. In fact, *that's where most of the heat comes from in high-pressure situations*. The fastest and most effective way to cool off hot people and heated situations is to seek out and then speak to the strengths of the people involved.

To illustrate what Drucker was talking about, I often set up a situation where you and I are working in a local auto repair shop. We repair automobiles for a livelihood and I'm your working manager. I'm working on my car in the stall next to where you're working on your car. One day, you walk into my stall and say, "Danny, I've got a problem. I've got a one-half-inch bolt here and I need to borrow your adjustable wrench." It always seems that the manager has an adjustable wrench.

If I am a weak manager, I will go ahead and loan you my adjustable wrench. If I'm a pathetic manager, I will go ahead and do the job for you. The healthy leader will recognize what is ultimately the best for you and, consequently, what is good for the organization, and assist you to locate your *own* half-inch wrench. Once that is accomplished, chances are good you will never come back to your manager in search of a half-inch wrench again. The next time you encounter a half-inch bolt, you will be equipped to handle it.

The intelligent leader will do whatever it takes to insure both parties are aware of how many tools are available to get the job done. It's not good enough that the leader knows or has a strong sense of what your strengths are. *You* must recognize your strengths as well. If you are not aware of your strengths, how can you use them fully? If you are not aware you have certain strengths, you might go looking to borrow someone else's strengths, like borrowing the one-half-inch wrench from your boss. When we understand this about ourselves, we are better prepared to help our people understand it about themselves.

It's Like Being a Plate Spinner

When my boss announced that the search was on for my replacement, I realized I didn't even have a good visual concept of what an effective leader looked like. The more I learned in my crash course, the more I began to visualize a leader as the plate spinner on the Ed Sullivan show. You've seen those performers who have 30 or so poles and proceed to keep a plate spinning on the point of each one.

There are a couple of parallels between the plate spinner and the effective leader. The first is the decision to spin plates at all. Nobody I've ever heard of ended up on stage in Las Vegas spinning plates by accident. He or she decided to attempt it. I'm also convinced that practice over time makes a person better at plate spinning, just like experience over time helps leaders become more effective.

Then comes the selection of the plates. A manager might select the best plates possible. The smoothest, best balanced plates with the lowest friction factor will get the manager's attention. But there are only a couple of plates with superior qualities. What about the empty poles down there? Too often, the manager settles for plates that simply *look* like the better ones. I call that hiring warm meat with a pulse. It's not a healthy and fair practice for you *or* the warm meat.

When you put plates up on the poles that never should have been there in the first place, whose fault is it when they don't spin as well as you would like? You just created more work for yourself as well because you have to spend the lion's share of your time keeping those unbalanced plates going. The time you spend with them is quality time you could be spending to develop plates that were a better choice to begin with. Too often, managers allow pride to keep them working on plates long after both the plate and the spinner should have cut bait and moved on.

What spins the person's plate is *communicating with his or her strengths.* When you spend your time away from your strongest plates, you run the risk of losing them or, at least, losing their edge. By the same token, a plate spinner can't get all of the plates spinning and then stand back to admire the spectacle. Before long, the plates or your organization, as the case might be, will come crashing down. Absentee management doesn't cut it. The leader/plate spinner must stay involved and stay in motion to be effective.

Taking an Employee's Eye View

As I rebounded from having one foot in the grave at one point in my career to eventually becoming a first vice president with that organization, I became increasingly creative. Strangely though, my people were not always excited about my terrific new ideas. To them, my great new ideas often were nothing more than additional work and complications. I *thought* my people would love the change of scenery. But I wasn't considering their point of view.

You might have seen the illustration of the tennis ball which is one color on one side and another color on the other. When you hold it up to show someone, you see the color that's facing you and the other person sees the other color. You can't see the other color until you place yourself where that person is or turn the tennis ball around.

Once I realized this, all the brainstorming and creating of new ideas had to include scrutiny from as many perspectives as possible. We would send staff on retreat from time to time to simply examine new ideas from as many angles as possible. We wrote all of the perspectives down and discussed them. Contrary to what many managers believe, they are *not* smarter than their people. If the manager is smarter than his or her people, then that manager hasn't staffed the organization very effectively.

If you're struggling with up pressure in your organization, a method for instant relief is to put your own point of view on hold for a time and genuinely examine your people's point of view. Even if you don't go along with them, feeling that their point of view has been given authentic consideration will ease tension.

As you examine all points of view, give your staff the credit they deserve for knowing their jobs and having the intelligence to know what works and what doesn't. All of your wonderful and creative ideas aren't worth any more than the level at which your people buy into them. As I mentioned earlier, nobody enjoys working on the lowest compliance level of motivation.

Letting Others Have Your Way

An effective leader really attempts to become as familiar as possible with how the people in the organization think. Here's the formula for getting a handle on how others process information: INPUT—EVALUATION—RESPONSE.

Input

The input the leader provides to the organization's thought process will influence the conclusions reached. The better the quality of the input, the more effectively you will influence the conclusions.

We are bombarded with input from the time we get up in the morning until the time we go to sleep at night. Radio, television, newspapers, magazines, billboards, and conversations with others are only a few examples of the data we're given to process each day.

The challenge to the effective leader is how much and what type of input to give people to help them understand the merits of the leader's thinking.

Evaluation

Next, you must allow your people to evaluate. The jury must be allowed to go out and deliberate on their own. If you keep their feet to the fire, they will not feel their conclusions are truly their own and will not invest themselves in the new ideas.

Give them good input and then give them time and space to process the information by mixing it up with their own thoughts and feelings. Everyone has a *Now Filter* that will prejudice his or her perspective. A person suffering from jet-lag will respond to the same input differently when he or she feels better. So the question often becomes, *Is now the best time to give my input?* Timing is important.

Knowing your people well is valuable in avoiding common mistakes, like giving a "morning person" a big frog to swallow late in the afternoon. All of us have unique features and it doesn't require a tremendous amount of scrutiny to figure them out. That's what listing strengths is all about.

The *Memory Movie* follows the now filter. The input is run through the now filter to determine how, in this moment, it should be received and processed. Once it is, our minds automatically submit the input for a memory check to determine if we've ever encountered anything like this before. If the input data has been experienced before, the memory movie will play back the experience, complete with how favorably or disfavorably it is recalled.

As a leader, you have the ability to not only turn another person's memory movie on, but to direct it as well. Think about John Wayne. See? I just switched on your memory movie and took you to a precise memory at the same time. Any input will trigger and potentially direct a person's memory banks. Sometimes this is necessary to help focus your organization.

Response

We use *imagination* to answer the question, "What am I going to do with the input I've received?" Will we use the input, ignore it, or what? If the leader delivers well-considered input, the people in his or her organization are likely to creatively put the input to use in ways that are consistent with the leader's goals for the organization.

The more effective a leader becomes over time at *hitting people's buttons*, or positively influencing their decisions through good input, the more cohesive and effective the entire organization becomes. The ability to deliver quality input is an acquired skill that improves with experience. However, if you understand the process, you're light years ahead of someone who is blindly stumbling across the truth.

More on Now Filters and Memory Movies

Influence can be negative as well as positive. I was flying with a guy once who knew how I thought. He flew in the back seat as a radar observer and really knew how to hit my buttons. Now that I no longer fly, I can confess that I used to spend quite a bit of time flying my supersonic jet fighter *inside* the Grand Canyon. As it went, I was playing cowboy one day, darting in and out of the maze of caverns and canyons.

I leveled off just above the canyon rim and noticed a steel tower ahead and to my left at the edge of the canyon. I kept my eye on it and asked my radar observer if he had any idea what it was. In his coolly calculated voice, he said he didn't know but there was another one just like it on the opposite side of the canyon.

The wings nearly tore off that jet as I yanked the control stick back into my belly to change our course from straight and level to straight up. We were pulling about a million G's when I noticed there was hysterical laughter coming from the back seat. A quick glance to the right revealed there was no twin tower as my now hysterical radar observer had reported.

He knew all too well how to switch on my memory movie and direct it. My memory check immediately recognized his input as high-power lines and my imagination kicked in to not only create the nonexistent second tower, but to string the nonexistent cables between them and visualize the disaster as I flew straight into the wires.

What did I do with the input? I took evasive action, much to his delight. He exerted tremendous influence on my behavior through extremely simple, but effective, input. This guy wasn't through with me though. On final approach to a base in New Mexico sometime later, he got me again. I tell you this story because it's fun and also to illustrate that we're *always* vulnerable to erroneous input.

I had never flown into this particular base before and wasn't familiar with the area, so naturally I was more cocky than usual. That 79,000 horsepower goes to your head pretty quickly. At any rate, as I turned onto final approach, I noticed some people standing beside the runway. I called the tower to confirm that I was on the correct runway. The controller in the tower that day was as cocky as I was. He said the people were a surveying crew but, if I needed a wider runway, he would try to find one for me.

That's all it took to get my attention. Everyone has their weaknesses and their Achilles heels and this tower operator had just found mine. You can do many things to a pilot he or she will ignore and let roll off of his or her thick skin, because, after all, pilots are bred to coolly handle crises. Just don't cast aspersions at a pilot's ability to land his or her aircraft. That's crossing the line. The controller knew it. My ego was now on a mission.

I felt I had no choice at that moment but to execute the most perfect landing ever witnessed by that tower operator and the surveying crew next to the runway. It felt as though my entire career, as well as the reputation of the entire United States Air Force, depended upon the precision of the landing I was about to make. However, I sealed my own fate by telling my radar observer my intentions. I told him my landing was going to be so perfect that we would have to ask the tower if our wheels had touched down yet.

There we were on short final and everything was perfect. My chest was swelling in anticipation as we approached the end of the runway at 220 miles per hour, which is about 10 miles per hour faster than the Space Shuttle lands. You had to fly those beasts down back then. I used to refer to my 20-plus-ton aircraft as a supersonic manhole cover. So we were moving right along as we crossed the numbers and a smile crept across my face. The air speed was bleeding off perfectly as we settled closer to the runway. Tears of joy began to form in the corners of my eyes.

We were about ten feet off the deck, only moments from the sweetest touchdown in history, when my radar observer made his move. "Danny, are you sure you put the landing gear down?" I panicked. Instead of gently kissing the runway with my tires, I *struck* the runway with my landing gear and bounced, not *once* but *three times*. Once again, my radar observer nearly wet his pants laughing. But he wasn't through.

As I taxied off the active runway, he said, "Danny, do you want me to log all *three* of those landings?" He could no doubt tell I wasn't amused because he tried to console me by saying, "If nothing else, you just impressed that surveying crew with how strong the landing gear is on an F-101."

Input—evaluation—response. In the two stories I just told you, I received input, I evaluated, and then I *reacted*. Kind of a knee-jerk reaction to be more exact. Please note that on *both* occasions, I set myself up to be victimized by his devious input. If I had used my *now filter* a little more judiciously, I would have placed myself in a better position to *respond* more appropriately.

The more familiar you become with your people, the better you are going to understand how they filter the *now*, what is stored in their *memory movie*, and how they are likely to *respond* to the input you provide. The effective leader is one who is sensitive to each of his or her people on each person's level of evaluating and responding to data. A good leader also recognizes that pressure and heat often stem from inappropriate input. We can take a potentially enormous amount of heat off of ourselves as leaders by paying more attention to the input we provide to those we report to and those who report to us.

"You're Fired!"

Never use those words. However, you will inevitably need to terminate people from time to time. So far, we've discussed the various aspects of building and developing a good team. There is no question how vital good people are, just as there is no question how vital effective leadership is. We've laid the foundation for effective communications and opened a discussion of motivation, which will be continued as we move into the next chapter on goal setting.

Whereas it is important for an effective leader to hire people who are better than he or she is, it is necessary to terminate the employment of those who can't or won't fit into the organization. It might sound contradictory for me to say this after suggesting you hire unorthodox and unconventional people. In attempting to assemble the best and get the best out of those you assemble, sometimes people wind up in your organization and it's simply not in their own best interest nor the best interests of the organization for them to remain.

At times, the individual simply doesn't know what he or she wants to do, but his or her attitude and productivity continue to defy any effort you can make to bring him or her into line with the rest of the organization. At other times, people are simply disruptive and won't respond to your counsel. Whatever the specific reason, it is incumbent upon the leader to determine when a person no longer belongs in the organization. Knowing you have explored all avenues to give this person a fair shot at adapting to the organization helps to reduce the guilt and anxiety that invariably accompany the termination of an employee.

It's also helpful to keep the goals and best interests of the organization and its people at the head of the issue, lest you begin to believe it's a personal issue with you. Where I grew up, we jokingly said, "You can't teach a pig to sing. It wastes your time and irritates the pig." There is some solid wisdom there. When you spend an inordinate amount of time trying to bring someone along, you are taking time from your good people and unnecessarily duplicating efforts.

When someone is simply not right for the organization and vise versa, nobody benefits. The leader's effectiveness is diminished, the person's coworkers are negatively influenced and the organization as a whole suffers. When fruit trees are pruned, they are sometimes cut back so severely the tree appears damaged. However, in time, you will observe a fuller and more productive tree than before. So it is with people and organizations. It may seem severe and harsh to let someone go, which is exactly why so many situations that call for termination are allowed to go unresolved for too long. Yet clean and precise farewells benefit both the organization *and the individual* over the long haul.

Hence, the Steps to Termination

Once you've decided to let someone go, follow a few simple guidelines that will help both you and the person you're terminating.

1. *Be discreet.* Out of respect for the individual, don't broadcast your intentions. Keep your agenda as private as possible. Ask for the individual to come see you at the end of a workday so he or she won't have to leave your office and face curious coworkers. Pick a time to terminate the employee when he or she can most quietly make an exit. Help the individual preserve his or her dignity in an emotionally vulnerable moment. A termination must be done in total privacy and in a climate of maturity.

2. *Be clear.* Don't chatter when the person comes to see you. Immediately state clearly that you have decided to let that person go in the best interests of the organization. You can even begin by saying, "As of this moment you are terminated." Don't engage in a debate with the individual. Your decision is the result of a carefully thought-out process and much consultation, even with the individual involved.

3. *Be honest.* State how you honestly feel. Stick to general terms in explaining the reasoning behind the decision. Assume part of the responsibility as a leader for the individual not meshing with the organization. You will no doubt be convinced the individual and the organization will benefit by parting company, so admit you believe in the decision. Wish them the best. But remain mindful of the best interests of your organization and the individual.

4. *Be brief.* Don't try to soften the blow with lengthy dialogues about this or that. You will probably achieve the opposite result. A termination is not pleasant for anyone involved. Brevity is kindness. Give complete information, but only necessary information. When the essential task has been completed, *stand up* and end the meeting.

5. *Be open.* Let the rest of the organization know what you've done and why you decided to do it. It's harmful to let the terminated person's former coworkers stew anxiously over what happened and why, hoping it won't happen to them. Keep everyone's eyes on the prize and you will no doubt be supported in your actions by the rest of your people.

Now that we've covered team building, it's time to move on to how *goals* focus your team's efforts and how advanced *motivation* propels the organization forward.

Chapter Four

The 2d Step–
Goal Setting When
the Heat's On

*"No person can lead other people except by
showing them a future. A leader is a merchant
of hope."*   —NAPOLEON

Eyes on the Prize

Whether the heat you're feeling is caused by down pressures, such as tightened financial demands, or up pressures, such as working conditions, you are likely to feel as if you're a firefighter attempting to lead a group of people safely out of a burning building without getting burned yourself. The attraction for you and the people you are leading is the promise of a future that's better than the moment.

Leaders truly are merchants of hope. Whether acting as individuals or in concert with others, we must intend *toward* something. Our natural tendency in high-pressure situations is to run *away from* whatever is troubling us. Effective goal setting changes our focus from that which we're trying to avoid to what it is we want to achieve. There is an enormous difference. Thoughts about what we're trying to avoid tend to be negative. Thoughts about what we want to achieve tend to be positive. Negative thoughts weaken us. Positive thoughts energize us.

You've heard all of the metaphors before. One of my favorites is the ship setting out to sea without a destination. It would be hard to be an effective leader and earn the trust and confidence of the crew and passengers if you had no idea where you were going. Up pressure would surely mount with each passing day. Attempting to lead an organization without well-established goals is like setting out to sea without a destination. Another thought that expresses a similar thesis says if you don't know where it is you want to go, any road will get you there.

The Real Reason Why *You* Work Hard

How do we fall into the avoidance trap? Have you ever found yourself not wanting to do some aspect of your job but *knowing* you had to do it? I recall feeling that way when I was prematurely ejected from the Air Force and found myself knocking on doors as a civilian trying to earn a living. Fortunately for me, I had a guy who took me under his wing. Everyone in the office warned me about this guy. They said he was meaner than a bear with a sore toe. Yet he was the one with all of the trophies and the plaques. I later began to suspect some professional jealousy, once I learned what that was.

One morning, he walked by my desk and said, "Danny, let's go out and knock on some doors." I didn't tell him how much I detested knocking on doors. Instead, I did what any reasonable person can be expected to do. I lied. I told him I just had too many things to do in the office. "What things?" he demanded. I wasn't ready for that one and babbled about this and that, but not very convincingly. He cut me off by asking, "What could be more important than finding somebody out there who needs our help and is willing to pay well for it?"

I had to admit I couldn't think of a thing more important than that, at least not without a little more time to think about it. He said, "Come on, then, let's go." I agreed to go, but he got to the car faster than I did because, while he was walking, I was dragging my feet. I still didn't want to go out "prospecting." But off we went. He sat proudly behind the wheel of his gold Cadillac Eldorado in his custom-tailored Italian silk suit looking every inch a success. By contrast, I was slumped into kind of a heap in the passenger seat.

As we drove, I asked, "Was there ever a time when you didn't want to do this? Be honest with me 'cause I'm about ready to throw in the towel." He told me he knew how I felt. But I didn't believe he could have ever experienced the kind of doubts I had at that point. Then he proceeded to describe the physical symptoms of doubt and anxiety, including the sweat on the upper lip, the queasy stomach, the weak knees, the tongue sticking to the roof of the mouth, and so forth. The shocker came when he told me he had felt that same way *only 20 minutes earlier!*

I immediately suggested we both go back to the womb-like safety of the office, reasoning that we had nothing to offer anyone given our pathetic emotional disposition. He replied, "Danny, that was twenty minutes ago. I don't feel that way now." Naturally, I asked him how he managed to climb out of his fear. "If I were to give you $500 right now," he asked, "what would you do with it?" I replied that I would pay bills. "Wrong!" he thundered. I knew right away my answer wasn't what he was looking for.

Being the quick study I am, I took another quick stab in the opposite direction. "I would have *fun* with it," I offered. Now we were connecting. "What would you do?" he asked. "Oh, I don't know," I stuttered. "What would you do?" he demanded. Obviously, I was losing the trail of his thinking again. It occurred to me he wanted me to be extremely specific about what I would do with the $500 to have fun.

As we drove, he nudged and prodded me to explain in great detail how I had been wanting to attend the air races in Reno, Nevada. The more vividly I pictured my pleasurable experience, the better. I described the airplanes and what they sounded like as they roared by. I described the hotel I wanted to stay in because of the balconies from which you can watch the sunsets over those rugged Nevada mountains and the lights of the city at night. He pressed me to describe in great detail my favorite restaurant and the terrific steak dinner I remembered getting there, right down to the freshly baked loaves of bread.

He then asked me to figure out what my commission would be if I could get a listing that day and sell a house. In those days, my share of the commission would have been just about $500. The difference between this man, who was the picture of success, and me at that moment became clear. Long before Tom Peters was ever commercially published, I had a blinding flash of the obvious. I just didn't know what to call it at the time. My associate *knew what he was working for* while I was just wandering out that day to see if I could get lucky.

That thought was worth a few sleepless nights for me. He had opened my eyes. As leaders, it's important to understand the value of helping our people open their eyes. If they only see through our eyes and not their own, it's easy for them to lose sight of our vision. However, once they have seen a personalized vision through their own eyes, they won't lose sight of it as easily, even when their eyes are closed. When people get in the habit of working on personal goals, they will automatically work on company goals.

Now Spread the Word

The vision we invite our people to share with us is the future as it best suits the organization and the people who make up the organization. Like Napoleon said, helping your people experience the future through their own eyes is critical to effective leadership.

Do you know what you're working for? Can you see it in great detail? If you can't, how can you help your people to see what they're working for? Helping your people truly see what they're working for is one of the greatest, life-long gifts you can ever give them. After the exercise in visualizing a piece of the future I was really working for that day, my associate asked how much money it would take to take my trip to Reno. "$500," I said. He then asked why I was so anxious to stay at the office that day and forfeit the $500 and my trip to Reno. He told me to think of what I would say to my wife that night if I were to go home and explain why I felt it was more important to stay in the office than to earn a trip to Reno for the two of us. I said, "Could you drive a little faster?"

In an automobile ride that couldn't have taken more than 15 minutes, my attitude had acquired new depth like drilling a well into an underground pool of hope and promise. I found energy and enthusiasm I never knew I had. The same will happen to you and your people when you learn how to embrace the future. Remember, motivation is a by-product of desire. Desire is present when we identify with the goal. My mistake had been to equate my hard work with paying bills. As a result, my hard work was about as much fun as paying bills.

The great twentieth-century philosopher, Alfred E. Newman, said, "Most folks don't know what they want but they're pretty sure they don't have it." Leading your team blindly without clear goals renders all of your sophisticated navigation equipment useless. Being driven by a sense of dissatisfaction with the present is not enough if there is no clear course established. This is to say a clearly charted course is the second best thing to a distinct goal. At least with a clearly charted course, you and your organization know in which direction you want to go. You are intending toward something, even if the something is not well-defined at the moment.

Go Boldly Where You've Never Gone Before

I can't tell you how often I've thought to myself, "I don't know where I'm going, but I am making good time." When I realized we can cover a lot of ground and make good time while going in circles, my appreciation for goal setting increased. The tragedy in too many organizations is that, in repeating yesterdays, they never make any progress. Management might crack the whip and increase the speed with which the organization moves around in circles. Management might attack the innocent by replacing the entire staff, only to set the new staff out on the same old track. Management will typically try this and try that, stopping every once in a while to scratch their heads and wonder why nothing's working. Unfortunately, managements that doesn't understand the obligation to be merchants of hope will scratch their heads bald before they figure out why, every time they set out for tomorrow, they end up at yesterday.

Every time such an organization reaches the crossroads, it takes the same wrong turn. As I touched on earlier, we know yesterday is safer and less threatening than tomorrow. So, without admitting it consciously, many of us might fall victim to *avoiding mistakes* rather than *breaking new ground*. This is why it's a natural tendency for people to repeat unproductive and uncomfortable behaviors. Rather than intend toward something unknown but promising, we feel *safer* repeating the familiar. The familiar might not be pleasant, but we know we can deal with it. When you see someone going boldly where no one has gone before, you're watching someone who is either courageous or lost.

Will your goals always live in someday? Before defining specific methods and techniques for effective goal setting, it's important to establish that goals must be achievable. The entire organization must believe the goals the leader helps to establish are attainable. Talking about goals without achieving anything reduces a leader's credibility and the organization's enthusiasm.

A Quick Session of Questions and Answers

I know a guy who graduated from not one but two reform schools as a youth. You could say he was twice as reformed as the next guy. His life is straightened out now. He made two multimillion dollar fortunes in two separate fields. He says he had a personal challenge to succeed in a second field because he didn't want people to say the first one was just luck. When I asked him how he did it, he replied that he, one, asked himself some questions and, two, *listened to the answers*. We can ask ourselves questions all day long, but do we really listen to our answers? Listening is the key. These are the questions he asked himself:

1. What do I really want?
2. What will it cost?
3. Am I willing to pay the price?
4. When should I start paying the price?

Question four is where the rubber meets the road. Answering the others is easy. If the time to start paying the price is *someday*, then the first three questions are moot. Someday never comes and dues to be paid someday never get paid. Scheduling your start date on someday insures you'll never get started. The time to start is every time you stand at the cross roads. The way to start is to take the road to tomorrow and not the one to yesterday. The only acceptable answer to question number four is *now*.

Okay, So Let's Deal with Why Not

Many people complain to me saying, "But, Danny, I've got problems." I'll buy that. So let's take a look at these problems and see how they fit into the goal setting picture. *Goals should not be just new things somewhere in the future, but a commitment to solve past problems that persist.* Many people tell me they had goals but they never reached them. When I ask why not, they say they aren't sure, but they remember feeling like their feet were nailed to the floor. When I ask what nailed their feet to the floor, they point to the problems they continually experience.

Pulling the Nails out of Your Feet

That experience tells me our first set of goals should be the elimination of present problems. Does that mean we're focusing on the negative past and trying to move away from it? No. I'm suggesting we focus on a future, free of the problems that plague the present. In short, we should intend toward pulling the nails out of our feet and moving forward.

Planning in order to merely *avoid disappointment* causes goals to be set too low. If a plan doesn't fail from time to time, you're probably playing it too safe and need to aim a bit higher. A buddy I used to fly with banged up an airplane pretty good once. He was okay so we kidded him about the incident. I'm glad we did because his response has stuck with me ever since. He said, "If you don't bang one up every now and then, you're not flying fast enough."

I do a seminar for major corporations called *Managing the Manager.* However, that's not the correct title. I intentionally misnamed the seminar because, if I had named it accurately, my clients wouldn't let me near their people. The seminar would be more accurately titled, *How To Pull Nails Out Of Your Feet.* I especially enjoy this particular seminar because it's a real boat rocker. By the time the seminar has ended, I know I've rattled their cages and they probably won't sleep for two or three nights after I leave.

Because it's strictly a high-level management seminar, only the top four to eight executives attend. The scene is always the same. We meet in the plush executive boardroom. The executives are dressed in expensive suits. The president sits at the head of the table. You get the picture. As the meeting begins, I turn to the president and ask if the company conducts problem-solving meetings. He invariably replies that this very group meets on a weekly basis in this very boardroom. Sometimes their problem-solving meetings last all day and they have food brought in.

I ask if anyone else attends. The president usually thinks a moment and then says there is always a secretary present to record the minutes of the meeting and distribute them to everyone attending. I ask if these minutes are kept on file. Everyone acknowledges their meeting minutes are filed away. I ask if everyone could go and fetch their minutes from last week's problem-solving meeting. Everyone begins to get up. I stop them and ask that they bring not only last week's minutes, but also a copy of minutes from six months ago, a year ago, two years ago, and so on.

Everyone sits back in their seats. By this point, it's obvious that, without saying it directly, the organization continues to cover the same territory again and again. The same problems are addressed over and over. They reach their crossroads every day and repeatedly turn down the road to yesterday. Such redundant behavior is so common in business I wouldn't be surprised to find a chapter on how to be redundant in business textbooks. Redundancy is as much of a common thread through American business as the profit motive.

A Problem by Any Other Name

We must all continually ask ourselves if we've been working on the same set of problems too long. Since this isn't a question we're used to asking *or* answering, it will be helpful to first examine what the term "problem" really means. The dictionary states that a problem is a perplexing question or situation, especially when a solution is not clear. That definition is very broad and will apply to most "problems" as we understand them. So let's move on to a self-inventory that will help each of us identify what we individually consider to be problems.

1. What is my biggest unresolved problem in *life?*

2. What am I doing about it?

3. If I'm not doing anything about it, *why?*

Who's Working on Problem Number One?

Believe it or not, I constantly do programs for companies which don't have an answer for the third question. If I ask what the company's biggest unresolved problem is, I'm often told that massive turnover in the sales force is considered the most threatening. I quickly ask who has been assigned to work on that problem and I'm told just as often that *nobody* has been assigned to work on the company's number one problem. The company can identify what its primary problem is, yet it has taken no action to specifically address it. This scenario is extremely common among the companies I deal with. Sometimes the company will throw someone at the problem until that person is reassigned or quits. But as a rule the problem is not being attacked, even though it has been identified.

Upon closer examination, I usually discover the company's efforts are being used to address problem number 13 or so. Problems number one through 12, it seems, are considered just too difficult or scary to approach. In most cases, the problems the company spends most of its time addressing are the most comfortable ones. I'd swear some people get their Ph.D.'s in worrying and stewing. They are really good at it. When I say, "What would you do if I could snap my fingers and resolve those problems?," the worriers get a panicked expression on their faces. Without unresolved problems, what would they do? The company wouldn't need them any more if there weren't any problems to worry about and stew over. Many people truly believe that unresolved problems represent job security.

A friend of mine asked me those questions while I was still flying fighters. He was at *my* house, eating *my* food, and still had the audacity to challenge me by asking what I thought my biggest unresolved problem was. Question one wasn't all that threatening so I told him that sonic booms and all the uproar they caused in the community were at the top of my list. There seemed to be no limit to the volume (in either sense of the word) of complaints caused by sonic booms.

Then my friend nailed me. "What are you doing about it?" he asked. I really couldn't come up with a very good answer because, at that time, the Air Force wasn't coming up with a very good answer. I finally said what I hear so many companies saying today, "We're just trying to figure out how to live with the problem." After a blinding flash of the obvious, I took it upon myself to become the sonic boom salesman I told you about in earlier chapters. I created that job and then filled the vacancy. There wasn't a line of people waiting to apply for a job selling a concept with as high an objection factor as sonic booms. I was the only applicant.

Intending to play on the locals' sense of patriotism and national defense, I entitled my 30-minute presentation "Better Boomed Than Bombed." I spoke to Rotary Clubs, Lions' Clubs, Elks' Clubs, churches, schools, and anyone who would have me. The first half of my presentation was always pretty well received. Before long it occurred to me why my audiences began getting restless at about the half-way point of my presentation. It was just about then they figured out I was not only the salesman for sonic booms, but also a distributor. They got that unmistakable look that said, "He's the one." It took every ounce of convincing I could muster to wave the flag in their face, play the Star Spangled Banner, and close with the Battle Hymn of the Republic before they could tar and feather me.

Believe it or not, I got tremendous gratification simply experiencing the effort of doing something about a problem I had a hand in creating. It's safe to say that most of us know the emptiness of leaving things unresolved. However, anyone who has had the experience of swallowing the biggest, ugliest frogs knows how liberating it feels to be part of the solution.

Learn to Distrust Effortless Solutions

There are none. Solving problems requires effort and investment. I think of effort as simply gritting your teeth and going for it. Working hard at something you love doesn't mean forgetting to work intelligently. I'm not suggesting you attack problems like a bull in a china shop. You should always bring the best of your experience and abilities to bear on resolving troubling issues. However, the most important component to your solution is when to make the effort. The answer to that is *now*. Another self-inventory helps to bring us to *now*:

1. Is your year planned out? Have you specified your professional and personal goals? Are your vacation times blocked out?

2. If not, why not?

3. When are you going to start?

I don't know about you, but, without asking myself tough questions and insisting on honest answers, I'm likely to find myself in a nursing home, unable to care for myself, still wondering when I'm going to begin realizing my full potential. That's what answering question number three with "someday" will do for you. *Today* is when we need to make the investment that will get us where we want to go. *Now* is not a moment too soon to begin. Authors and business consultants Al Ries and Jack Trout talk about the need for immediacy in terms of *Monday morning*. Their challenge to leaders at retreats and seminars who identify problems and set goals is, "What are you going to do about it *Monday morning?*"

As leaders in hot situations, a little historical research will usually confirm we're in hot water largely due to neglected problems and unresolved issues. Taking a look back through our daily planners will reveal how much time we scheduled to attend to tasks directly related to goal setting and fulfillment. While we wait for problems to go away on their own or for an easy solution to miraculously appear out of nowhere, a river of opportunities is flowing past us. There will be no special day when fireworks go off and sirens sound to announce it's time to safely set out toward your desired goals in life. Please trust me, that day never comes. You might as well get down to business now or grow old waiting on life's sidelines.

There's No Escape from Neglect

By *not* setting specific goals for your organization and your personal life, you actually *are* setting a goal to not realize the potential within you and your organization or to enjoy the things you like most from life. In the random selection of the universe, the odds are extremely remote you'll stumble across the opportunities and conditions under which your dreams will be fulfilled.

There are no magic mornings when it all comes together and no fairy godmothers to wave their wands and make it all come true. Failing to set goals is equal to believing in the mythical phenomena I just described. This all might sound to you like motivational hype, but I don't know of any line of reasoning that has more practical value. If you don't like to be accused of believing in fairy tales, then give me a logical argument for why your goals have been neglected.

Concentrate on Effective Goal Setting

Dr. Alexis Carrel once said that "Life leaps like a geyser for those who drill through the rock of inertia." Goals are the drill bits that cut through the rock of inertia. The more exciting the goals, the faster they penetrate. If goals are the drill bits, then self-discipline is the drive shaft. Dr. Carrel went on to say that, "Self-discipline is always rewarded by a strength that brings an inexpressible joy. Therefore, goals that motivate us have gifts for us in the form of accomplishment."

If a look back through your daily planner doesn't reveal much conscious effort toward setting and achieving goals, then how about a look ahead? Do the future entries in your daily planner reflect a more concerted effort to devise and execute an effective plan for the balance of the year? Anyone who answers "no" to those questions is practicing what I call an *on the ropes* style of management.

These managers allow all sorts of fires to break out and then expend all of their energy chasing them and putting them out. Because these people feel so overwhelmed with continual crisis, they are likely to tell you they simply don't have the time to spend on planning and goal setting. Instead of being *on the attack*, these people are *on the ropes*. Instead of being *on their toes*, these people are *on their heels*. Instead of operating from a *position of balance*, these people are continually *off balance*.

Remember your modeling relationship with the people in your organization. If the leader is operating off balance, on his or her heels and on the ropes, how can the rest of the organization be reasonably expected to operate any differently? The goal: adopt behaviors to infect your entire organization. I stated earlier that your organization is going to get whatever you've got, good or bad, and that idea is certainly no less true for goal setting.

Accept the Risk and Face Up to It

There's an undeniable risk in goal setting. However, the risks are far, far greater if you don't set goals. By not setting goals, you're truly leaving the future of your personal and professional affairs completely to chance. Going into the office each day to "see what happens" is a greater risk than going in and attempting to carry out a well-thought-out plan, no matter how ambitious.

It's impossible to grow and realize new potentials if nobody pushes the envelope. Pushing the envelope is what risk-taking is all about. Behind every major breakthrough is a series of perfect failures. It wouldn't hurt any planning session to routinely ask the question, "Are we pushing the envelope on this?" It's even better still to ask, "Am *I* pushing my envelope?" In fact, I would recommend you put it on your wall. If you find that you are never answering "yes" to that question, then you shouldn't be surprised if your organization doesn't seem to be growing or going anywhere.

Three Steps to a New Reality

A *new reality* is an *achieved goal*. We are headed into the future at the same rate the second hand sweeps around the clock, whether we like it or not. We can't hold back time. So, given that the future is coming, how are we endeavoring to shape it? What are we doing *now* that will leave our mark on our future? Here are my steps to shaping a new reality:

Visualize Your Goal Vividly. You must clearly see what you are intending toward. Generalizations about your intended goals do you no good. The greater the clarity of your vision, the more focused and efficient your efforts toward it will be. The more diffused your vision, the less efficient your efforts will be. I don't know of anyone who wants to waste effort.

Break Your Goal Down into Do-able Daily Tasks.   When goals loom enormous on the horizon, it's natural to feel intimidated and to become reluctant to even approach them. Be realistic about what a human being can accomplish in a day and don't expect any more of yourself or others. Realizing goals is far less dramatic this way, but you will get there eventually.

Act on Your Goals Every Day.   I don't mean you should work seven days per week. But don't let a workday go by without even a small step that moves you closer to your goal. Progress is progress, no matter how small, and the feeling of accomplishment is just as sweet in many small doses as it is in one large one. However, the feeling of disappointment at never achieving the big goal will not be minimized by breaking the task down into smaller disappointments. A goal is like a dream and an unrealized goal is no more than a fantasy.

Guidelines for Goal Setting

Goals should be:

1. Measurable
2. Realistic
3. Challenging

Time divisions for goal planning:

1. *Short-term goals* range from the immediate to one year.
2. *Mid-term goals* range from one to five years.
3. *Long-term goals* are more than five years.

The goal planning process:

1. Make a written list of your goals and divide them into the appropriate *short-, mid-* or *long-term* categories.
2. Establish a *time table* for each item. If the steps seem unreasonably large, break them down further. Don't fall prey to the myth that a goal that's not achieved by an exact deadline is no longer worth achieving.
3. Concentrate on *results.*
4. Begin and *don't stop.*
5. *Celebrate* when a goal is achieved and *simultaneously* replace it with a new goal. If you forget to celebrate the dawn of a new goal, you and your

people are likely to experience a letdown. Something must always be out there to be anticipated if we're to keep the spring in our step.

6. *Evaluate your progress.* When? For personal goals, evaluate each year on your birthday. It takes courage to write yourself a letter outlining all of your goals for the next year and to seal it up to be read one year later. For your organization's goals, birthdays can be hourly, daily, weekly, monthly, and so on.

Some Common Roadblocks to Goal Achievement

The following roadblocks might be impeding your progress without you being fully aware of their presence. An effective leader is vigilant and monitors the organization for signs of frustration and loss of interest among the staff. When roadblocks are detected, there are several remedies available.

1. *Goals are not understood by everyone or seem unattainable.* First of all, if goals aren't understood or seen as attainable, better communication is called for. If due diligence has been adhered to in the planning process and the goals *are* understandable and attainable, clearer instruction and information is called for. It's critical that each member of the team understand and accept what is expected of him or her.

2. *The effort doesn't appear to have adequate rewards.* When rewards don't seem forthcoming or consistent with the level of effort required, it's time for the leader to start selling. Actually, the time for selling is when the goals are being established. If the team members feel the prize doesn't match the effort required, the leader must evaluate the equity of the situation and then either correct the imbalance or, if the effort and reward are in balance, frame the goals in such a way that the reward becomes clearer, thus increasing motivational influence.

3. *Procedures for goal achievement are too rigid.* Flexibility is one sign of a confident and creative leader. Too many people impose rigid structure on their organizations because they lack basic confidence in their own abilities and the abilities of their team. Focusing on results instead of methods will open the door for your people to contribute more of their own originality. Have the courage to let them run with the project and apply gentle guidance at most. Good people will develop good methods.

4. *Success is feared.* Many people are much more familiar with mediocrity than they are with success, and therefore lack the drive to pursue goals. Fear of success is natural if you have little experience with it. Remember my salesperson who was afraid to earn any more money than his

father? To contradict the frightening aspects of actually doing what your organization sets out to do, you can broaden the sense of accomplishment to include the whole team and reduce the uncomfortable spotlight on those who have a problem with attention.

More importantly, you can continually encourage your people through promoting personal growth. Helping people to push their personal envelopes will prepare them to not only enjoy success, but to expect it more often. Good coaching of the team will prepare them to enjoy winning. When some of the members of your team grow and expand their horizons, the others will notice and, hopefully, internalize that desire. A team that internalizes the expectation and enjoyment of success will become synergistically greater than the sum of their parts.

A Case in Point: Improving Company Productivity through Personal Growth

I know of a company that adopted these principles for goal setting and put them into practice. The result was an unprecedented increase in productivity. More importantly, the increases were not short-lived. The application of these principles established enduring improvements. Bear in mind these principles have broad implications and applications far beyond the world of business. Parenting and teaching are two of the most obvious applications that come to mind.

The leaders in this organization made a commitment to become involved with the personal growth of their people, as we've already discussed. The leaders engaged in personal and consistent counseling. Without consistency or personal interest, the counseling efforts would have been meaningless. Many managers, parents, and teachers tend to get uncomfortable at the thought of personal counseling. They prefer to keep an arm's-length relationship and focus on bigger goals and accomplishments, or perhaps problems and other issues that shift the focus away from personal growth.

One reason these people, and you might be one of them, experience such discomfort is that taking a personal interest in the personal growth of another requires an investment in one's own personal growth. That other person isn't going to get any better until you do, remember? Facing one's own personal roadblocks can be downright terrifying. I know. I used to avoid personal growth issues with myself and others at all costs. Yet you can't become an effective leader without an investment in the welfare of your people. It simply can't be done. That's why courage is on that list of leadership characteristics I discussed earlier.

You should now have a clear image of a leader who is secure enough in his or her own personal growth to extend him or herself to others in order to help develop theirs. I'm not suggesting you remove the boundaries that separate a leader from others in the organization. Your roles are different. However, the principles which guide your conduct are not. There is no room for double standards in effective leadership. Likewise, becoming inappropriately close to your people on a personal level, such that you begin to lead a dual relationship, is not fair to you, not fair to the individual involved, and certainly not fair to others in the organization.

We dispelled the notion early on that people work primarily for money. This is where that knowledge is extremely helpful. If a leader doesn't demonstrate care and concern for the personal growth of his or her people, it's unreasonable to expect the individual to truly care about the best interests of the organization. You would be amazed at how many managers I encounter who think people work only to collect a paycheck. Nobody who thinks that way is getting as much out of their staff as they can. That kind of thinking leaves unrealized potential buried deep.

The sample company I'm referring to began with a very simple goal. They wanted to make each month more productive than the month before. They approached the goal on an individual basis. The individual goals were *measurable, realistic,* and *challenging*. Here are some of the specific techniques my example company used to build up their people:

1. Individual counseling sessions were held monthly between the manager and each member of the team.
2. Each individual's production was *never* compared to anyone else's production. The only issue was how much that individual had improved since the previous month.
3. When individuals had their best month of the year, they received a letter from the vice president. If every month was better than the previous one, those people had a lot of letters.
4. When an individual had the best month of his or her career with the company, he or she received a letter from the president.

I can already hear some executives saying, "I've got more important things to do than write letters to my people just because they earned more money for the company this month than last." To these executives I say, "Nuts!" There isn't any more important or productive use of your time than to help your people grow and develop. There is no more effective way to insure the growth and prosperity of your company. In a nutshell, that's what leadership's all about.

Refusing to get involved with people on that level makes me suspect an executive isn't in touch with his or her personal growth issues. The organization will get better as soon as the leader does. People love to break their own records, and I believe that applies to leaders as well.

Take the Time for a Personal Moment of Truth

If you want to test yourself and determine how strongly you are committed to personal growth and goal achievement, answer these questions as truthfully as you can.

1. What were my major goals in the past 12 months, both personally and professionally?

2. What were my major personal and professional achievements in the past 12 months?

3. Did my achievements match my short-term objectives and/or move me closer to my mid- and long-term objectives?

4. In what ways do I need to improve?

5. What do I need to do to improve?

6. What changes would I like to see in my personal and/or professional life?

7. What can I do to make these changes occur?

8. Which personal and professional strengths do I feel I'm not using?

9. What is my plan for growing as a leader over the short-, mid- and long-term?

10. What's my next step up and who will I choose as my replacement?

11. How do my peers feel about my reaching my goals? Are they correct in feeling that way?

12. My *next* step to achieving my goals is to _____.

If these questions are answered truthfully and you truly listen to your own answers, you can't help but be propelled toward improved goal setting and increased efficiency in fulfilling them. With that much truthful information about your personal and professional affairs, it would require a conscious effort to ignore the obvious and stay on your treadmill. The greater your ability to get in touch with your honest needs and desires, the more effectively you will be able to set and achieve meaningful and worthwhile goals.

My final thought for you on goal setting: if you don't have a goal, make finding one your first goal.

Chapter Five

The 3d Step— Time Planning for Higher Productivity

*You can transform something important into
something urgent, if you wait long enough. "*
—THE AUTHOR

Putting Time into Perspective— Words from the Funny, the Fictional, and the Philosophical

Robert Benchley was more than a great comedian. He was also bullish on human determination when he said, "Anyone can do any amount of work . . . provided it isn't what he's supposed to be doing at the time." There is a valuable management secret in that for all of us.

Want more wisdom? Henry David Thoreau said, "It's not enough to be industrious, so are the ants. What are you industrious about?" I think Andy Capp, the great twentieth-century British philosopher and cartoon character, said it best: "The trouble with time is that it disappears while you're trying to figure out what to do with it."

Want some prose to frame on your wall and help you live and work more effectively? Figure 5-1 is one of my favorites.

Another helpful insight from an anonymous source helps me to keep time in perspective:

If you had a bank that credited your account each morning with $86,400 carried over no balance from day to day, allowing you to keep no cash in

Today Is Here

Today is here, I will start with a smile and resolve to be agreeable. I will not criticize. I REFUSE TO WASTE MY VALUABLE TIME.

My time is equal to all others'. Everyone draws the same salary in seconds, minutes and hours.

Today I will not waste time because the minutes I wasted yesterday are as lost as a forgotten thought.

Today I refuse to spend my time worrying about what might happen. My time will be spent making things happen.

Today I am determined to improve myself so that tomorrow's opportunity will not find me lacking.

Today I begin by doing, and not wasting time. One week from now I will be more than the person I am today.

Today I will not imagine what I would do if things were different. Things are what they are. I will succeed with what I have.

Today I will not say, "If I could only find the time." There is no hidden time. I must take what's available.

Today I will treat others as if this were my last day on earth. I won't wait to be what I have dreamt about being tomorrow, for tomorrow never comes.

                                                              –Author Unknown–

Figure 5-1.

your account, canceling all unused funds at the end of each day, what would you do?

You have such a bank. It's called time.

Every morning, each person's account is credited with 86,400 seconds. Every night, each second not put toward a good purpose is canceled. Time carries no balance forward. Nor does time allow us to borrow against future allocations.

We can only live on today's deposit and invest our time toward the utmost health, happiness and success.

How many sports teams, who were defeated by a shot at the buzzer or a field goal with no time remaining, wish there was one more period to play? "If wishes were horses, then beggars would ride." The good news is we can all essentially gain that extra period by starting to play more effectively from the beginning. Time management is more about good starts than miracle finishes. Figure 5-2 lists some of my own thoughts on the birthplace of a brighter future. In addition, the following injunction was found in the pages of *Boardroom Reports:*

> All you can do with time is *spend* it or *waste* it. Find the best ways to spend available time and the appropriate amount of time for each task. Concentrate on the best ways to spend time, instead of worrying about saving it.

The skilled time manager I'm describing accomplishes 95 percent of his or her work in 25 percent of his or her time. He or she accomplishes a great deal and knows it. He or she feels comfortable with a slower, steady pace. These people have quality time for family and friends, as well as themselves, while finishing more quality work than others, who work longer hours at a more frantic pace.

Time and productivity are inseparable issues. Whereas a passive-aggressive type of individual might give us enough rope to hang ourselves with, the good Lord virtually always gives us enough time to correct our errors. We have all memorized the maxim, "There is never enough time to do it right the first time, but there's always enough time to do it over again." The truth in that statement hits me in the wheel house. How about you? Speed might not always kill (as the popular saying goes), but it usually will cost you plenty in the long run.

Doing it right the first time requires time planning, or darn good luck. If you're like me, good luck is a rare commodity—certainly not common enough to stake a career on. It has also been said that making your own luck is simply a matter of doing the necessary things in order to be ready and available when opportunity appears. In just a moment, I'll start listing those things necessary for effective time planning.

Birthplace of a Brighter Future

As I concentrate on each word of this thought, "now" slips by me into the past. My past is nothing more than a history of how well I dealt with each irretrievable "now." So if yesterday is history and tomorrow is prediction, only the present exists.

The future is nothing more than an approaching series of "nows." During each of those "nows" I will make a decision whether or not future "nows" will be different. A brighter future grows out of a brighter "now." Therefore, my future improves only as I make better use of the current moment.

It's the time remaining that counts. My willingness to accept responsibility for improving my time will determine the quality of the rest of my life.

The speed at which "now" becomes the past is staggering. Yet, if I commit my God-given strengths to improving each of these approaching "nows," the faith in my bright new future will be exhilarating! For I realize the same velocity that carries this "now" into the past can carry me at the same rate toward exciting moments of the future when ever increasing goals become reality.

A year yet to be is unborn, untarnished, and full of promise. One of those brand-new years, bright with potential, accomplishment, and joy, will be delivered to me tomorrow at dawn. My choice is to accept it as it is given or, through habit, mold it into the shape of years past.

The challenge is clear. The choice is mine.

Figure 5-2.

Why People Don't Plan Their Time

As a diagnostic tool, I first want to list some of the most commonly given excuses for *not* planning time so we'll all feel at home. More importantly, it's the meaning *behind* the excuses that helps us to understand how we often tend to get ourselves all tangled up.

1. "It takes too long." Which really means, "I would rather focus on a day-by-day or short-term basis."

2. "I don't have enough information to plan well." Which really means, "I might fail and failing would draw attention to me."

3. "It's impossible to predict the future." Which really means, "I would have to give up acting on impulse and develop new disciplines."

Four of the Biggest Time Wasters You'll Ever Encounter

In a recent survey of business managers, people named their own lack of time management for 92 percent of the failures among those under their supervision. This raises the ominous question, "How do managers waste so much time?" Several primary reasons top the list:

1. The most common contributor to wasted management time is *doing an employee's job for him or her.* This occurs much more frequently than we might think and can easily cost a manager one-third or more of his or her efficiency.

2. Another cause of lost productivity in management is *doing tasks that can be handled by someone with less responsibility.*

3. It's not uncommon to find a manager *spending a disproportionate amount of time on a "favorite" or "pet" project* at the expense of items which are more valuable to the organization as a whole.

4. *Repeating instructions* is another time killer. The lesson employees learn from this misguided practice is that they don't have to take action until the boss instructs them for the third time.

Let's never forget to turn lemons into lemonade whenever the opportunity presents itself. For example, the practice of favoring pet projects could be turned into a motivational maneuver by scheduling favorite activities at the end of the day or upon completion of another project or task.

The headline in all of this is:

MOST PEOPLE WASTE TIME THE SAME WAY EVERY DAY!

Minor Corrections for Major Improvements

The good news is minor corrections can mean major improvements. For example, if a manager figures out a way to save only 10 minutes every work day, that savings will total 42 extra hours gained at the end of a year. What would the bean counters say to cutting an entire week off of everybody's vacation every year? To them, that would represent one heck of an increase in productivity. All from just 10 minutes per day.

What are some of the most valuable expenditures of a manager's time? Training new people, for one. Equally, if not more important, is the continued nurturing and development of veterans within the organization. We must never forget our obligation, both to our people and the organization as a whole, to keep the furnaces stoked in our human "fleet."

Then there is planning for the future. Whether it's next week, next month, three years, or more down the road, a ship under a full head of steam isn't very useful to anyone if it has no destination. Seeking out new opportunities, challenges, and markets are productive uses of management time. How about establishing new personal and business goals? Organizing a better system for your business and your home? Creative and innovative thinking are time investments for a better tomorrow.

Would You Believe It If Peter Drucker Said It?

Peter F. Drucker, the great management expert, has many suggestions for ways in which we can all profit from liberated time. Here are three of his most salient:

1. *Record your time.* Don't count on your memory for an accurate assessment of how you spend your time. Would you trust your memory more than the register in your check book? I promise you that documenting your time usage for three days will convince you beyond any doubt how much you need time planning.

2. *Manage your time.* Peter Drucker was so convinced of the importance of time management that he said, "Until we can manage time, we can manage nothing else." Managing means being aware of and proactively appropriating time to tasks rather than letting time "get away from us."

3. *Consolidate your time.* Group chores together for the most efficient execution. In other words, instead of merely planning your time, also time your plan.

Stop Doing What You Know Doesn't Work

Doing away with the unnecessary and inefficient is the first step toward higher achievement. However, most people continue to repeat ineffective patterns, even after they've become aware their efforts are not working. In fact, the *Muddling Manager's Law* specifically states, "The more unsure you are of what you're doing, the more you need to do it." How often have you watched that proverb being repeated over and over again?

Once, during a counseling session with one of my more cynical employees, I paradoxically asked him to give me a scenario of how *not* to make money in the business we were in. He grinned at me and asked, "You want me to tell you how not to make money here?" I nodded. "That's easy." He continued, "I do that every day." Then I stumped him. "In that case, what do you have planned for tomorrow?" My question wiped the grin off of his face.

In a moment of gratifying revelation and contrition, worthy of the *Old Testament* or a Jimmy Stewart movie, he looked at me and said, "I just realized I was planning to do what I already know doesn't work *all over again.* That's not going to happen." Believe me, we all repeat yesterday far too often, frequently with full knowledge that yesterday was not successful.

Ask Yourself Some Simple Questions— and Answer Them

To help gain more from your time, you can answer a few simple questions for yourself. They are "What am I pretending *not* to know?," "What's not being done in my organization that should be?," and "What's being done that *shouldn't* be?" How about, "What's being done that should be done more often?" These are questions we should use to periodically challenge any standard operating procedure. We can ask ourselves, "If I had to do this in a whole new way, how could I do it better?"

Looking at your daily "to do" list in your daily planner, ask at each item, "What would happen if I didn't do this at all?," "What things could be done just as well or even better by someone else?," and "Knowing how many of these items are unproductive or inefficient, how many will I repeat anyway?" Ask people who work with you, "What things do I do that waste your time and/or inhibit your productivity?"

Obviously, one needs the thick skin that comes with personal confidence and commitment to the organization to successfully process some of the possible answers to these and other probing questions. If you can't take the heat of the kitchen, you shouldn't be cooking.

What's Your Time Worth, Anyway?

I've heard it said it's impossible to lead a successful life. The best we can do is lead one successful day after another. I personally think even that is too much to chew. In fact, *people fail or succeed in 15-minute segments.* That's right. We can all benefit from drastically reframing our sense of time.

Are you aware that, to a person earning $5,000 per year, one minute is worth five cents? Multiply it out for yourself. A person earning $10,000 per year is earning ten cents per minute. At $100,000 per year, each minute is worth one dollar.

This is all a means of *drawing perspective* on the question we should be aware of throughout the day, "What is my time worth?" Or, better yet, "What do I want my time to be worth?" Questions like these should be tattooed between your index finger and your thumb, written on the back of the name plate on your desk, on the face of your watch, and on a sticker in the cradle of your telephone. At the end of the day, if you wrote yourself a mental check in the amount of what you thought that day was worth, how much would it be?

Invest Something in the Time Management Process

A big step in time planning is purchasing a large, week-at-a-glance daily planner. Sounds simple, doesn't it? Yet I frequently ask people if they plan their time, only to watch them produce an itty-bitty month-at-a-glance calendar with postage stamp-sized squares for each day. Write down "pick up the laundry" in one of those squares and it looks like you've got a big day planned. The larger, more detailed daily planner shows you the holes in your day where you can plan more activity.

Organize Your Space

Next, take an early morning, evening, or weekend and organize your work space, your attaché case, and your car (if you use it in your work); be *merciless* in throwing low-priority things away. Put things most frequently used in the most accessible places. Set up a file system that makes sense to *you*. Divide up your job into parts and decide which of those parts needs the most organizing.

The Right Way to Do a "To Do" List

Lay out a step-by-step plan (or master "to do" list) of organization, with a deadline for each part, and GET STARTED. The master "to do" list should contain all of the tasks you want to complete, both high- and low-priority. Your plan should be *written, measurable, expressed in results* (*not activities*), *realistic/attainable,* and *based upon a date of completion.* The value of a good plan is summed up in the carpenter's advice to "measure twice and cut once." The "to do" items should be labeled in three categories:

1. Do today.
2. Do today, if possible.
3. Do today, if time is available.

The tendency is to load up the "to do" list with nothing but high priority items for the day, excluding low priority items. Wrong. The little things can be ultimately important to our sanity, and accomplishing them is a good way to sustain a true sense of perspective. Remember the frogs? Swallowing the biggest one first is the way to start. But the job is not done until the little guys go down as well.

Almost nothing motivates us and elevates our mood as effectively as the sense of accomplishment gained from crossing items off of a "to do" list. It's cheap therapy. Of course, the list clearly reveals what remains to be done. And a closer look can reveal if the list is going to outlive the day or vise versa, giving us a time reference.

Make Setting Priorities a Priority

How is the priority system set up? First of all, we need to answer the question, "Am I doing an efficient job on unimportant work?" It is always possible to be efficient without being effective. Some people have called this "job security." Don't overkill low priority items with planning energy. The planning energy spent should match the priority of the task.

Always remember Dwight Eisenhower's revelation, "Urgent things are seldom important and important things are seldom urgent." (A secret that your overnight mail service wants to suppress!) Urgent tasks require immediate attention, but frequently have little or no impact on long-term goals, while important tasks *are* valuable to achieving long-term goals.

Peter Drucker gave us another jewel when he said, "It's more important to do the right thing, than to do things right." Accordingly, we should focus first on getting the right things done and worry about efficiency second. This isn't a license for shooting from the hip or otherwise being irresponsible. Rather, it is simply intended to liberate us from the legacy of being penny-wise and pound-foolish.

Ten of Your Best-Spent Minutes

I believe the difference between a successful person and the "also rans" can be as little as two well-planned hours per day. To this end, I recommend you take at least 10 minutes at the end of the day to plan tomorrow's activities. Those who already engage in this practice know how gratifying it feels to wake up in the morning with a head start on the day.

Allow Some Flexibility in Your Planning

As a planning strategy, allow 10 percent more time than each task should realistically require. If you're just getting started with time planning, don't attempt to plan any more than 75 percent of your work day. Advanced time planners only plan 90 percent of their working hours. There will always be spill-over and interruptions that need to be accommodated.

According to Phillip Musgrove, formerly of the Brookings Institute in Washington, D.C., everything takes longer than expected. 2.71828 times longer, to be exact. Don't ask me how he measured that, but I prove it just about every time I book myself too tight.

Make the First Hour Count Double— Do the Worst Things First

Strive to make the first hour of your work day the most satisfying by remembering to swallow the biggest frogs first. Another way to think of it would be to have frog for breakfast everyday! Hopefully, there won't be any left by dinner time. Do the three things you *least* want to do first. If you leave unpleasant tasks for later, they tend to negatively flavor or just plain stink up everything that precedes them.

If you're like me, you've played the avoidance game a time or two. I'm talking about our occasional fantasy that, if we ignore ugly tasks long enough, they will simply disappear. More than once have I had a real foul odor around my office for days and even weeks at a time. It sounds easier than it really is. But believe me when I tell you that the *best* way to have fresh air in your office is to get those stinky jobs done quickly and thoroughly.

Inventory Your Efficiency

I agree with the countless successful people who are absolutely convinced the first few hours of the work day are the most fertile and productive. So, when planning your time, schedule the most creative and demanding work during the time when you are at your personal best. For some people, their personal best time is in the middle of the night. Our biorhythms vary. Take a self-inventory and try to determine during what part of the day you are the most efficient.

Your self-inventory can be very simple. Just keep a log for one month, both at work and at home, documenting what part of the day is the most productive. When do you feel you are accomplishing the most? When are you tired? When are you alert? During what times of the day do you get along the best with other people and when do others respond the most positively to you?

For most people, the first two to four hours of the work day are the most productive. The lull seems to come through the middle of the day, with productivity resurging into the evening. Your own personal record should inform you whether you are stronger early or late. You might discover a quick cat nap in the place of eating lunch gives you a burst of energy through the afternoon, when you formerly felt bogged-down for hours.

A Mini-Strategy for Combatting Unexpected Problems

If a problem interrupts your best efforts, don't simply bear down on it harder. Do what Peter F. Drucker suggests. Back off and look at the situation from a variety of angles. Bend over and look at it backwards and upside down between your legs. After gaining a broader perspective, break the problem down into its component parts and grade them in order of priority. *Then* move in and begin to work on the most important aspect of the problem.

A Self-Test for Each Task Taken On

Prior to each task, give yourself a 30-second test by asking the sequence of questions shown in the Figure 5-3 flow chart.

It's pretty obvious how you can save yourself quite a bit of unnecessary effort by doing a quick review of your activities from time to time. Don't be surprised if you find yourself doing many unnecessary and inefficient tasks. Most people resist asking simple questions such as these for fear of discovering how much their routine needs to be altered. Does that sound true for you? If so, it's time to loosen up a little, for your own good.

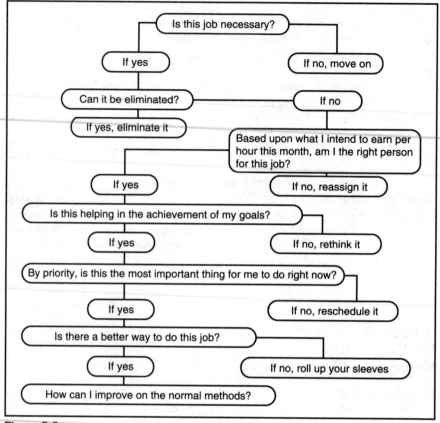

Figure 5-3.

Learn to Say No

Before you say yes to a commitment in the future, ask yourself, "Do I have time for it *now?*" If you don't have time for it right *now,* you probably *won't* have time for it later on.

One of the principle reasons that 20 percent of the people invariably do 80 percent of the work is that the 20 percent either have an inflated concept of their abilities or, more likely, they simply don't say "no." (The 80 percenters don't want you to learn these time efficiency techniques because the work load will automatically shift more equitably across the staff!)

According to *Executive Productivity* of Boca Raton, Florida, saying "no" is one of the five key steps to eliminating executive time wasters. Here's their list:

1. *Doing work beneath your abilities.* (On average, executives spend 53 per-

cent of their time performing secretarial or clerical tasks. If it *can* be done by someone else, it *should* be.)

2. *Tolerating too many interruptions.* (Schedule your availability *and* your unavailability. Set aside a "quiet" period each day when you absolutely prohibit all visitors and phone calls. And another period when your door is open.)

3. *Handling trivial assignments while keeping the big job on "hold."* (Attack the most important project first thing in the morning, and work on it as long as you can. The payoff: by 11:00 A.M. you'll feel as though you've accomplished a whole day's work.)

My interpretation is, of course, by 11:00 A.M. you shouldn't be staring at any more frogs.

4. *Working without a plan.* (Take a few minutes at the start of each day to outline your objectives and priorities. By helping you organize your working day, those minutes will save you many hours.)

5. *Saying "yes" too much.* (Make "no" the automatic response to demands on your time. "Yes" should be the exception.)

Do not be discouraged if there are items left on your list at the end of the day. Many people really beat themselves up emotionally for not finishing everything. Sometimes that is just not a realistic or reasonable expectation. Why clobber yourself unreasonably? Take comfort in knowing that, with good time planning, you've made the most out of the time available to you.

Conduct a Brief, Daily, Personal Productivity Survey

Take a few moments at the end of the day to evaluate your productivity. Schedule the time for this evaluation. It's important to be aware of how you're doing. No, not so you can beat yourself up for doing poorly, but so you can assess where you can do better and appreciate your own efficiency.

A Case in Point: A Lesson from One Awesome Australian_____

I know an Australian who was illiterate at the age of 26. By the age of 49, he was one of the 10 wealthiest men in Australia. He now reads five or six books per week. People like this fascinate me and I asked him, "How do you get so much out of your time?"

He replied that he evaluates his day on a daily basis and showed me a special daily planner he had printed. Each page represented one day and there were four squares at the bottom of each page. To grade himself every day on a 100-point system, he writes a score in each box each day. His four categories, each one worth a maximum score of 25 points, are:

Simplicity (1–25)

On simplicity, he grades himself by asking, "Did I keep my day simple?" and "Did I stay on top of my agenda or did it overwhelm me?" The beauty of watching masters at work is often found in how skillfully they keep disruptions and problems from knocking them off track.

Desperation (1–25)

When he named desperation as his second category, I asked him to explain. He replied that he asked himself, "Do I understand I don't get this day back?" That's an important question, he continued to explain, even if it's a day off, spent with my family at the beach. Simply stated, he was telling me we need to make the most of each day because we will never relive this particular 24 hours again.

Planning (1–25)

How good a job of planning was done? Most of us know the difference between truly thinking something out in advance and "winging it." Everyone spends some amount of time flying by the seat of their pants. I've done it in supersonic fighters and I'm here to say that it's no smarter at 60,000 feet than it is behind your desk or on a sales call.

Job Action (1–25)

Job action is defined as *actually making a profit*. Isn't it funny how profitability becomes the farthest thing from our minds while at work? Profits are made when plans go into action. Job action is probably the most vital category. I believe strongly that hard work without talent is a shame and talent without hard work or "action" is a tragedy!

Eyes on the Prize—Cultivate a Sense of Profitability

My Australian friend is not alone in keeping profitability in the forefront of his consciousness as he moves through his work day. Almost every successful person I know has a keen sense of profitability. In a practical sense, they are valuing their 15-minute intervals the way we discussed earlier. This doesn't mean we should become obsessed with profitability. It means we need to be driven, in part, by awareness of how our efforts transform into dollars and sense.

Dealing Decisively with Interruptions

I can't think of anyone who isn't frustrated by interruptions and the loss of time they cause. However, as we've already discussed, we often make the same mistake over and over and over again, contributing to our own dilemma.

Our most common mistake is focusing too much attention on whatever lands on our desk, and whoever drops in or calls on the telephone. Usually, we will stop in our tracks and spend high-priority time attending to low-priority items. Another way to describe this phenomenon is that we allow others to plan our day for us whenever we allow them to interrupt and rescramble our priorities.

There are several methods which can help minimize interruptions in your work day:

1. Rearrange the furniture in your office so your desk does not face traffic as it flows by your door. Disrupt the line of sight between you and passersby.

2. Reduce the number of chairs in your office and keep them as far away from your desk as possible.

3. Place a clock (or clocks) where it is visible to you *and* anyone who is visiting your work space.

4. Don't automatically look up when someone walks in. This is a toughie. However, if you appear to be concentrating, people with unimportant business are less likely to interrupt.

5. Keep an interruption log for a week. Make columns that identify who caused the interruption, what time they came in and left, and the total time of their visit. Finally, note briefly what you think you could do to maintain better control over your time.

DATE: _____

WHO	TIME IN	TIME OUT	TOTAL TIME

6. Schedule a quiet hour when you don't see anyone or accept any calls. Do it for the whole office if you can. Some recent studies on quiet time

in the office indicate the amount of work that formerly took three hours can frequently be accomplished in one.

7. When someone asks, "Do you have a minute?" learn to say "no." Another toughie! You'll be surprised at how understanding people can be when you're up to your elbows in alligators. Saying "no" from time to time is not an eternal severing of communications with a person or persons. Rather, it is an effective way to establish appropriate boundaries that help everyone function more effectively.

8. If someone has a chronic habit of coming to you seeking advice or help, learn to respond by asking them what *they* think. You're being asked to do their thinking for them. So don't! If you refuse to do someone else's thinking, they will eventually stop asking. This doesn't mean that you shouldn't offer a word of encouragement when they have a good idea. That encouraging word can also help them stand on their own capabilities, while maintaining an appropriate boundary and allowing you to get back to your tasks much faster.

9. If you have difficulty terminating a conversation in your work area, simply walk the person back to his or her work area and leave them there. Excuse yourself to go back to work. The message is subtle, but clear.

10. Don't be part of the problem. The interruptee can become an interrupter. I sometimes catch myself insidiously slipping out of a work mode and into a social mode. Once again, excuse yourself back to work.

Thank You, Alexander Graham Bell

Thank you, Alexander Graham Bell, for that marvelous discovery, the telephone. Perhaps the greatest development in the history of telecommunications rests not in technology, but in our ability to maintain control over and not allow ourselves to be controlled *by* the telephone. Here are some techniques based upon Stephanie Winston's book, *The Organized Executive:*

1. *Establish time limits* when talking on the telephone. When someone asks if you have a "few minutes" and you determine that you do, go ahead and say something like, "I've got about three minutes." Avoid using common blocks like five or 10 minutes. Using short and odd time segments will focus the caller's attention on being brief and to the point.

2. *Foreshadow the end* of a telephone conversation by saying something like, "Jerry, before we hang up . . ." What I just politely told Jerry was, the end is near.

3. Don't hesitate to inform a talkative caller you're in the middle of an

urgent task and you'll have to call him or her back. Then, call back just before quitting time. People often use the telephone to take up time and make 5:00 come more quickly; don't let someone recruit you in his or her effort. Calling back at quitting time will usually result in a quick conversation.

4. Ask the caller in advance how much time he or she needs to complete your conversation. Then, suggest something a little shorter.

5. How about *steering the telephone conversation toward issues important to you*, rather than following the caller's agenda? By asking a question the caller can't answer, it is possible he or she will appreciate that you're involved with something more important than what he or she had to talk about. He or she will probably graciously let you get back to your work.

6. Then, of course, there is the old stand-by of *having your secretary call* you on another extension if the caller is just too persistent to get the hint.

7. You can save yourself a great deal of time by *using a conference planner.* Draw squares on a standard sheet of paper. Draw the squares in a variety of sizes because conversations vary in complexity and length. Write the name of the person you want to talk to at the top of each square and note the points you want to cover. This will help to keep you on track while you're on the telephone and will prove helpful in quickly recalling your original agenda when someone, who isn't initially available, returns your call hours or days later. (See Figure 5-4.)

8. Accept long distance calls whenever possible and *talk on the other party's money.*

Make an Effort to Recall the Times You've Done Things Right and Analyze Why

Everyone experiences time emergencies and these experiences can serve an educational function in our lives. For example, review an experience when you were called upon to complete a task in a shorter amount of time than you originally thought you had. Perhaps a deadline was moved up, but you got the job done in spite of the additional pressure. The big question is, "How was I able to accomplish that in less time than I had budgeted?"

Sprinting

Many people are engaging in what is called "sprinting." All this means is they look at tasks which are scheduled to take a designated amount of time and decide they're going to accomplish them in half that time. What customarily takes a full day or a full hour will take only half a day or half an hour, and so on. Sprinting through a day or even an hour will demonstrate that tasks can be accomplished in shorter periods of time without the pressure of emergency.

A nonthreatening way to approach sprinting is to do it for a day and then return to your customary pace. My only caveat here is to beware that, once you've experienced how much you can accomplish, you will probably be reluctant to accept your former, slower pace any longer. Even when you drop off of your sprinting pace, my bet is you will have increased your personal speed and will concentrate your action.

Try This "What-If" Exercise

How would you change the way you do your job if a medical emergency forced you to work only half days? Which tasks would you drop completely? Which tasks would you delegate or distribute to others? How would the role of family members, part-time help, and other staff members change? Which people you give time to would you avoid under greater time constraint?

Speed-Reading Is Alive and Well—Do It

There are many organizations that are anxious to take your money in exchange for teaching you to read faster. Your public library can tell you who offers speed-reading courses and for how much. If you really don't think you can spare the time or make the effort to attend a formal course, then simply adopt the practice of moving your index finger or the point of a pencil under the text you are reading as fast as your eyes can keep up with it, and you will at least DOUBLE your reading speed.

Practice "jumping" your finger or pencil down the page. You will soon begin to pick up entire phrases, major ideas, and concepts, without having to read every word. The bottom line is you can spend less time reading each day, or read and understand more in the same amount of time, by learning some basic techniques for "processing paper."

1. *Selective Reading.* I recall how comforting it was to learn I didn't have to read everything that came across my desk. Neither do you. Prove this to yourself by throwing away anything you don't consider absolutely vital at first glance. See if the world truly comes to an end.

2. *Never Pick Up the Same Piece of Paper Twice.* Never pick up a piece of paper unless you intend to do something with it. Tackle it or toss it, just

```
┌─────────────────────────────────────────────────────────────────┐
│                    TELEPHONE  TRAFFIC  LOG                        │
├─────────────────────────────────────────────────────────────────┤
│ NAME_____ NUMBER(   )_____DATE_____ │
│ COMPANY_____ TIME ON_____TIME OFF_____ │
│ ITEMS TO COVER:                                 TOTAL TIME_____ │
│ 1._____│
│ 2._____│
│ 3._____│
├─────────────────────────────────────────────────────────────────┤
│ NAME_____ NUMBER(   )_____DATE_____ │
│ COMPANY_____ TIME ON_____TIME OFF_____ │
│ ITEMS TO COVER:                                 TOTAL TIME_____ │
│ 1._____│
│ 2._____│
│ 3._____│
│ 4._____│
│ 5._____│
├─────────────────────────────────────────────────────────────────┤
│                       CALLS  TO  RETURN                          │
├─────────────────────────────────────────────────────────────────┤
│ NAME_____ NUMBER(   )_____DATE_____ │
│ COMPANY_____ TIME ON_____TIME OFF_____ │
│ ANYTHING TO NOTE?                               TOTAL TIME_____ │
│ _____│
│ _____│
├─────────────────────────────────────────────────────────────────┤
│ NAME_____ NUMBER(   )_____DATE_____ │
│ COMPANY_____ TIME ON_____TIME OFF_____ │
│ ANYTHING TO NOTE?                               TOTAL TIME_____ │
│ _____│
│ _____│
├─────────────────────────────────────────────────────────────────┤
│ NAME_____ NUMBER(   )_____DATE_____ │
│ COMPANY_____ TIME ON_____TIME OFF_____ │
│ ANYTHING TO NOTE?                               TOTAL TIME_____ │
│ _____│
│ _____│
├─────────────────────────────────────────────────────────────────┤
│ NAME_____ NUMBER(   )_____DATE_____ │
│ COMPANY_____ TIME ON_____TIME OFF_____ │
│ ANYTHING TO NOTE?                               TOTAL TIME_____ │
│ _____│
│ _____│
└─────────────────────────────────────────────────────────────────┘
```

Figure 5-4.

do something with it. Don't put it back down to clutter your life again in the future.

3. *Preview* material for key words and phrases by reading the first and last sentences of each paragraph. If you're interested, go back and read more. If you're not interested, move on.

4. Immediately *separate and organize* all high-priority correspondence and respond quickly, even before you sort through low-priority materials.

5. Whenever possible, write your reply on the original page and dispatch. If you feel a little guilty at treating your message and the other party with such apparent informality, then get a rubber stamp or a sticker that reads, "Hand written for immediate response. *Promptness before formality.*" The other party will be suitably impressed (especially if you bring it to their attention with your rubber stamp) and you will save yourself and your clerical assistant a great deal of time. File a copy of the letter with your response, thus cutting the amount of filed paper in half.

Time-planning consultant, Alan Lakein, has listed some of the most helpful tips on handling paperwork I've ever read. Figure 5-5 summarizes some of his most valuable tips.

Respect the Time of Others

Depending on your situation and personal style, many of these methods and techniques will not only make your efforts more time-effective, but also increase your respect for others' time. Practice what you preach. Lead by example.

1. Don't conduct a $1000 meeting to address a $100 problem.

2. Be prompt to your appointments and don't keep people waiting to see you. Promptness helps everyone's morale, including yours.

3. Boil down your information to its most vital and salient points.

4. Speak in headlines. If people want to know more, they'll ask.

5. Sum it up FIRST, not last. Begin at the end.

Time Planning and Leadership

Now—Lie Back and Enjoy the Benefits of Good Time Planning

It's important to frame all of this time-efficiency information properly, lest you think I'm suggesting you take on more work, more responsibility, and

---

SCREENING

1. Screen out items that go directly into the trash can and dump them.

2. Use carbonized interoffice memos with a space for replies.

3. Have requests for a decision submitted in a way that you can answer with a simple "yes" or "no."

4. Attach previous correspondence to current letters and attach relevant background material as an appendix.

5. If you want to see advertising mail, collect a week's worth before reading it.

PROCESSING

1. Highlight important ideas with a pen or highlighter, so that you don't need to read the whole thing again when referring back to the document or asking someone else to read it.

2. Force yourself to be brief in your response, two paragraphs or less in most cases.

3. Allow your secretary to draft letters whenever possible.

4. Include your secretary in processing your paperwork and resolve each piece of paper as you go.

5. If an item goes through the system three times without action, put it in the dead file.

IMPROVEMENTS

1. Develop ways that your secretary can lighten the load for you.

2. Get off mailing lists.

3. Eliminate unnecessary *For Your Information* copies and reports.

4. Train your staff to submit a recommendation whenever submitting a problem statement.

5. Require a summary on any report longer than three pages.

Figure 5-5.

literally burn yourself out. The fact is these time-management techniques, when employed properly, will reduce your stress level, lower the amount of pressure you are experiencing, and generally improve the quality of both your personal and professional life.

Perhaps most important of all, you will relate better and more meaningfully to other people, rather than allowing ineffective time use habits to

smother you. Ask yourself, "Would I be more drawn to someone who confidently has it all together or to someone who is constantly under pressure
and on the verge of losing control?" Note the word "confidently." The
proper use of these techniques will help transform personal and professional panic into self-assurance.

Strive to be more like the person who you are attracted to and respect,
whether that person exists in fact or only in your imagination. Others will
respond in kind. What better definition for a great leader could there be
than someone who truly behaves in a fashion consistent with his or her personal beliefs and values, constantly seeking newness in effective living?

It's important to understand some people are driven by a need
to achieve as a compensation for their own lack of self-esteem and self-
confidence. Others are truly attempting to live life for all God meant it to
be. The difference between these two motivations is most easily seen in how
each person treats others along the way. One person appears to be running
scared in everything he or she says and does, while the other person wel-
comes others into his or her world with open arms.

Without dashing off on a psychological tangent, it needs to be said that
there are healthy and unhealthy reasons for achieving. The substance of
our motivations, healthy or unhealthy, is usually evident in the degree of
satisfaction we receive from our successes, in addition to how confidently
we can accept our failures.

All of us must look inside of ourselves and conduct a self-inventory to
answer these questions. Just remember, few people apply the term "overworked" to something they love doing. Such terms are reserved for tasks we
feel we are being forced to do against our will. I'm encountering more and
more people these days who have learned the difference. Moreover, such
insight is helping to change lives.

Time for Yourself

Leisure time is very important to me for many reasons, and effective time
management improves both the quantity and quality of leisure time. One of
the most beneficial features of leisure time is the opportunity to "recharge
your batteries." There is a point of diminishing returns in an overworked
individual, and a case of burn-out can render a person useless to him or
herself and others. Working oneself to death out of a personal compulsive
need is not beneficial to anyone.

To avoid the erosion of morale and a general decrease in effectiveness,
I've learned to schedule leisure time for both myself and my entire staff.
Setting a good example when it comes to rest is just as vital as being a good
model for proper work habits. Mental and physical renewal are vital components of a quality work ethic. Here's my "two-step":

1. Plan some QUIET TIME ALONE each and every day. Even the most

die-hard, compulsive workers will accomplish more if they take time away on a daily basis. If you can't decide when you most need a break, or simply forget to take one, post a reminder to yourself to break two hours after you begin working, at midday (whether you eat lunch or simply walk around the building), and again two hours before you're scheduled to go home.

2. Break tough jobs down into more easily accomplished tasks. The result is a more immediate feeling of accomplishment that reduces the ominous burden ahead. It's important not to become overwhelmed with the task at hand. Breaks between finished segments help to keep a realistic perspective of "do-ability." Don't forget to acknowledge your accomplishment by rewarding yourself when a tough job is completed. The "Salami Theory" states that slicing a task into small parts will *not* speed it up, but it *will* make the task easier to complete.

Remember the great story, "Cheaper by the Dozen"? The father in the story said something like, "If you are awake for 16 hours per day, that's 960 minutes. Devoting a minimum of 9.6 minutes, or one percent of that time, to making someone else happy will brighten all of your hours."

The Right Way to End Your Day

There is even a right way and a wrong way to end your work day. The right way is to end on a high note or a point of accomplishment. Doing so promotes satisfaction, improves the quality of your relaxation time, and helps you return to work the following day more refreshed and eager.

If you must end your day with an unresolved problem, then write down a clear summary of the problem as it stands when you leave it. Before you leave, clear your desk or work area from clutter and distraction so you can attack the problem when you first walk in the following day. This gives you a good framework for pondering your situation in the hours away from the work place. The answer might come when you least expect it.

These preparations will also serve you well prior to breaking for lunch, so you'll get back up to speed more quickly and with less effort after your break. Reorienting yourself after breaking requires energy that can be saved with a little forethought prior to your break.

Employing these time-management techniques should help you avoid working on weekends, holidays, and vacations. I'm not suggesting you take on more work than you should in light of your personal goals and professional responsibilities. I am trying to help you accomplish more in less time so you can live a more balanced personal and professional life.

What's It All for Anyway?

All too often, personal relationships with friends and family suffer because we are simply "overloaded at work." This is too high a price to pay for success if you ask me. What's it all for anyway? As I mentioned earlier, if work is simply a device to avoid personal responsibilities, then you would be better served to deal with the personal issues that are driving you to compulsive and self-destructive work habits.

Work effectively and then take your vacations, all of them. I used to pride myself on never taking vacations until a mentor taught me that I was simply demonstrating my own lack of effectiveness in getting my work finished. Never having time to take vacations is not a badge of honor, as much as it is a mark of ineffective time management.

Keep Your Leisure Time Leisurely

Take your time and relax. As I mentioned, you'll be a better worker, and more valuable to yourself and everyone else when you have been recharged. This also means avoiding the urge to turn leisure time into a mini-military drill. Relaxing means spending some time alone and engaging in mindless activities. Ordering yourself and your family into a tight schedule is not relaxing. Rigid, compulsive structure might seem comfortable to you at first blush, but it's not going to leave you refreshed. Relaxation takes different forms for different people. However, it must take you out of your working pattern to be truly therapeutic.

Some Closing Thoughts

Finally, some mythology of time management:

> We trained hard. But it seemed that every time we were beginning to form into teams, we would be reorganized. I was to learn later in life that we tend to meet any new situation by reorganizing. And what a wonderful method it can be for creating the *illusion of progress* while producing confusion, inefficiency and demoralization. [emphasis mine]

These words were written by Petronius Arbiter in the year 66 A.D. The regrettable truth is that, in many organizations, the same thing can be said today. So much for learning from history. Human nature hasn't changed much in leadership. *Mad* magazine masthead Alfred E. Newman stares at us from the newsstand and declares, "Just because it's changed doesn't mean it's different." The great playwright, Somerset Maugham, advised us to "live life, don't portray it!" To me, that means aspiring to the highest and best use of our time. The difference between the self-made president and the self-made pauper can probably be found in how each person uses his or her equally allocated time.

Chapter Six

The 4th Step–
Keeping Morale High
When the Heat's On

"Morale is a lot of little things."
—BENJAMIN FRANKLIN

Make High Morale
a Priority Mission

That maxim is the nugget of a high-performance/high-morale organization. The fact is you can't have a low-morale/high-performance organization or a low-performance/high-morale organization. If you think you do, you don't have the level of productivity you could have, or you might be unaware of how deteriorated the overall morale of your organization is. The chicken-and-egg debate goes round and round over whether friction heating is caused by poor morale or poor morale is caused by friction and pressures from within the organization. No matter the answer, the story always ends up with the leader on the hot seat.

Morale is generally accepted to mean a state of mind, involving one's sense of confidence, courage, hope, or zeal. High or good morale is positive and people want to stick close to it. Low or poor morale is negative, and people generally want to get away from it. Staff turnover is the tip of the low-morale iceberg.

Some people make the argument that turnover is good for an organization. Their logic is that new blood keeps creativity and innovation high,

111

because people naturally stagnate over time. Some people even feel the experience of seeing others around you lose their jobs will keep you on your toes. Others believe staying with the same people for a long time promotes a sort of incestuous promotion cycle that weakens the bloodlines of the organization. No matter what the reason, I have some fundamental problems with this kind of thinking.

When we have problems with our kids we don't send them away and go get some more. As a parent, I've know the temptation, but the reality is we do our best to get the best out of who we've got. We don't merely give up on them. As I've already discussed, there are situations when it is in the best interests of the individual and the organization to part company. However, when I hear someone tell me an organization must hire new people in order to gain new ideas, I'm troubled all the more. The myth that new ideas can't come from people inside the organization is an indictment on how the role of morale is being recognized. Besides, why would any truly creative person want to join an "idea-less" organization anyway?

Somewhere along the way a leader has to plant his or her feet and commit to raising and maintaining the morale of the organization. A commitment to improving the morale of an organization is a commitment to the people. The morale of your staff members is directly proportional to the quality of their experience of being a part of your team. In fact, the level of morale is a good barometer of how each of your people is experiencing your leadership.

Heed the 10 Warning Signs of Low Morale

Low morale can exist without anyone, including the leader, fully realizing it. One of the responsibilities of effective leadership is to keep a vigilant watch for signs of deteriorating or overall low morale. Here are a few biggies:

1. Uncooperative attitudes
2. Lack of enthusiasm
3. Absence of commitment
4. Fault finding
5. Increasing complaints
6. Growing tardiness and absenteeism
7. Deterioration in the appearance of the work area
8. Breakdown in discipline
9. Long faces
10. Low morale as a rallying point

Uncooperative Attitude. Generally, an *uncooperative attitude* is detectable the moment you walk into a place. Somehow, you can sense very quickly there's something wrong, even if you can't place your finger on it immediately. One of the most obvious indicators of a generally uncooperative attitude is how helpful people are toward you. Do they make you feel as if you're imposing on them? Does doing little or nothing appear to be more important than dealing with you? The second you come into contact with a person who has a cooperative attitude, you'll recognize the difference. It's unmistakable. I believe people are fundamentally cooperative by nature. It's only when the environment is somehow contaminated that they become unfriendly.

Lack of Enthusiasm. A *lack of enthusiasm* can sometimes be perceived as a pervasive sense of boredom. Once again, I don't think people enjoy being bored. They must have a reason to avoid doing more interesting things. Either that, or they're being restricted from doing more interesting things. True, an activity one person might really enjoy might bore someone else. However, in an organization with high morale, we can assume the leader has done an effective job of matching people up with tasks and responsibilities that are consistent with their individual interests.

Absence of Commitment. When there is an *absence of commitment* or general sense of melancholy about what the organization is supposed to be doing, chances are good the same opinions are reflected in the organization's leadership. If the leader is not committed, then there could be a host of problems, such as poor communication, incorrect assignment matching, and so forth. As we already know, it's highly unlikely that team members are going to have or maintain any sort of commitment if the leader isn't committed.

Fault Finding. People who are not happy will tend to *find fault* in anything, everything, and everybody. When morale is high, even mistakes are not dwelled upon in an orgy of negative thinking. When morale is low, even the greatest victories might be picked apart and talked down. A person who is consciously committed to finding the good in people and their efforts will not be trapped in the quagmire of fault finding, which is nothing more than a cycle of negativity feeding on itself. In an imperfect world, there will be an inexhaustible supply of faults to find in even the best people. Therefore, if someone chooses to be a fault finder, he or she will have enough material to last an unhappy lifetime.

Increasing Complaints. When *complaining* seems to be a favorite activity, you can bet folks aren't having a good time. I challenge you to show me a happy complainer. In an organization where there hasn't historically been much complaining, a noticeable increase is an indication that morale is slipping. Complaining usually takes place quietly, out of the leader's hearing. By the time the leader becomes aware of complaining, it has usually had time to become fairly serious.

Growing Tardiness and Absenteeism.   Blatant *tardiness and absenteeism* are generally grounds for termination and, at the least, an overt discipline problem requiring immediate attention. However, if absenteeism and tardiness appear to the leader's vigilant eye to be on the increase, they can be considered a subtle indication that morale is slipping. People who love what they do can't get enough of it and can't seem to stay away. Once again, the difference between people who love their work and people who are discontented is clearly evident in punctuality and attendance.

Deterioration in the Appearance of the Work Area.   Some very creative and productive people don't keep their working space very neat. So how is a leader supposed to know when a *change in the appearance of the working area* indicates an erosion of morale? That depends on how well a leader knows his or her people as individuals. The key word is *change* in the appearance of the working area. People who are customarily neat and tidy are sending a clear message of dissatisfaction if they become sloppy and unkempt. I'm referring not only to the work area but to the individual's appearance as well. On the other hand, if someone who is usually somewhat less tidy and, possibly, less fashionable suddenly spends most of his or her time cleaning and straightening up, it could be a sign that he or she is bored or uncomfortable about something.

Breakdown in Discipline.   The key word once again is change when *discipline* breaks down. There is a normal range of fluctuation in all things and an effective leader will have a sense of how an organization operates on its best and worst days. Discipline will vary greatly from one organization to another, depending upon the type of business being conducted, where the business is located, and many other considerations. However, if overall discipline appears to be breaking down over an extended period, the leader will want to begin checking out possible causes.

Long Faces.   *Long faces* can mean many things. An individual's temporary low energy and sour expression can be caused by physical discomfort due to illness, emotional discomfort due to tension in the family, or any number of other nonwork reasons. The leader's concern should be primarily limited to how an individual's attitude affects that person on the job as well as others. Once again, a good relationship with each individual team member goes a long way toward diagnosing when a change in attitude requires attention and how much. Personal problems brought to work can become a problem for more than just the individual, and the leader has to be an effective counselor who shows genuine concern for each person's situation, while keeping the overall best interests of the internal or external customer in sight. The subtle art of leading is, in part, the ability to read faces, voices, posture, and other indicators of unhappiness. A long face on everyone in the office, everyday, is something else again.

When Low Morale Becomes a Rallying Point.   When the people within an organization *begin to talk* about how lousy it is to work in the organization and reach a general consensus on the subject, the leader and the organization have a real problem. Typically, discontent will effect different members of your team at different rates and with different intensity, due to the range of personalities involved. As with the increase of complaints, any collective discontent that virtually all of your people agree upon and openly discuss represents an advanced stage of discontent and is worth the leader's attention. When your people make no attempt to conceal their negative feelings, you can bet there is something wrong and whatever it is poses a real threat to your organization's long-term morale. No manager worth his or her salt would miss an indicator as obvious as consensus discontent in the ranks.

Interpreting the Signs

As a leader, you will probably never encounter just one sign or no signs of low morale. When morale is strained or threatened, there will probably be a combination of signs. Even when there is high morale, someone or something might emit signs of low morale, which really don't pose an immediate threat. An effective leader is good at reading and properly interpreting signs. Much of your sign-reading confidence will come from experience. However, knowing what you now know will give you a tremendous head start.

I once heard a company refer to upper management as the "morale suppression team." That is unfortunate. Yet, when you stop and think about it, there are many organizations that appear to be committed to flattening out any improvement of morale. Some managers and executives give every appearance of hunting down good attitudes in their organizations and punishing them. I don't believe smothering healthy attitudes is a conscious goal for anyone, but some styles of management seem to have the effect of nipping enthusiasm in the bud whenever and wherever it's found.

A Case in Point: Flying the Not-So-Friendly Skies _____

(This is *not* a story about United Airlines.)

My seminar and speaking schedule takes me on the road for over one hundred appearances per year. As you can imagine, I spend a great deal of time on various airlines. One day, not so long ago, I was seated in my first-class seat waiting for departure when a woman came and took the seat beside me. We didn't talk as we waited for the plane to be pushed back from the gate. When we were ten minutes late and nobody had said anything, the woman and I glanced at each other. After another ten minutes passed without a single announcement, and we still had not moved, several of the flight attendants gathered in the forward galley, only a few feet from where the woman and I were seated.

Although they drew the curtain, their conversation was easily overheard. In fact, we couldn't have *not heard it* if we had tried. The flight attendants were emphatically renouncing their loyalty to the airline. They were trying to top each other's accounts of what a lousy company it was to work for. We were late taking off and I was hearing the airline described in such a way that I was becoming more afraid of flying by the moment. For an ex-test pilot, that's shaky. To hear these flight attendants talk, you wouldn't think this outfit ever bothered to change the oil in the engines or check the air pressure in the tires.

After overhearing a large dose of this negative conversation, the woman beside me turned and sheepishly said, "They really shouldn't be talking like that." I told her I agreed the discussion was inappropriate within earshot of the customers, but I had to concur with the flight attendants' assessment of the airline. I proceeded to recite my own litany of horror stories about lost or delayed baggage, poor punctuality for flights, and other complaints about that particular airline.

I was a bit surprised at how intently she listened to my complaining. "You sound like a person who is concerned about customer service," she observed. "I conduct seminars on the subject," I replied. Then I asked her what she did. Much to my surprise, she told me that she was in charge of customer service. Much to my embarrassment, she said she was in charge of customer service for *that airline!*

I apologized for laying into the airline so severely. However, she said she appreciated hearing what people thought about their service. She went on to tell me that much of her job was to reply to the complaint letters people sent in. Apparently, she wrote a personal reply to each one. The way this outfit was going, I wouldn't have wanted her job for all the tea in China. Then came the shocker.

I asked her what she did with the complaint letters after she had replied to them. She told me she kept them on file in her office. "You don't give a copy to anyone else?" I asked. "No," she replied, "I've been instructed that upper management doesn't want to see them." I couldn't believe my ears. Yet, in an instant, it all became clear. This was an organization that intentionally buried its head in the sand and then left its employees twisting in the wind to catch all of the flack for a poorly run company. A company that desperately needed to close ranks and communicate effectively up and down the line appeared to be doing everything possible to alienate their own people as well as their customers. I had to assume upper management simply didn't know how to address morale and productivity, and therefore avoided the issue. The real tragedy is that such an example is not uncommon in American business.

The way to absolutely avoid such a miserably counterproductive scenario in your organization is to recognize signs of low morale, such as those I just outlined, and to understand the causes of low morale that I'm about to discuss. Most of all, investment in high morale must be a *priority* for leaders, not an incidental afterthought. The good attitude or the poor attitude leaders demonstrate toward company morale and customer relations will permeate the entire organization.

Get Familiar with the Causes of Low Morale

Detecting the warning signs of low morale is only the beginning. To fully address the morale issue, an effective leader must understand what causes a decline in attitudes within the organization. Only after the causes of low morale are determined can the process of morale building begin. Without knowing the cause of low morale, a leader might try in vain to correct the situation and never get to the real issue.

Here are some of the most common causes of low morale:

1. People's failure to understand their jobs

2. Unrealistic or ever-changing goals

3. Poor communication

    a. Constant criticism or *Big Brotherism*

    b. Inaccessible or absentee management

    c. Erratic and inconsistent discipline

    d. Being thought of as a number

    e. A manager's lack of growth as a leader

4. Over-inflated organizational structure

5. Over-staffing

6. Misemployment

7. Poor psychological work environment

8. Management that is not people-oriented

9. Lack of performance appraisal and feedback

10. Continuing education that is dull or nonexistent

This list is by no means complete. There are many variations on these and other causes of poor morale, depending on your unique situation and combination of people involved. However, I've found this list generally covers most categories. In looking at each one, it should be clear how attitudes within the organization can suffer, and it should be equally as clear why and how attitudes about your organization from the outside can deteriorate.

When People Don't Fully Understand Their Jobs

It is critically important for leaders to help their people fully *understand what's expected of them.* There are few things more frustrating than to be left in the dark about what it is you are expected to accomplish. What is even worse is the tendency on the part of some companies to keep their people in the dark as to their job expectations and then come down hard when a person fails to perform at a level which has never been defined.

If you don't think training is important, think again. Corporate training and continuing education is your best hedge against misunderstandings and the resulting dissatisfaction when job expectations are not clear. I'm referring not only to the organized training activities of your organization but also to the ongoing personal counseling relationship between a leader and his or her individual team members. Make sure that each of your people fully understands what you expect and how their individual goals fit into the larger picture of the organization's objectives.

When Goals Are Unrealistic or Change Too Often

As I described in Chapter Four, *goals must be realistic.* If they are not, then you will pay the price later in damaged morale. It's not fair to expect people to achieve unrealistic goals, and people who are treated unfairly don't stay happy for long. If you wonder how your people feel under such circumstances, simply consider how *you* feel when someone demands the unreasonable from you. By the same token, if goals are constantly changed, your people can't be expected to take them very seriously. What would be the point of working hard on a goal if it's highly likely it will be changed or abandoned? The result of changing goals and expectations is usually frustration and, of course, decreased morale.

When Communication Efforts Fall Short

Poor communication seems to be at the core of almost any problem, in the work place, the home, the school, or anywhere else. Poor communication in the context I'm using means difficulty in sending and receiving not only accurate messages, but also damaging messages. For example, there is not much mistaking that criticism is a clear expression of disappointment and negativism. In that respect, criticism is clear communication.

Criticism and Big Brotherism.   However, *criticism is poison.* The more clearly and effectively it's communicated, the more painful and damaging it will be. Nobody enjoys being criticized. Yet we are so exposed to it as children, at home and/or at school, it seems completely natural to bring it to work with us. The net result of constant criticism is the pervasive feeling that nobody can do anything right, which is simply not true. Take Ken Blanchard's advice and make it a priority to catch people doing things right. You'll be surprised at how much good is being done once you take off your criticism-colored glasses.

Inaccessible or Absentee Management.   As I also covered in earlier chapters, *an effective leader is available* to his or her people. The point is not to do their work for them or to hold their hand, but to be as invested in the organization's efforts as anyone else. You simply can't join in your people's investment if you're isolated or absent altogether. Every organization is different. How close you are to your people's efforts and how much space you allow them is a function of the unique dynamics between you and your team members. The bottom line is, if your people don't feel you care, why should they? You can't pay people enough to care.

Erratic and Inconsistent Discipline.   If the *rules are always changing* or *the enforcement of company policy is inconsistent,* the result will again be frustration and an overall sense of unfairness. Morale will be damaged if your people can't count on consistency from their leadership. It's difficult to be consistent with discipline because we naturally feel differently toward different people. However, if the leader keeps the best interests of the entire staff in mind, consistency in discipline will improve. Don't give a favorite person extra and undeserved slack at the expense of the other hard workers in your group. The others will be troubled by your inconsistency and their morale will suffer as a result.

It is said that *the manager sets the mood,* whether it's good or bad, for an office within the first fifteen minutes of his or her arrival. I believe it. People have their unconscious radar antennae up constantly and you really can't hide your mood from them. Be honest with your people if something is troubling you. Don't leave them in the dark while making them suffer from your ill temper. As the manager's mood swings, so will the mood of the office. When a manager is in a bad mood, he or she and the team both suffer from it for the day. However, the team continues to suffer from the uncertainty of the manager's moods for at least three additional days. This is not to suggest you need to be unreasonably cut off from your feelings. It is simply important to be aware of how the leader's emotional mood swings affect the organization and to act responsibly. Your people tend to go up or down as you do. Accept that you have that power as a leader.

Being Thought of as a Number.   When people feel they are *thought of as a number,* the resulting depersonalization is depressing. Naturally, morale will suffer if people don't feel appreciated as distinct and unique individuals. Walt Disney understood this and said, "The larger a company grows, the more personal it has to become." Don't be fooled that personal relationships within an organization are merely a function of numbers. I've seen large companies that are extremely good at engendering healthy relationships among their people as well as small companies that are cold and impersonal.

A Manager's Lack of Growth as a Leader.   One of the very first things I talked about in this book was the concept that people within organizations get better as soon as the leader does. The point here is that, if the *leader lacks personal and professional maturity,* it's simply unreasonable to expect any better from the organization. When a leader promotes or merely allows pettiness, cliques, resistance to change, instruction to be ignored, etc., he or she is setting the stage for terrible morale.

As I mentioned in the previous chapter on time planning, if the course of performance in your organization is to wait until the manager asks for something the third time before it is acted upon, the manager suffers unnecessary hardship right along with the organization. Remember that an individual's peers are constantly briefing him or her right along with the manager. Low morale and immature work habits on the part of the leader will come around through the organization full cycle and turn up the heat another notch. Everything will be late, which increases pressure and friction.

When the Organization's Structure Is Overinflated

An *over-inflated organizational structure* as well as *over-staffing* cause inefficiency and often confusion within an organization. When job boundaries begin to overlap and there are *too many chiefs and not enough Indians,* the atmosphere is likely to heat up with tension and suspicion. All of this instability will result in an erosion of morale. Top-heavy organizations experience up pressure from resentful people in the ranks who feel as if they are disproportionately burdened with work while the "fat cats" on top aren't pulling their fair share of the load. In over-staffed situations, people often simply bump into each other and confusion reigns. Eventually, the self-starters will take over and the others will fall by the wayside. Before long a few people are doing most of the work and the unavoidable resentment and hostility occur.

When Misemployment Occurs

I also discussed earlier how important it is to recognize when *an individual and the organization are not right for each other* and to act accordingly. When a person winds up in a job he or she is not right for, the leader must act to correct the situation in the most appropriate manner if damage to overall morale is to be avoided. The airline I just described at least had the sense to put the pilots in the cockpit and the flight attendants in the galley. If they didn't, I don't want to know about it.

When the Work Environment Is Psychologically Depressing

A *poor psychological work environment* can be created by allowing any combination of these morale-killers to exist or persist for very long. If you step back and really examine your working environment, you should be able to determine whether or not the atmosphere promotes good and positive feelings among the staff. The mood of a place will impact an individual's psychological well-being over time.

When Management Is Not People-Oriented

One of the best ways to insure the atmosphere is healthy and uplifting is to place a high priority on *people-orientation*. In an atmosphere where objects and accomplishments are held in higher esteem than people, it shouldn't be surprising that people will not feel affirmed. Morale hasn't got a chance where people are down on the priority list.

When Feedback Is Lacking

Performance appraisal, not criticism, is an effective method to communicate with and counsel your people. The result of quality, individual *feedback* is affirmation that the individuals in your organization *are* important and vital to the company's success.

When Training Is Not Adequately Covered

Companies often publicly acknowledge a need for *training and continuing education,* only to withhold the strong emphasis such activities deserve in the organization. In my experience, the companies that place the appropriate emphasis on training and continuing education by elevating them to their proper role in the company's hierarchy realize a tremendous return on their training investment. The antiquated thinking that training expenses represent money down the drain costs companies dearly. Unfortunately, most companies persist in relegating training and continuing education to the background. Training and continuing education can, at the very least, communicate the hopes, dreams, and ambitions of the company's culture to everyone in the organization. Training and education can be one of your most effective tools to generate synergy in your organization.

Putting Into Place the 10 Fundamentals of a High Morale Environment

Which specific elements contribute to high morale in your organization depend in large measure upon your individual situation and the particular challenges your organization faces. In other words, no two organizations have exactly the same equation for high morale. However, there are some fundamental principles which apply to human nature, regardless of what your particular business is. These ten elements of a high-morale environment are primary and can be mixed and blended in a variety of shades and colors.

1. Keeping a job interesting
2. Welcoming new ideas
3. Fostering a sense of accomplishment
4. Recognizing effort
5. Treating people fairly
6. Being responsible
7. Offering fair and appropriate compensation
8. Supporting personal growth
9. Promoting a sense of belonging
10. Providing opportunity

Keep Other People's Jobs Interesting

Some *jobs are interesting* all by themselves, while others are only meaningful when considered within the larger picture of an organization's activities. An effective leader will be sensitive to the fact that some tasks are mundane and sometimes just plain boring. Why does the leader care? Because the morale of the work force is at stake and even the most boring jobs are vital to the success of the organization.

As a former test pilot and a current frequent flier, I appreciate that those people who put rivets in airplanes take their job seriously. Have you ever looked at how many rivets there are in a big jet? It must be boring as all get out to put those things in every day at the factory. However, if the rivets do not get put in properly and something falls off of the airplane in flight, quite a few people are going to have a bad day, including the company that built the airplane.

This example might sound silly unless you're reading this book on an airplane. If you're cruising several miles above the earth right now, you no doubt appreciate that even the most uninteresting jobs, like putting rivets in airplanes, are often vitally important. Flying the airplane will always be a more interesting job, but everybody can't fly the plane. So it's important to include the riveter, or anyone in a mundane job, in as much of the overall picture as possible. How?

1. Consult with everyone on the team for suggestions regarding a more efficient approach or methods for quality control. In other words, involve them.

2. Give constant feedback to people at all levels to keep them abreast of how their function contributes to the overall success of the organization.

3. Rotate mundane tasks as often as it is possible and practical, without losing the benefit of special training and skills where necessary.

4. Use the methods on the current high-morale list, such as recognition and personal growth, to demonstrate how you genuinely value your people.

5. If a boring or mundane task is not necessary or vital to the organization's success, get rid of it.

Keep an Open Mind with Regard to New Ideas

The way some people are treated when they come to their managers with *new ideas* would make you think they are asking to burn the factory down. The fact is, if a manager has not reached an adequate level of personal maturity and confidence, he or she might feel threatened when approached with new ideas—not necessarily by the person bringing the new idea, but by the change in the organization the new idea might bring about. If people feel stifled, they're going to cut off the creative part of themselves and not be able to wholly experience their responsibilities.

Don't simply keep your door open to new ideas, actively encourage and solicit them.

Foster Individual Feelings of Accomplishment

A *feeling of accomplishment* is basic to our human nature. From the time we're toddlers, we want to sense that what we do has some meaning and contributes in some way to the world around us. There is no argument whatsoever that people will work harder and more effectively if they feel there is some good that will come from their efforts, even if it's a small contribution. The need to feel a sense of contribution never goes away. If the entire organization feels they are accomplishing something and each individual has a role to play, your morale will be high.

Affirm Accomplishment with Recognition—Formal or Informal

It's difficult to maintain an individual sense of accomplishment without some sort of *recognition*. I feel management sometimes misreads the desire for recognition as a desire to blow one's own horn or have someone toot it for you. A more accurate reading reveals that people want their contribution to the accomplishments of the organization to be recognized and affirmed. Recognition is confirmation that what we do is helpful, not necessarily validation that we are good people.

Napoleon said essentially that, if you gave him enough medals to distribute to the troops, he could win any war. He wasn't saying he had an army of narcissists. He was acknowledging that the contributions of individuals to the greater purposes or goals of the organization must be recognized. When people expect their efforts will be noticed, they will pay better attention themselves and the quality of work will increase along with the morale. Remember high morale goes hand-in-hand with high productivity.

Develop a Clear Idea of What's Fair and Make It Central to Employee Treatment

The issue of *fair treatment* runs to the point I made earlier about consistency and discipline. I don't believe there is any evidence that people resent rules and regulations that are appropriate and enforced fairly. Rules and regulations become controversial and divisive when they are unnecessary, inappropriate, cumbersome, and/or create a double standard. Once again, our sense of fairness comes from our infancy and is a constant issue throughout our childhood. If you've been the parent of more than one child, you probably have a keen sense of how children demand fair and equitable treatment. People can handle all types of regulations and controls as long as they are proved to be necessary and, more importantly, justly applied across the board. Favoritism in any arena will generate resentment and damage morale.

Match Responsibility to Competence

Just as an individual is motivated by a feeling of accomplishment and recognition, he or she will respond with enthusiasm to the assignment of *responsibility*. It's important to specify that the responsibility needs to be assigned on the basis of the individual's ability and competence. Loading somebody down with responsibility that is inappropriately heavy or out of proportion with the rest of the team will not engender high morale. In the correct context, responsibility is the raw material of accomplishment and recognition. If responsibility is the alpha, recognition is the omega.

Compensate Effort Fairly and Appropriately

Compensation is a litmus test of how honestly management backs up its expressions of recognition and fair treatment. The studies confirming issues such as recognition and working environment are more important to workers than money don't entirely dismiss the importance of fair and equitable compensation. Appropriate levels of compensation vary with geographical region, type of job, health of industry, level of training, and other factors. However, the bottom line is that compensation, benefits, and incentive plans will either accurately reflect the relationship management has established with the individual team members or expose it all as false and misleading.

Invest in the Personal Growth of Your Work Force and Let Them Invest in Their Own Growth

Personal growth is not a casual option. It is the antithesis of shrinking as a person. When a muscle is not used, it doesn't simply continue to exist in its previous state. Atrophy takes place. In the same way, if people aren't growing and maturing, atrophy takes place. We begin to forget what we have learned and to slide back into older and less healthy habits. An investment in the personal growth of your people is an investment in the morale and productivity of your organization.

Lay the Groundwork
for a Sense of Community at Work

Many people expend a great deal of energy attempting to isolate themselves from others. I'm no psychologist, but these are not the type of folks you want to build your staff with. People have a strong, innate sense of community and attempts to run against that indicate problems. *A sense of belonging* is far more natural and faithful to our human nature. More specifically, it's a sense of community we want as people and a sense of community we want as an organization dedicated to accomplishing something. The sense of belonging produces not only improved morale, but also synergy.

Maintain a Focus on Opportunity

Opportunity simply means an ongoing sense of being alive with hope for the future. When people sense they have nowhere to go and nothing more to accomplish, they begin to atrophy in a variety of ways. Although it's not generally known, some astronauts from the early and middle days of our space programs, especially those who made major accomplishments, have experienced tremendous emotional letdowns because there is no sense of opportunity left to them. Younger astronauts have taken over, and those they replaced will never return to the level of adventure, accomplishment, and public recognition they once enjoyed. When opportunity is removed from the picture, morale will dwindle and eventually disappear altogether.

Putting It All Together

It's a combination of these elements that will produce high morale. It would be a highly unusual and unreasonable expectation if you attempted to weight each one of these elements equally or expected them to have the same meaning to each and every individual. However, the more of these elements you have and the larger the dosage, the higher your morale and your productivity will be.

Singling Out the
Personal Growth Element

Abraham Maslow said that there are four levels of learning. I've listed them for you with the highest level on top and the lowest level on the bottom, in addition to one I added myself. You might prefer to call it a *ladder of learning*. The reason I've chosen to hit this element of a high-morale environment harder than the rest is because personal growth is a primary determinant in whatever we think, say, or do in our lives. The levels of learning are:

Level 5—Conscious Unconscious Competence (mine)

Level 4—Unconscious Competence

Level 3—Conscious Competence

Level 2—Conscious Incompetence

Level 1—Unconscious Incompetence

Level 1.   Another way to describe *unconscious incompetence* is well-fed, dumb, and happy. (This is my example, not Maslow's.)

Level 2.   *Conscious incompetence* is the level good old Ticky reached the moment he picked up that hot horseshoe in Orie Hyfil's blacksmith shop. At that point he had no question that he had messed something up. He was definitely conscious of his error. Others announce when they've reached this level by saying, "A-ha. There *is* a better way to do this."

Level 3.   *Conscious competence* is achieved when you're doing things correctly, but you need to focus a great deal of attention in order to remain competent. This is an exciting level because a person who invests so much focus on a job has either just recently become competent at it or loves it so much he or she wants to think of nothing else. Doing something you formerly could not do is exciting to most anyone.

Level 4.   The ability to do something correctly without even thinking about it is *unconscious competence*. This can become your personal auto pilot. However, there is potential danger here. When a job has ceased to become a challenge, things like complacency and boredom set in and quality begins to drop. You might be a person who has changed jobs in order to find something more challenging. I say you can challenge yourself right where you are by identifying aspects of your job you don't do well. If you go somewhere else to do the same thing, you will end up bored and changing jobs all over again. When you realize you are at the level of unconscious competence, it's time to make the conscious move to the fifth level I added.

Level 5.   Becoming *conscious of your unconscious competence* reveals a great deal about you. For one thing, you're at another crossroads. You have some choices to make. You are committed to stimulating increased excitement about your own personal growth and development. One of the first steps is to identify those areas in which you need the most improvement. When you've identified such a skill and worked to become increasingly competent at it, you bring yourself up through Level 3 again. When you experience conscious competence again, you reexperience the excitement that accompanies it. It's fun to try new things that work, no matter how high in the hierarchy you are.

Putting the Levels of Learning to Work

When you become unconsciously competent with your new skill, it's time to challenge yourself with another area that has been traditionally weaker in your personal inventory. If you need a list of areas in which you can improve and experience the excitement of making new things happen in new ways, go back through this book, begin with the characteristics of a great leader, and work that list and every one that follows, right up through the elements of high morale. There will be something for you to improve at and doing so will energize you and benefit the entire organization.

Turnover in an organization occurs at the fourth level, when things cease to be fun and challenging. To cut turnover and stimulate unprecedented productivity in your people, get to work counseling them on their own growth on the ladder of learning. Learning, growing, and developing are the primary functions of training and continuing education. If your training and continuing education are boring your people to tears and never seem to make any difference in the organization, my bet is you haven't got people climbing the learning ladder. People get excited whenever they learn something new. You might want to make another sign for your wall that says:

"What have you tried today that's new?"

The more we learn the more we realize how much we *don't know*. The result is a world of wonder. Of course, a little knowledge can be a dangerous thing. So keep learning! As models to organizations, it's important that leaders invest in their own personal growth. Don't expect anyone in your organization to make an investment you're not willing to make. There is a *little* truth to the maxim that it's lonely at the top. More importantly, it should be *exciting* up there.

Keeping Your Top Achievers Happy

I've found top achievers are characterized for the most part by the following three characteristics:

1. They are driven toward self-fulfillment.

2. They love solving problems.

3. They love discovering new and better ways to do the job.

Top achievers are not characteristically patient people when it comes to accomplishment and seeking out new challenges. Therefore, you need to follow some ground rules to provide them with the most fertile environment possible.

1. Give them room to grow and develop their potential. When you recognize the difference in ability and ambition among people, don't ignore it. Support their quest for personal and professional growth by subsidizing training and continuing education through seminars, conventions, college, and technical classes, as long as the result is enhancement of the company's direction and goals.

2. When a major change is about to be instituted, discuss it with your high-achievers first. Involve them in decisions whenever possible and at the highest levels practical. Their input and support can make or break your plans.

3. High-achievers, like thoroughbred race horses, enjoy running the race. They want to stretch and strain against their own limits and they enjoy the challenge of the competition. Make sure you give them those opportunities, lest they get bored. Help them to discover new opportunities within the organization when they get too comfortable with the old ones. Encourage them to take on as much responsibility as possible without reaching their point of diminishing returns. Involvement in creative projects seems to have a stimulating and renewing effect on almost everyone.

4. Don't depend on higher salaries and larger commissions alone to keep your high-achievers happy. Money is important. But praise, recognition, and relationships are the very substance of motivation.

5. Above all, keep the high-achievers challenged. The effective leader understands the driven person needs to keep stoking the furnaces. The fuel will be different with different people. Know your people and keep them in good supply of what drives them.

10 Easy Ways
To Get Your Morale
Campaign off the Ground

Recognizing that everyone is surrounded by individual issues that affect attitude and morale, the effective leader must be as well acquainted with each individual equation as possible. Factors can be negative or positive.

The leader's challenge is to multiply the positive influences while minimizing the negative. Factors that influence morale, either positively or negatively, include:

1. Family
2. The training program
3. Economic conditions
4. Peer pressure
5. Clients/customers
6. Pride in the team
7. Contests
8. Meetings
9. Counseling sessions
10. Termination techniques

1. Take Your Objectives into the Home

The *family* exerts enormous pressure, which can be either positive or negative. The families your people leave at home each morning and return to each evening will be either a major ally to what you're attempting to accomplish or a deterrent. If the family sees their loved one coming home frustrated, exhausted, and/or irritable, it might well encourage him or her to leave your company and find somewhere that suits him or her better. One company became aware that new commission sales people were likely to experience some resistance at home because the rewards are delayed in commission sales, especially at first.

Resistance to the delayed compensation from commission sales might not be the most important issue facing your organization. However, you can probably benefit greatly from what this particular company did to bring the family into the picture. The first thing the company did was to invite the families to attend an open house where they could become more familiar with how the company operates and the benefits they could expect from having a family member employed there. This is important not only during training of new employees, but also periodically throughout a person's career. By sending a video or audio cassette tape home with the employee during training, including the homework for the following day (so that the tape is sure to be played), the company sends its plans and benefits right into the home, where the family members are likely to hear them along with the employee. The result of including the family as a team member will be increased support and encouragement for the employee's efforts at work.

2. Reach Them
on the Training Ground

The initial and ongoing *training program* you have at your company is another factor that influences morale. Make the commitment that your people will never be out of a training program. All of us are constantly learning things, so you might as well invest in an effort to teach those things which will best benefit the organization. The relevancy of your training and continuing education, as well as emphasis on tangible benefits, will help keep your training efforts on the positive side of morale building.

3. Help Them Cope Successfully
in the Larger Economy

Although *economic conditions* in the country or the world are not under your control, you can help your people be educated as to how changes in the economy can and will affect them on the job and at home. You can also smooth over rough economic times by teaching your people how to budget and manage their own resources. How many people who feel as if they must earn more money could be helped by some education in how to do more with what they have? This information can help morale at home and, consequently, in the work place.

4. Make Constructive Use
of Peer Relationships

Don't be fooled into thinking people leave *peer pressure* behind in the school yard. Peer pressure is one of the most powerful ongoing influences on the morale of your organization. Peer pressure is constant and can have either a positive or negative effect. The peer pressure issue prompts me to say an effective leader must have radar hearing that constantly sweeps across the work area to pick up what's being said. The radar is to pick up positive comments as well as negative comments.

When a positive exchange is heard between two or more of your people, the manager should materialize at the scene as soon as possible to reinforce what's being said, thus building up both the giver and receiver by amplifying the compliment. If negative pressure is detected between team members, the manager needs to appear as soon as possible and say to the negative party, "It sounds like you're having trouble, why don't you come into my office where I can listen to your problem and you won't have to burden anyone else with it." About the third time this individual is invited into your office to explain how bad things really are, he or she might figure out that complaining to peers is going to wind up in a trip to the manager's office. In Chapter Five, I already set up some guidelines for how you entertain such discussions in your office.

5. Get Morale Mileage
from the Client Relationship

Clients and/or customers will influence your people's morale. It's wise to establish creative and effective methods for dealing with customers and clients in order to exert some measure of influence yourself on the degree of influence they will have on your people. Specifically, I can think of one company who recognized the relationship between customers and employees and addressed the issue right in the waiting room at the company's office. The company made the waiting area as comfortable as a living room, complete with current magazines and newspapers, coffee, and personal conversation with the branch manager about the client's needs and why he or she had chosen that particular company to do business with. A great deal of helpful information was generated while the customer was made to feel personally cared for. The result was a positive working relationship which, in turn, built morale.

6. Take Advantage of Team Pride

Pride in the team is always important to morale. In the office I practically destroyed early in my management career, we ended up with all sorts of plaques and trophies around the office for the excellence we ultimately achieved together. This is important to point out because I used to feel that when I briefed a new team member, it was his or her final briefing. Not so. My briefing was the *next* to the last one. In observing the trophies and awards in the office, the new person received a clear message that excellence was *expected* in that organization. The evidence of our success as a team provided a nonverbal, but extremely effective, briefing.

7. Build Esprit de Corps
through Friendly Competition

Contests are a fun way to keep everyone focused on the goals of the organization. While contests are most common in sales organizations, they can be effectively used in many other situations as well. If it's important to complete a design with minimal flaws in a short period of time, prizes for measures of accomplishment might help keep everyone pulling in the same direction. If creativity and new ideas are called for (which they should be anywhere) contests can help bolster those efforts as well. No matter what you do, you should endeavor to make it fun and rewarding, with both immediate gratification—such as a prize—and long-term benefit considerations.

I learned the hard way that, if you shout long enough and loud enough about something you feel needs rectification, you will probably get to be in charge of the committee to rectify the situation. Such was the case with the way our company was running contests. I complained and promptly got the job of coming up with new ways to run contests. Here is my list of *Cox's Contest Rules:*

1. Develop a theme that reflects the goals and objectives of the organization. Use a name that is a good metaphor for the nature of the desired accomplishment.

2. The contest should target the middle 60 percent of your staff. The top 20 percent are fired up without any assistance and the lowest 20 percent require motivational efforts on your part which are disproportionate for the return.

3. The length of the contest should be consistent with the goals sought. It's important to keep the contest duration shorter rather than longer in order for the intended emphasis not to be lost. Sales contests should typically run from 30 to 45 days.

4. Keep the rules simple. Each person should receive a printed copy of the rules as well as a list of the prizes. It might be good to send these to the employee's home in order to involve the family.

5. Make sure the prizes are worth working for.

6. Make it fair to all by using appropriate handicaps based on past performance or direct impact on the desired goals.

7. Set goals just out of your team's reach, but not out of their ability.

8. Have numerous winners. First place through fifth, for example, recognizes the efforts of more than just one person. If there's only one prize and one person leaps ahead early on, the rest of the people will lose interest. Sometimes, the whole team should share equally in the prize if it's a team challenge.

9. Offer a choice of prizes for each winner to generate more incentive because of the increased personalization. Be careful when using money as a prize that you don't inadvertently create a morale backlash after the contest has ended. Trips are a better choice. Even small trips make good rewards.

10. Give each person the opportunity to be recognized for his or her efforts, even without receiving one of the big prizes.

11. Promote the contest prizes with enthusiasm. If the leader has no interest in the contest, neither will the staff.

12. Keep promoting throughout the length of the contest, not just at the kick-off.

13. Keep an up-to-date contest progress display in the office as a reminder of how things are advancing.

14. Send out fliers during and after the contest, announcing the leaders and the winners. This works well especially when someone who might not be expected to perform competitively is leading or doing well.

15. Announce the winners when you originally promised to. Always make your announcements as close to the end of the contest as you can.

16. Take pictures of the winners, with their prizes or on their trips, to use in promoting the next contest.

17. Keep a file of past contests with the rules, participants, results, etc., including how well it succeeded in reaching its goals, to review when developing new contests. Relying on your memory for what worked well and what didn't is not adequate. You should complete your critique of a contest as soon as it ends.

18. Major contests should not be held more than twice per year. You don't want to condition your people to feel like everything the organization does is intended to win a prize. A healthy working atmosphere is an ongoing prize for everyone in the organization.

8. Boosting Morale through the Proper Conduct of Routine Meetings

Even if your organization never has occasion to hold contests, you probably have *meetings*. Meetings are another major factor in the morale of your organization. The more frequently you hold meetings, the more you must concentrate on effective elements of good meetings. So here are some of the most time-tested techniques for effective meeting planning:

1. It will help you to keep a personal planning book in a three-ring binder. The divided sections should include:

    a. *Meeting themes* for the future and support materials. Ideas for future themes can come from a variety of sources. You can wake up in the middle of the night with an inspiration which you should write down immediately and put in your binder the following day. You can clip ideas out of newspapers and magazines.

    b. *Personal experiences* will help to illustrate and support the goals and objectives you're seeking in your organization.

    c. *Attention getters* help you get your people's attention. Ideas for these devices should be listed here. I once used a head of a cabbage on the table in front of me to illustrate how I was going to help my salespeople to make more money. Of course they initially equated cabbage with money. However, my point was: to *close* a *buyer*, be *aggressive*, *gentle*, and *enthusiastic*. Get it? Another good attention getter for salespeople when teaching telephone techniques might be to wrap a telephone on the desk with dollar bills or tens or hundreds to illustrate how important the telephone is in selling. As attention getting devices and ideas occur to you, they should be listed in this section of your meeting planning book.

    d. Keep a list of *meeting places.* Meeting in a variety of atmospheres might help keep your meetings interesting. Try to match the environment with the issue to be discussed. I know of one sales manager who met with his people one out of every four times at his home, which was set beautifully on a golf course where the atmosphere was relaxing.

    e. A list of *speakers other than yourself* should be kept in its own section in order to give you some variety with who is available to make presentations to your people.

    f. *Past meeting notes* should be kept in their own section so you can be clear about what has been covered at each meeting and how successful it was. With good meeting notes to refer to, you can quickly assess if progress is being made or if you're covering the same territory over and over again.

2. With the help of your meeting planning book, lay out your meeting plan.

    a. Decide upon a theme.

    b. Select points to support the theme and form the outline for the discussion.

    c. Add support material for each point: how a person can use this information, why these ideas work, etc. Use illustrations or personal experiences whenever possible.

    d. Select three to four questions to ask your people, the answers to which reflect the theme you've chosen. Asking questions is also a way to break the ice and get the meeting started.

    e. Select devices to get attention.

    f. Construct visual aids for the meeting.

3. For a 45-minute meeting, the manager should spend two to three hours preparing throughout the previous week, not the night before.

4. Arrive an hour before the meeting is to begin.

5. Arrange the chairs in the room to maximize everyone's attention and minimize distractions. Arrange everything else in the room with the same purpose in mind, including projectors, hand outs, visual aids, name tags, etc.

6. Have the coffee and refreshments ready to go well in advance so as not to delay the start of your session.

7. Music is a great way to set a lively tone for a meeting while people are coming in and getting settled.

8. It's not necessary to start a meeting with a joke. Too many people try, and too many people stumble right out of the gate. Be yourself and leave the jokes to Bob Hope. Use your attention getter instead. This is also the time to use your opening questions.

9. Be sure to talk *with* your people, not *at* them. A good meeting has the tone of a discussion rather than a lecture.

10. Always expect the unexpected. There is usually one sort of distraction or another at every meeting. The best way to keep your crowd's attention is to walk away from a distraction in the room and get quieter rather than to move toward it and get louder.

11. Stay relaxed throughout the meeting. You will appear more friendly and credible.

12. Plan a powerful close that includes an inspirational challenge with a quick word of appreciation and thanks. I've been known to say, "We can do it. We have a strong team. I love working with all of you. You make my job easier. Now, let's go make something happen."

To insure you're conducting the best meetings possible, do a self-critique after each one. Tape recording the session and listening to it later is helpful. After you listen, answer these questions:

1. Was I really prepared?
2. Did I start the meeting exactly on time?
3. Did the people respond freely and easily to my questions?
4. Did I keep the meeting on track?
5. Did I refrain from lecturing or playing "the expert"?
6. Did I maintain a healthy control of the meeting?
7. Were distractions handled properly, without magnification?
8. Did I keep their interest throughout the meeting?
9. Did I make full use of visual aids and other tools?
10. Were the outlined points covered thoroughly?
11. Did I answer everyone's questions clearly?
12. Did the majority seem to enjoy the meeting?
13. Were they given something to really think about?
14. Did I close the meeting on time?
15. Did *I* learn something from the meeting?

9. Counsel Them One-on-One

The individual *counseling session* is one of the least understood, yet most powerful, tools a leader has to educate and motivate his or her people. A counseling session is a prime opportunity to initiate many positive changes. According to management expert Jim Rohn, people want to change most often because

1. They are uncomfortable with the current state of affairs. When the pain gets bad enough, they will commit to making something new happen.
2. They simply want a change because they're bored with the same old way of doing things.
3. They get excited at the mere discovery that things *can* change.

Many managers fumble the ball and miss a great opportunity at point number three. When you see a positive change and the resulting increase in morale and productivity, don't sigh and say, "Thank God for small favors" and then move on to something else. The moment something new and positive happens is the moment you should introduce that person to another possibility and then another and another and so forth. People get excited about their own growth and the leader should feed that excitement.

Pinpoint the Skill to Be Worked on/Start the Session on a Positive Note.   Perhaps you're aware one of your people is having difficulty with time planning. Before that individual arrives for the counseling session with you, make a list of ways you think he or she could better utilize time. Then put your list aside until the person has arrived, you've closed the doors, and thrown bouquets at him or her about how much improvement there has been since the last counseling session. Literally praise that person's success. Talk about the improvement. Make no other comparison than to his or her individual growth since the previous session.

Establish Your Understanding of the Personal Situation.   Talk to that person about why he or she is working so hard. Talk about his or her goals. What are the time frames involved? If a son or daughter is going off to college in a few years, that's a measurable length of time in which to accomplish some things. Then break down the goals into easily understandable units. For example, how much money needs to be set aside to get the son or daughter through college. Break down the goals into smaller units to demonstrate how much you understand their unique situation.

Reveal the Area Targeted for Improvement.   Only after you have established how well you understand the situation and have helped that person to get excited about his or her ability to reach desired goals, do you introduce areas that can be improved. Always remember to *attack the problem, not the person.* Your purpose is to open the door to discussing issues where this person needs improvement, not to shut him or her off with negative criticism. Tell the person you're counseling that you have some ideas to help him or her reach the goals you've been discussing sooner and/or with reduced effort.

By introducing time planning ideas as if they are your own, you don't tell the person you feel he or she is lousy at time planning. That is a comment sure to get a mental door slammed in your face.

Keep on Track.   Once you've opened the discussion, follow some rules to keep you on track:

1. Get to the point quickly.
2. Describe the problem you want to correct.
3. Listen to how the employee describes the problem.
4. Get agreement on what the problem *really* is.
5. Explain your ideas on solving the problem.
6. Have the employee sum up the problem and the solution.
7. Schedule a follow-up meeting on this issue.
8. Schedule your next follow-up session.

Item 7 is *not* the next monthly counseling session, but a "how's it going?" kind of follow-up. A follow-up on the issue you've discussed is vital for a couple reasons. First of all, you need to see if any improvement is being made and the sooner the better. Second, the employee needs your feedback if there is no improvement and desperately wants recognition if improvement is happening. Therefore, if you schedule a follow-up session one week later at a specific time (as you should), *keep your appointment.* Imagine the letdown your employee will suffer if there is improvement to be celebrated and your secretary calls him or her to reschedule. The leader has to make every effort to support the efforts of his or her people to improve, especially when requested to.

Come Full Circle/Set the Stage for Monitoring.   Finally, at the close of your counseling session, bring the discussion full circle by returning to the individual's stated goals. Reminding that person of how the new information discussed will promote the accomplishment of those goals will open the door to monitoring. Once the importance of, say, time management has been established, ask if that person wants a reminder if you notice old habits threatening the progress he or she has made. The employee will no doubt encourage you to monitor his or her growth in that area, thus opening the door to further coaching for improvement.

10. Mastering Termination Situations—a Morale Minefield

Termination techniques are methods more for *keeping* employees than for getting rid of them and are forms of leadership counseling. Once again, I'll refer to managing salespeople. However, the principles have broad application for virtually all staffers in a wide variety of organizations. A recent study identified a tendency I have labeled the "90-day-I-want-to-quit-syndrome." For whatever reason, some employees tend to lose sight of the future pay-offs of a job and become overwhelmed with a sense of hopelessness approximately three months after joining the company.

The "Drown Them in Affirmation" Approach to Employee Retention

If you've been managing for very long, you've had them enter your office before announcing they have decided to resign. These are usually extremely good people you don't want to lose. So when you hear the words, "Can I see you for a minute?," you feel a chill on the back of your neck.

Use the Element of Surprise. Once inside the office, an individual says something like, "I don't exactly know how to tell you this, but I've decided to leave." At that point, you say, "Congratulations and welcome to the team!" With that said, the employee's mouth should be hanging open and you know you have his or her undivided attention.

The person standing in your office might feel as if you didn't hear correctly and tell you again that he or she is leaving your organization. You tell that person you not only heard correctly the first time, but you *anticipated* this conversation because *everybody* goes through these feelings. What you're trying to do is communicate that what this person is experiencing is common for people in their circumstances. You can point to someone else in the organization who has experienced a similar dilemma and risen above it to succeed. Through means of identification, the individual in your office might no longer think that such feelings are unique to him or her and go back to work. However, it's usually not that easy.

Apply the "Conveyor Belt" Principle. The individual in your office might acknowledge that, even though others had similar feelings, he or she still wants to leave. That's when it's time to explain what I call the "conveyor belt principle." The conveyor belt principle simply states that all of the work someone has done to date is in process and, even though the fruits of labor are not presently evident, a little more patience will soon be rewarded. If this person understands the virtues of waiting for the benefits to cycle back to him or her, yet still insists on going, it's time for the heavy artillery.

Play Your Trump Card. Say to this person, "What's really going to hurt about this is the fact that I'm going to have to assign somebody else to carry on in the area or territory where you have been working so hard. That new person is going to enjoy the benefits you should be receiving for the hard work that you've invested." It's human nature to want rewards and recognition for work we, ourselves, have done. However, your employee might be *really* set on leaving. What then?

If All Else Fails . . .   It's time for "the-grass-is-always-greener-on-the-other-side-of-the-fence-but-it's-just-as-hard-to-cut" segment. You say, "I don't understand why you think you're going to be happier or work more successfully at a second or third choice employer." Hopefully, your employee will realize that grass here is just as good as grass anywhere else. Of course, you might have an individual who has his or her mind set on leaving and new grass is as good a reason as any. What do you do then?

Take It to the Team.   Use your top people to influence the one leaving. Look at the employee standing in your office and say, "I've invested a great deal of coaching and counseling in you and I want you to help me protect that investment by granting me one more hour. Not 90 days, but one more hour. Have lunch with me and (so-and-so) so we can say goodbye and hear more about why you feel you have to go." So-and-so is the person who you identified earlier as the individual who once had the same desire to leave but thought better of it and went on to become very successful within the organization.

Your deal with so-and-so is to buy lunch if he or she will share a personal "90-day-I-want-to-quit-syndrome" experience with the person leaving. The lunch hour itself will be one of the most difficult hours you will ever endure, because you must keep your mouth shut, except to eat. You've set the scene. Now let the team members exchange their ideas about the organization. It should be clear that the person leaving hasn't considered all the angles yet.

Call for a Moratorium Period.   If, at the end of the lunch, the individual is still leaving, take him or her back to your office and say, "I think you need to take some time off. Take the rest of the week off and get away with your spouse to the desert, the mountains, the river, the ocean, or wherever you want to go and think about what you want to do with your future. Then come back Monday and tell me if you still think your wisest choice is to leave. If you still feel this way next Monday, we'll process the papers at that time." If the person has truly been working hard, the time off will sound extremely inviting.

If You Really Value a Person, Always Leave the Door Open.   If the person comes back Monday and still wants to quit, do you process the papers? Not quite yet. First say, "The reason I hired you is because I sensed some real potential within you and I believe it's still there. I hope the new manager you're going to work for sees that potential too. If he or she doesn't, you could be losing out on the good coaching you would have received here. Go ahead and give your new job your best shot. But, *please* stop by from time to time and have a cup of coffee with me. I want to know how you're doing. If it turns out not to be as good as you thought, you can always pick up your stuff and come back *home.*" If you've done your job right, you should have that person in tears. He or she might even soften enough to admit that your organization *does* feel a little like family. Your final hurrah should be a sorrowful account of how you'll have to go out and tell the rest of the "family" that this person is leaving. If the "90-day-I-want-to-quit" person survives this process and elects to stay with you, chances are good he or she will never try to leave again. The process is simply too exhausting to experience twice.

P.S.—If You've Shown Leadership in Your Hiring, It Would Be Contradictory to Neglect Leadership in Retention.   I'm sure many people reading this feel my methods are melodramatic and lack professionalism. They might even smack of manipulation to some. I can almost hear voices saying, "It's not worth it. If they want to quit that bad, who needs them?" or "That's ridiculous. It would never work with my people." To these folks I say a leader must believe in the value of working for his or her organization. Furthermore, I have used the process I just described more times than I can recall, with tremendous success. I became known for my reputation of turning people around at the door. The bottom line is some people have to be drowned in affirmation to counteract their innate sense of failure and, once turned around, are new people who are changed forever. Some of my brightest, long-term superstars went through this process with me and went on to tremendous success with our organization.

The Farewell Interview:
It's More Than Just Goodbye

In spite of the long and arduous process I just described for keeping good people on the job, it's incumbent on the leader to diagnose if the terminating individual is a symptom of a deeper and wide-spread dissatisfaction on the part of your staff. If the individual has weathered all of your attempts to keep them on the job, your focus should turn to the farewell interview as a study in how to make improvements where possible within your organization.

Even Terminations Serve Team Goals.   Although it might sound strange, the first order of business in the farewell interview is for the leader to explain the long-term goals for the organization. Then you ask the person who is leaving to help you achieve those goals by answering a few questions.

It's often best to do this over lunch or somewhere outside of the office where people feel less inhibited talking freely. Here are the questions:

1. What are *your* long-term goals?
2. Why did you pick this time to leave?
3. What did you like most about this job?
4. What disappointed you the most?
5. How does your spouse and family feel about your work?
6. Why did you pick our organization in the first place?
7. What are you being offered there that you can't get here?
8. How do you feel about the training you received?
9. How could we have helped you more?
10. Did we let you down in any way?

If this is a person you really want back if possible, be sure to ask what can be done, if anything, to get him or her back. Be sure to listen with all of your receptors open to the information this person gives you. This data is invaluable in developing a sense of what people are thinking and experiencing inside your organization. But what if the person is gone and you *still* would like to get him or her back? Even though he or she might be working for someone else, all is not lost.

Maintain Post-Termination Contact. Send a letter every month to that person's home. Be honest and say you hope things are going well and you're pulling for him or her to fully realize the potential you always felt he or she possessed. Invite that person to stop by your office to say hello whenever possible and share some conversation over a cup of coffee. Keep these letters going for at least three months because this is the time period over which that person and his or her spouse are going to be questioning the decision to make the move. Your letters convey to the former employee and his or her family that you still care and take a personal interest in his or her success. Chances are your concern will exceed that of the manager he or she is currently working for.

If the Prodigal Does Return, Enlist That Person As An Ally. If the former employee decides to return, kill the fatted calf and have a celebration. Never say, "I told you so." However, it's important to let everyone in the organization know this person has decided to return. The message should be clear to others in your organization who are tempted by the "grass-is-greener" syndrome. Now you have someone who can assist you with personal testimony the next time someone else decides to leave.

Specific Tactics for Improving Morale

Send a Letter of Recognition to the Employee's Home

Including the employee's family as much as possible in recognition for good work expands the overall impact of the recognition. It also helps to acknowledge the employee's support base and the contributions family members make to success at work. You often see schools involve the family in recognizing quality efforts by students in the classroom. Taking similar action for quality work in business follows the same principle. People sometimes wish their spouses or children were more aware of what they do on the job. This technique helps not only to inform the family, but also to bring them into the picture.

Call Your Employees at Home on Thanksgiving

Wishing your people well and acknowledging their family life keeps the leader and the team members more conscious of the important link between an individual's personal and professional lives. Any way a leader can show respect and genuine compassion toward the people in the organization will engender a more positive and productive atmosphere and build morale.

Take One Person Out to Breakfast or Coffee Per Week

The point of spending some time away from the office one-on-one is to communicate clearly that you have an authentic interest in your people as individuals and not merely as an obligation to apply new management techniques. I constantly encounter situations where managers are instructed to take a more active role in their employee's affairs. The result is that managers too often simply make their rounds and ask questions they really don't care to hear the answers to or emerge from their offices at the appointed time each day to mechanically slap everyone on the back and then disappear into the dark recesses of their offices again. People *know* if your interest is real.

Recognize Employment Anniversaries

Many companies are good at awarding some sort of trophy, pen, watch, trip, or other token of appreciation when a person reaches a milestone in his or her tenure with the company. You can easily program electronic personnel files to remind you when a person has reached an anniversary. In fact, it can become so easy that many recognitions of this type become mechanized and lack any personal meaning. Even the boss taking a person out to lunch to award the trophy can be a stuffy experience. I applaud and encourage these methods of recognition. However, the most important point I can emphasize is that all of these efforts on the part of management will only seem as genuine and rewarding as the pervasive quality of the day-to-day relationship between a leader and his or her people. A fountain pen placed in the hands of someone who truly feels appreciated will mean more than a Hawaiian vacation presented to someone who is bitter over being a number for so many years.

Encourage People to Personalize Their Offices

Obviously, whether your people receive clients in their offices and/or are in highly visible positions will present some limitations on how outrageous decorating can become. However, within the context of reason, it's always to your benefit as well as the individual's benefit for all of your people to be as comfortable *where* they work as it is for them to be comfortable with what they're doing. An effective leader wants his or her people to be as personally invested in their work as possible and to create a familiar and comfortable environment that promotes the cause. Care must be taken to avoid one individual's tastes becoming offensive to others. As a leader, you are a sort of "village chief" who needs to protect best interests of the greatest number of people in the organization. However, while making people conform to cookie-cutter images and placing them in little identical cubicles might appear to be productive and orderly, it is probably costing you a great deal in morale and individual enthusiasm.

Encourage Outside Activities, Such as Fitness

The more ways you can help your people express themselves and more wholly experience the multiple dimensions of life, the stronger your morale is going to be in the work place. Not only is physical fitness a worthwhile goal with positive benefits at work, but the sense of positive fellowship and community sets a tone that carries over into the work environment. Sports is not the only form of organized activity. Encourage people to form car clubs, hiking and camping trips, theatre and movie clubs, etc. The more you can encourage people to invest in activities that reflect their personal interests, the more completely they will open up to creative and innovative developments at work.

Take the Rap on Occasion for Good People

Two key words here are "occasion" and "good." Even your best people are going to foul up once in awhile. If you are willing to step in and bail them out instead of allowing them to suffer alone, people are going to understand how much you appreciate the good things they do. This should not be a regular practice nor should you bail people out who don't deserve it. That would produce a very different and less positive message. It would even be a slap in the face to your people who try harder. Yet the well-placed and well-timed intercession on behalf of someone who is a solid contributor will make a stronger statement than almost any other gesture.

Promote Community Projects

Businesses don't exist in isolation. Your staff lives in the community as well as your customers. The community could be a neighborhood or the world. Regardless of the scope of your effort, it's important to promote community involvement among your people. You can offer company facilities for community meetings, blood drives, scout meetings, bible studies, CPR training, and a wide variety of activities which reflect the needs and quality of life in your community. Donations and sponsorship of worthwhile causes are also important. We are known by our actions as business people just as we are known by our actions as individuals. It's best to involve team members at all levels in determining how and to what extent the organization will become involved in supporting the community. You'll be proud when you see some of your people featured in the local news media.

Photos and Stand-Ups

Some companies put a portrait of high-achievers in the lobby or some other prominent place. If budgets permit, you can even have a life-sized stand-up done to make the recognition more dramatic. One caveat here. Most work places are not filled to the brim with narcissists. As a leader, you must be sensitive to whether or not public recognition for your people might make them nervous or self-conscious. Being aware of individual feelings within your organization can help minimize embarrassment or, possibly, help to prevent team members from intentionally lagging behind in order to avoid being put on display.

Reserved Seats

By setting aside special seating in meeting rooms for high-achievers and rotating the honorees each month, you can make sure each achiever feels a sense of recognition in front of his or her peers as well as promoting a sense that his or her ideas are receiving special attention in staff meetings. Take-home namecards on chairs also give that impression of special treatment.

Video Recognition

Use high technology to produce a "Day in the life of _____" for a super high-achiever and present it as a gift. By making a small production out of an individual's activities, you are not only honoring that person, but also reaffirming those aspects of his or her efforts that are most beneficial to the organization. This type of gift gives the individual the opportunity to share his or her accomplishments with friends and family. This video gift can also be used to reward an entire department. Don't forget your company newsletters and newspapers are other valuable media resources for recognition.

Trinkets, Tickets, and Other Giveaways

For individual or team efforts, concert, movie, or sporting event tickets make good prizes. T-shirts, coffee mugs, or other items with appropriate mottos, slogans, and/or personalized congratulations are appreciated in direct proportion to the amount of personal investment the leadership has in the individual or team effort. Sometimes, when recognition is in order, an advertisement in an appropriate trade or general publication extends your sincere congratulations.

Look Behind the Scenes

Don't overlook the contributions of those people whose tasks might not be as spectacular or visible as others. A good policy to adopt is to recognize someone in a nonvisible support role each and every time you recognize someone in a more visible position. Recognize them together whenever possible to promote the awareness among your people of how synergy works and how the efforts of everyone in the system contribute to the big picture.

Keep an Accomplishment Yearbook

Establish an annual publication that details who did what over the past 12 months and set the tone for the following year. Include pictures and case histories. This is a good opportunity to deliver much needed recognition in the context of the organization's overall goals. The impact of the annual publication can be increased by associating awards with it and even an annual awards dinner.

In the Name of . . .

Another clever idea is to name a space or an object in the building with a small sign for someone who is a deserving recipient. Such acknowledgment can range from naming a cafeteria after someone who is an inspirational contributor to the best interests of everyone in the organization to naming the photocopier after the secretary who has a special knack for keeping it running. This is yet another way that the workplace can be personalized while, at the same time, providing recognition.

There can be as many ideas for a list such as this as there are creative people and concepts. Your own situation might well give rise to other means of providing recognition. Don't forget the most reliable source of information when it comes to what makes your people feel appreciated is *your people*.

Conclusion:
Don't Forget Number One

If the organization gets better after the leader gets better, then the leader needs to practice what he or she preaches! I've spent a great deal of time establishing the need for leaders to model the principles they set forth for others to follow. Morale and overall attitude are probably the most important examples a leader can set. I'll go so far as to say the leader's morale and attitude, positive or negative, is the most powerful force at work in any organization.

The leader not only sets the mood and the tone for the entire organization, he or she establishes the momentum. If the leader isn't as invested as he or she expects everyone else to be, all the speeches and trophies in the world won't improve morale. Worse yet, if the leader's heart isn't in it, the speeches and trophies are resented for their hollow and manipulative nature. Your people will most likely respond positively to the same things you do. I had an employee once who told me her favorite feeling came after solving a tough problem. I felt the same way, but was less aware of it until she taught me.

The most powerful way I know for anyone to improve his or her own morale is to climb out of the rut we find ourselves in when we insist on repeating yesterday. Top achievers not only love to solve problems and seek self-fulfillment, but also enjoy the search for new and better ways to get the job done. Improved morale at the top stimulates creativity and carries with it a productivity-enhancing momentum.

Here are some practical methods for *you to use* to achieve higher levels of self-fulfillment and enhanced personal and professional growth:

1. Lay out a new list of goals. Be sure to break down each goal into daily tasks to assure accomplishment.

2. Go for a walk in the park, on the beach, or in the mountains. In short, get away to your own thoughts and hear what they have to say.

3. Read several books on a variety of topics to stretch your mind around someone else's thoughts and ideas.

4. Get away for the weekend, to a luxury hotel or spa, and pamper yourself.

5. Exercise and get into better physical condition.

6. Buy something for yourself you've always wanted.

7. Invite interesting people who are not in your field over to your home for dinner.

8. Listen to good music and sing along at the top of your lungs.

9. Get your office and/or home totally organized and enjoy the moment.

10. Go see a funny movie.

11. List your assets and achievements.

12. Talk to somebody who always makes you feel good.

13. Take up a hobby.

14. Give help to someone who needs it. Invest one percent of your 16 waking hours of the day (approximately 10 minutes) in making someone else happy.

15. Take five-minute daily vacations to renew your energy.

If you can't manage to get yourself out of your bad mood by the time you reach the office, pull a 180-degree turn and get out of there. The last thing your people need is a leader with an infectious bad attitude. Remember, positive or negative morale begins with the leader. Everything in this chapter is first and foremost for *you!*

Chapter Seven

The 5th Step–
Creativity When
the Heat's On

*"The (person) who follows the crowd will
usually get no further than the crowd. The
(person) who walks alone is likely to find
himself (or herself) in places no one has ever
been before.*

*Creativity in living is not without its attendant
difficulties, for peculiarity breeds contempt.
And the unfortunate thing about being ahead
of your time is, when people finally realize you
were right, they'll say it was obvious all along.*

*You have two choices in life: You can dissolve
into the mainstream or you can be distinct. To
be distinct you must be different. To be different
you must strive to be what no one else but you
can be."*
—ALAN ASHLEY-PITT

When the Heat's On,
Creativity Is Your Fan

When the heat is on, creativity is a necessity, not a luxury. If what you have
been doing was thoroughly working, you probably wouldn't be on the hot
seat. Therefore, it is likely that treating creativity as an option is what helped
to create the pressure in the first place. As Ashley-Pitt points out, creativity
is not always greeted with open arms in an organization and people tend to
avoid it as a result. However, the bottom line is that when old ways get you
into trouble, new ways are what you need to get out.

Creativity lays the foundation for solving problems and managing change. It's important to understand what creativity is, how it helps you to be the most effective leader possible, and how you can stimulate it in your organization. Nobody I have ever met wants his or her organization to "dissolve into the mainstream." As I share ideas, methods, and techniques on creativity, bear in mind the goal is to be distinct in realizing your full potential and the potential of those you lead.

Creativity Likened Unto a Coffee Bean—A Short Parable

George A. McDermott, Jr., in the *Executive Idea Stimulator,* put it this way:

> One day . . . a long time ago . . . in, say, a million B.C., somebody figured out that you could put things in water and boil them, then throw out the water and eat the things.
>
> (Somebody also figured out that that was called *cooking,* but that's minor-league creativity.)
>
> Well, Cooking was very nice, but it was still a relatively new invention, and they hadn't worked all the bugs out yet. For instance: coffee beans, even after people cooked them, still tasted crummy.
>
> So everyone gave up on coffee beans . . . at least until some genius had a flash of inspiration.
>
> "Hey, maybe Cooking doesn't always work the same way," he said. "Sure, the *beans* taste lousy, but we haven't tried drinking the *water* we cooked them in."
>
> If that doesn't sound like significant genius to you, ask yourself these questions: Have you ever tried eating coffee grounds? Would the taste inspire *you* to drink the water?

Profile of the Creative Mind

Characteristics of a creative person:

1. Child-like sense of wonder

2. Consistent openness to alternatives

3. Unthreatened by new ideas

4. Eagerness for the future

5. Ability to test new ideas

6. Ongoing flexibility

Never feel as if you are not a creative person. Creativity is not a genetic trait. Anyone can develop creative abilities by understanding what creativity is. For example, a creative person is, first and foremost, curious and inquisitive. He or she is likely to read, travel, and explore a great deal. The creative person is likely to have some unique hobbies. Creative people truly enjoy the child-like experience of discovery.

Creative people don't find satisfaction in limited alternatives. They want to discover as many alternatives as possible. This can be a problem for the leader who has creative people in his or her organization. If you don't decide at some point which alternative to go with and refocus your people's attention on new tasks, they will keep coming up with new alternatives into the next millennium. The good news is that a constant openness to new alternatives will often lead you and your organization out of the proverbial woods, especially during a forest fire.

Some people stifle their own creative potential by caving in to fear of the unknown. The business world is loaded with self-stifled people. For whatever reason, these people believe what they're currently experiencing, as unpleasant as that might be, can't be as bad as an unfamiliar alternative. By contrast, creative people feel that, however good the present is, there is always a better future waiting to be discovered. They are not threatened by the unfamiliar. Creative people seek the excitement of discovering the previously unknown.

If the present is familiar and therefore comfortable, then, to creative people, the future will also be familiar and comfortable. Creative people are drawn forward into uncharted territory by an eagerness for the future. To them, what lies ahead is bright and beautiful.

Henry Ford said, "Some of our best ideas have come from letting fools rush in where angels fear to tread." Don't encourage your people to be timid angels when it comes to creativity. There is plenty of time to be angelic when your organization gets involved with community service projects. The "fools" Mr. Ford talks about are really just normal people with permission to be a little unconventional when the urge strikes them. Eva LaGallienne said, "Innovators are inevitably controversial."

As an effective leader, you should see to it that creative people get quality feedback on their ideas. They are eager to test new ideas to see how they work. You could say the moment of truth or the peak of excitement for creative people occurs when they actually *try* new ideas. A major joy in the creative process is seeing a new idea work. Of course, to truly creative people, as soon as a new idea works, it becomes an old idea. In an organizational context, it's always good to get feedback from others before a new idea is launched, providing the feedback does not block or stifle the creative impulse.

Creative people are not typically *married* to any one concept or idea. They don't develop sacred cows. Whereas less creative people tend to cling desperately to the past or existing ideas, the more creative people are willing to scrap something that doesn't work and move forward. Flexibility is driven in part by curiosity and eagerness for the future and maintained by the sheer delight of moving on to new things when the opportunity arises.

Five Fundamentals of Cultivating Creativity

If Henry Ford and Eva LaGallienne are correct, creative and innovative people might be thought of as controversial fools. If you have experienced resistance or criticism during your creative moments, don't be surprised or discouraged. More flack received may indicate greater creativity. However, in spite of all the potential difficulties, you are committed to creativity because you realize it's an essential component of personal and professional success. So here are some ways to go about becoming more creative:

1. Schedule more uninterrupted private time

2. Use the "kaleidoscope" approach

3. Be gullible

4. Anticipate mental conflict

5. Continue to look at far-fetched ideas

Buy Yourself Some Thinking Time. When I was told my boss was looking for my replacement, I took some private, uninterrupted time to be by myself at the beach. At that point, I was at a loss for what else to do. I didn't have the information then I'm sharing with you now. Even though I initially stumbled across the correct action to stimulate my creativity, I can now recommend such isolation to anyone who is experiencing major problems. Most people in the heat of battle will feel they can't abandon the fight. Believe me, staying in the struggle with no ideas or anything else to offer won't do anyone much good.

The point is you need to place *more* distance between you and the problem, not *less*. It's possible and all too probable to lose perspective by staying too close to difficult issues. Going to seminars doesn't accomplish this. Going on crowded cruises won't do it either. In order for isolation to have any positive effect, your mind needs a chance to clear itself and get beyond the everyday clutter.

Unrelated Pieces in Motion. I often recommend to partners in a company that they get away to a mountain cabin together and write out a description of their company five years into the future. Isolation allows you to observe your situation through a longer lens. You can actually see the life return to someone's face who has managed to put some distance between himself or herself and the problem. You can then return to the struggle refreshed and with something new and valuable to offer.

You remember looking through a kaleidoscope as a kid, watching the colors and shapes tumble and change. I look at creativity the same way, as pieces floating around in no particular order or formation. When I start to move the pieces around in my head, exciting thoughts begin to form. My wife refers to my creative time as "being on the mountaintop" even though I'm usually in my own library. If you have the pieces in motion but haven't seen a good picture yet, keep turning the pieces. It will happen if you give it enough undistracted time.

Go Against the Grain of Skepticism.   Being gullible is like being the unconventional fool who rushes in where angels fear to tread. In short, don't be afraid of being fooled or being called foolish. Many people simply never allow themselves the luxury of being wrong. The fact is we are wrong most of the time if we're committed to being creative. It's those rare moments when we're right that make the world go around. No inventor has ever had more successes than successful failures. People who are afraid of being wrong don't trust new ideas. The creative person trusts each and every new idea until there is a solid reason to reject it. Just think of what a different world this would be if great inventors and pioneers throughout history didn't trust ideas others held no stock in. Don't give up your new ideas out of hand just because others might find them a bit unorthodox.

Expect Pressure to Accompany Progress.   Anticipate mental conflict during the creative process. Anticipate it so strongly that, if you don't experience any internal or external conflict, you can assume you're not as invested in the creative process as you might think. Dr. Robert Schuller tells us that conflict is the *birthplace* of creativity. A personal inventory of your life would probably reveal that when you experienced the greatest conflict you were also being the most creative.

Unfortunately, many people stare helplessly at the conflict and say, "Oh, woe is me." That's when you need to throw the conflict logs on the creativity fire because *there is no progress without pressure.* You can carry the argument a step further and say that moments of conflict are when you are most effective as a leader if you have the appropriate commitment to creativity. I know many readers are scratching their heads right now and thinking that, given the amount of heat lately, they must be especially creative and not even realize it.

Be Careful Not to Throw Away Ideas Too Hastily.   Look at illogical and far-fetched thoughts with credibility. The reason most people will so often dismiss a new thought is because it doesn't fit neatly into the existing scheme of things. Remember that all of those illogical thoughts rolling around in your kaleidoscope will eventually fall together in such a way as to create a great new *idea*. Just because an idea doesn't immediately represent the entire answer at the moment doesn't mean it's not a valuable component of the larger solution. Don't discard a thought that might serve as a springboard into a new idea.

Know What Makes an Idea Successful

The fellow I learned these principles from lost his job as a young newspaper reporter because he "lacked good ideas." His editor back in Kansas said that he was "void of creativity." Strangely enough, nobody knows the name of that editor. However, almost everyone in the world eventually learned to equate the young reporter's name, Walt Disney, with creativity. In order for an idea to become successful, Walt Disney maintained that it needs:

1. A *uniqueness* factor
2. A *word-of-mouth* factor
3. A *flair* factor

Ensuring the Uniqueness Factor.   The first criterion for your creative endeavor is to make sure it's *unique*. Why should anybody get excited about something that's ordinary? Walt believed that, unless something is truly unique, there is no reason to go out of your way for it. The question to keep asking throughout the creative process is, "How is this different from what I'm already doing?" Or you could ask, "How is this going to make things different in the future?"

Tapping into Natural Excitement to Generate Word-of-Mouth Promotion.   The *word-of-mouth* phenomenon Walt lists as his second component of a successful idea proceeds naturally from the excitement people feel when they discover something unique. When people have a positive new experience it's virtually impossible to keep them quiet about it. It could be a new book, a movie, a car, a piece of furniture, a pair of shoes or anything else that makes a significant impression because of an unexpectedly pleasant experience. The big question we should ask ourselves in business is, "Am I a unique and positive experience to the people I work with or sell to?" If the answer is yes, then you are successfully integrating creativity and uniqueness into your interactions with others, and the people you work with or sell to are probably talking you up to others.

Capitalizing on the Flair Factor.   The *flair* factor Walt Disney talked about means doing it *big*, doing it *right*, and giving it *class*. It only makes sense that something which is truly unique and generates the enthusiastic endorsements of others should be done with style. The reasons people get so taken with an idea can vary. Some might be impressed with how well planned it is. Others might be impressed with how effective it is. Yet others might be impressed with the image it conveys. All in all, people want to associate themselves with something classy.

A Four-Part Process for Creativity Enhancement

I think of creativity as the *voice beyond silence*. I've already talked about isolating yourself to experience a clear mind. In the silence of isolation will come the voice that is creativity. I built the library onto my home because I collect rare books and that library has become a sort of retreat for me. There are times when I can go into my library and induce creativity. There are other times when I have to stop eating in the middle of a meal and start taking notes because thoughts begin to erupt.

Whether or not you are able to induce creativity or it simply happens when the time is right, there is a four-step process to follow that will help you make the most out of your creative experience:

1. Preparation
2. Incubation
3. Insight
4. Verification

Do Some Homework

If your intention is to create a new product or method for doing something, it's important to learn everything you can about that subject. In other words, do your research. Too many people think the birth of a new idea is enough. To make the new idea more meaningful, it's part of your responsibility to *prepare*. When Thomas Edison wanted to get creative in some aspect of his varied interests, he read about other people's experiments. In doing so, he learned from the mistakes of others and didn't have to repeat as many failed experiences. He put pieces that other people came up with into his kaleidoscope along with his own before he began turning them. If you look only at your own knowledge, your picture will be that much less complete.

Observe an Incubation Period
as the Idea Takes Shape—
Mulling It Over

A new and creative idea begins to cook in the *incubator*. Once a new and creative idea has been born, it needs time to get a grip on you and vise versa. The incubator is a mysterious place. Nobody is really sure why things grow in there, but they do. Have you ever pondered a new idea only to sit up bolt upright in bed at 2:00 A.M. with the completed picture clearly before you? The incubation period is a time when an idea takes root or withers. Whether it takes root or withers is out of our mortal hands. That's why, when an idea is incubating, we're really not able to actively or consciously manipulate it. The kaleidoscope will often turn itself while we sleep. When the correct picture appears, we are awakened instantly.

Await and Recognize
the Moment of Insight—Eureka!

Insight is the moment you receive a new idea. That moment when you sit bolt upright in bed is a moment of insight. We sometimes refer to insight as an innate quality some people seem to have. What we're really saying about that person is that he or she has discernment. Insight is really that elucidating glimpse at the suddenly clear and illuminated answer.

Objectively Confirm the Worth
of the Idea—Coming Down to Earth

Verification is not fun. Creativity flourishes in a mythical environment that has no boundaries. The process of verification brings it all back to reality and begins to establish boundaries. It's difficult to exist in both worlds at the same time. Fantasy and reality don't mix. Nevertheless, any idea born in the realm of creativity must be brought into the world of reality before it can be of any use to anyone. Therefore, verification, although not very entertaining, is a necessary evil if we intend to benefit from creativity.

There are three steps to verifying a new idea:

1. Suitability: Will it solve the problem or simply be a "stop gap"?

2. Feasibility: Is it affordable and practical?

3. Acceptability: Who will support it?

Is It Suitable?   When evaluating the *suitability* of an idea, you must first determine if a permanent solution is required or if a temporary fix will suffice. This doesn't mean that every creative idea needs to be a solution to an existing problem in order to be valuable. However, it's important to determine if the idea has long-term or short-term implications. When a problem exists, the question must be raised as to whether or not the idea specifically helps to bring about a solution to the problem at hand. When the idea is not problem-related, it's still important to determine what tangible benefit the idea will bring about and whether the benefit is long- or short-term. Is the idea appropriate for the organization?

Is It Feasible?   *Feasibility* is really an issue of ability. Your team needs to answer the question, "Can we do it?" When budgets meet effort, there can be a great deal of discussion. This is a discussion that is particularly important to have with your people. The suitability of an idea can be determined independently by the leader, even though I recommend always including your people in decisions that affect them. An effective morale killer is the autocratic decision that an idea is do-able. Few things are more annoying to people than to be given an assignment without any input. Managers might be more concerned with costs than the other team members. However, the practicality and amount of effort involved with carrying out a new idea directly impacts the people in your organization. They are extremely concerned with feasibility.

Is It Acceptable?   *Acceptability* raises several questions, including "Who has the final word on this?," "Will the people who have to carry out this idea accept it?," "Will this idea have a positive impact upon the people who matter most, like our customers?" It's not hard to see how acceptability for some people might not matter if other, more important, people don't accept the idea. The people who say yes or no need to accept an idea if it's going to become reality. The people who have to carry it off must accept it if their efforts are going to be productive. The ultimate beneficiaries must accept the idea if everyone else's acceptance is to mean anything.

If you want yet another wall plaque, the verification process can be capsulized like this:

"Is it *us?*"

"Is it do-able?"

"Will they buy it?"

Dismantle the Four Greatest Barriers to Creativity

Knowing what blocks the creative process is helpful to any leader who is committed to being as creative as possible, as well as developing and encouraging creative growth in every member of the team. If an individual or group of individuals seems to resist creativity or simply won't engage in creative activities, chances are one or more of these four blocks to creativity is operating:

1. Habit

2. Fear

3. Prejudice

4. Inertia

"We've Always Done It This Way."   *Habits* are hard to break, assuming we even *want* to. Some people will say they are just not creative. What that comment really means is they are more comfortable with how things have always been than with how good things truly could be. Habits mean hanging on to the status quo like a needle sticking on a phonograph record. The result is to continually repeat yesterday, which we've already determined is the opposite of growth and creativity. The rallying cry of habit-bound people is "We've *always* done it this way."

"Why Can't We Leave Well Enough Alone?"   *Fear* often explains why we stick with habits and other repetitive behavior longer than we should. You hear people constantly cautioning others that it's better to "leave well enough alone." As I've already mentioned, many people opt to remain in an uncomfortable yet familiar situation rather than to take the risks involved with breaking into the unknown. Fear of what *might* happen keeps people immobilized far more than fear of something known.

"That Wouldn't Work Here."   Fear and ignorance frequently team up to form *prejudice.* As I travel across America promoting creativity and new ideas, I encounter a great deal of prejudice. Prejudice exposes itself when you hear people say things like, "That's not the (*company name*) way." Or, "That's not how we do things here." I hear some form of prejudice in virtually every organization I speak to. After I've delivered my message and moved on, I get letters from virtually every organization saying, "Hey, it *does* work here!" Every letter like that makes me proud to be a *prejudice buster.*

"Don't Rock the Boat."   *Inertia* stops creativity—cold. If our fear is strong enough to immobilize us, we will hesitate to make any move or shift our weight in such a way that might rock the boat. Heaven forbid if we should tip too far and get wet. We would have to climb back in the boat. Even if an organization is following a specific road with its creativity, it's important not to exclude the possibility there might be other directions worth exploring. This is especially true of individual growth and creativity.

Storyboard Your Concept

A tool that helps launch ideas into concrete actions is the storyboard. The concept of storyboarding is not new to people who create film and video productions. I learned it from someone I met two weeks after my boss announced the search for my replacement. Needless to say, at that point I was receptive to almost any new idea that came my way. This person, Mike Vance, had worked for nine years with Walt Disney, who is credited with developing the storyboard concept.

Usually a storyboard is a large bulletin board with the title of the project across the top. Disney might have used one that said, for example, "Mickey's Day at the Park." With the storyboard posted, his creative people could walk by and see the title. Immediately, images would come to mind about what Mickey could do in the park. The creative people would go away and sketch their ideas, bring them back and pin them to the storyboard. Walt would then call his creative people together and conduct what was called a "gag session." During the session they would put the ideas together and form a story, noting what the strong points were and where they needed to fill gaps.

A Case in Point: The Rain Parade

Walt himself figured out one day that storyboarding could be useful for more than making cartoons. After that, the storyboard method was used for everything from finance to development of new attractions for the theme parks. Several years after Walt Disney died, Walt Disney World in Florida was ready to open. Shortly before the opening, Mike Vance was walking through the nearly completed park with Walt's brother, Roy Disney. Roy noted that, unlike Disneyland in California, the sidewalks on Florida's Main Street were covered because of the frequency of rain in that part of the country.

Roy was concerned that, in the event of rain, people would leave the park. My friend had a blinding inspiration with one of the shortest incubation periods in history. While they were still walking down Main Street in Walt Disney World, he suggested having a "Rain Parade." Roy looked at him quizzically and asked what he meant. My friend went on to say that, when it rained, people could stand on the covered sidewalks and watch this special parade rather than go home. Roy said he liked the idea and instructed my friend to begin a storyboard to develop it.

The result was yet another innovative Disney concept that turned a negative into a positive. Once the storyboard was in place, the ideas came flooding in, so to speak. One person in the organization suggested the costumes for the Rain Parade *not* be water-proofed so the crowd could see the characters having fun getting wet. Such creativity! They were so successful at turning a negative situation into a positive situation that visitors to the park who saw the Rain Parade went home and told others about it. The word-of-mouth popularity of the Rain Parade was testimony to the creativity of the organization, aided by the storyboard process. Where else would people tell their friends they hoped it would rain during their vacation?

The same type of creative genius was used on the West Coast when Disney imagineers developed a method for keeping people at Disneyland on cool summer evenings. Almost everyone in America has seen or heard of the Main Street Electrical Parade. The parade is promoted all day long and I defy anyone to attempt taking the kids home before the parade goes by at 9:00 P.M. It's practically unthinkable. Once again, the storyboard technique brought many creative minds together in an environment where creativity is not only allowed, it is encouraged and rewarded.

How to Storyboard in a Business Setting

After my friend, Mike, shared the concept of storyboarding with me, I began applying the concept to my office. Before long my managers started hearing me say, "Let's Rain Parade it" every time a problem came up. "Let's take all of these negatives and turn them into positives," I would say. They thought I was off my rocker at first, but pretty soon the departments were bringing in their storyboards and new ideas were popping up everywhere. The one thing a manager doesn't want to take to the meeting is an empty storyboard if he or she has been given the task of assembling new ideas.

This is another example of how negatives turn into positives and conflict engenders creativity when the leader knows what methods and techniques to apply. Any significant issue facing us became the title for a storyboard. We had our own gag sessions and began to string new and exciting ideas together into workable plans. I caution you not to rank the unresolved problems at the top of your storyboards from greatest to least. Simply identify the unresolved problem. It's important not to plant ideas in the minds of your people as to what's most important and least important, lest they disregard problems you feel need attention, even if those problems are not the most critical in *your* mind. Also, you might want to keep storyboards on extremely sensitive topics at home where the information won't be disruptive to the people in your organization.

One of the reasons storyboards work so effectively is because they keep the issues up in front of people in such a way that the issues are always in the conscious mind. Usually, in a business situation, the ideas that go up on a storyboard are written on index cards. However, ideas can come in the middle of the night, at a restaurant, at the ball park, or anywhere at any time. Therefore, don't be surprised to see storyboards with napkins, backs of envelopes, torn-off corners of team rosters, or most anything else pinned up there.

In Figure 7-1, you see a storyboard for a sales meeting on telephone techniques. I generally use adding machine tape to make my title banner across the top and then use smaller strips to mark the subsections. For a recruiting storyboard, the columns might be titled: "Career Night," "Brochure," "Advertisements," "Competitors' Ideas," and other categories where we want to create new ideas. Many people ask me why I want to be constantly reminded of my competitors' ideas. The answer is that, to be constantly reminded of how the competition is thinking, my people are better prepared to eliminate all ideas that don't top our competitors'.

Don't expect people to line up outside of your office to contribute creative ideas. Unless you're in a business that's driven by creative activities, like Walt Disney's company, it's likely your people will have to be encouraged to participate in *idea storming*. The leader is typically the primary source of ideas. Once again, the leader's model is the track others will follow.

One company I worked with on storyboarding provided each of their salespeople with a little pocket-sized flip chart of all the objections they were likely to encounter on the telephone. As they were making calls to set up appointments, they encountered objections. All the salesperson had to do when he or she heard the objection was to spot it on the index, flip open the chart to the appropriate page, and read the prepared response. There was also a section for appointments and a record of how the call went. The entire flip chart concept was the result of a storyboard process. As you read the following chapters on solving problems and managing change, remember that storyboards are invaluable to these activities.

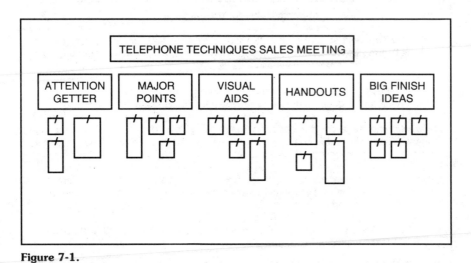

Figure 7-1.

"Imaginars" for Systematizing Team Creativity

Walt Disney had his imagineers; I developed what I came to call "imaginars." These weekly meetings with my managers were, appropriately, held in our district's *imaginar room*. While most companies were having seminars, we were having imaginars. A sign hung in our imaginar room that read:

> "None of us are as smart as all of us."

Our theme was a constant reminder that no one individual could offer as much as the corporate effort of the entire group. My people went in there with the express purpose of discussing solutions to problems and creating new ideas to put into action. Creativity was not only allowed, it was encouraged. Creativity was our first order of business. When we really wanted to dig deep into ourselves for ideas, we rented a room in a local resort and got away from the clutter of daily activities altogether. We covered the walls with sketch pad sheets, filled with thoughts and ideas we later verified and put into practice.

We found a genuinely creative environment allowed us to go beyond the ordinary, everyday questions most businesspeople ask themselves and to go deeper into the real *meaning* behind what employees and customers said they wanted and needed. As a result, we were able to gain a much better perspective and solve problems much more effectively and permanently. Major issues which faced our company, such as a high rate of turnover in salespeople, dropped dramatically.

Basic Rules for the Imaginar

1. *Set a time limit* so that you don't wind up wasting your group's efforts by not completing the process. Give the group enough time to spin new ideas, but then move along to organizing and verifying the ideas as well.

2. Don't begin the verification process too soon. *The quantity of ideas is more important than the quality of ideas* during your idea gathering phase.

3. *Avoid criticizing, complimenting, or questioning ideas* during the idea gathering phase. You don't want to chase good ideas back inside of people's minds for fear of embarrassment or feelings of inadequacy.

4. *Encourage free-wheeling and piggy-backing.* One person's idea can stimulate thoughts in someone else. Keeping the proceedings orderly and linear can stifle creativity.

5. After the idea gathering phase is completed, *prioritize the top 10 ideas* prior to beginning the verification process.

Figure 7-2.

Another company I consulted wanted to start a franchise, but wanted to avoid the type of failure many franchises have experienced. We held an imaginar, got down to the core issues facing a franchise attempt, and really had a handle on the proposition before the company proceeded. Another situation called for the development of a training program on the toughest jobs in managing managers. This imaginar focused on what happens when a manager leaves the job he or she knows well and steps up a notch into an unfamiliar position. We started by approaching upper-level managers about their experiences when they made the move. The result was an extensive list of issues and experiences that served as a springboard for a new training program filled with improved methods and techniques for handling promotions. This imaginar process worked for studying the difficulties of job transitions at all levels in the organization. Figure 7-2 lists the five basic rules for conducting an imaginar.

Creating a Creativity-Inducing Environment

Creativity flourishes in an environment of:

1. Experimentation
2. Playfulness
3. Spontaneity

Creativity Calls for Experimentation. *Experimentation* is risky business. Creativity can create heat for the leader by stimulating up pressure *and* down pressure. A leader is likely to meet resistance from his or her own people as well as those higher in the organization, since the thought of doing something new or different terrifies some people and mildly frightens the rest. Yet the leader courageously asks, "Why don't we try this?" The answer is almost automatic from his or her people: "Because we've never done it that way before." To me that's just not a valid reason to block creativity. Yet, you'll hear it virtually every time a new idea is mentioned.

The larger the company, the more likely the manager is going to be pressured from above not to venture out in new directions or to adopt new methods and techniques. During the years I spent with a large organization I was told many times not to alter course. So I learned to fudge a little. When the chiefs came around and asked what I was doing, I told them I was doing what we had always been doing. My answer pleased them very much and they moved on. Yet, in those early days, I used to wonder to myself why, when the old ways resulted in poor productivity, upper management continued to discourage new thinking and approaches.

That's when I fudged. After telling upper management I was doing things the company way, I then met with my people later and said, "This is what we're *really* going to do." We tried new things at first because I was the boss and my staff had to do what I said. But soon they began to get excited when our new ideas started to show results. Then, when upper management came to visit again and praise us for our improved productivity, I gently let them know what we were doing that produced the positive results and they gradually began to loosen up. So don't be surprised when you race into a meeting saying your organization needs to try new things and you are met with blank and even annoyed expressions. People don't want to hear that stuff, at least not at first. There is long-term value in the ability to be discrete and diplomatic. Softening the hearts of upper management and your own staff to creativity takes a gentle hand, not a sledgehammer.

Creativity Calls for Playfulness.   An *environment of playfulness* simply means an environment that grants permission to have fun. In fact, it encourages people to have fun with what they do. Urge your people to play the "what if" game and kick new ideas around. Some bosses will catch people brainstorming a new idea and demand they quit goofing off and get back to work. What poor, misguided souls. People were engaging in one of the most valuable exercises to improve production, and they were nipped in the bud.

Creativity Calls for Spontaneity.   Take the "what if" mind set seriously. Keep the door to new ideas open constantly. Encourage innovation whenever possible. I know a retail merchant who started what he calls the "One Idea Club." Each month, my friend selects about a half-dozen employees, making sure every job level and description is represented regularly, and drives them as much as two hours away to observe a store where customers are served well. The next day, the team that traveled together meets and each team member stands up and shares one new idea learned on the trip to use in their own store.

A Final Call to Creativity

In discussing creativity and its value to any organization, I've covered characteristics of a creative person, environments where creativity flourishes, how to become more creative, what makes ideas successful, the creativity process, how to verify a new idea, what blocks creativity, and how to turn negatives into positives by invoking the "Rain Parade" theory and "Imaginars." The thread running through all of these topics is creativity. More precisely, creativity is a stimulant to growth. The organization with no new ideas stops growing. The organization that stops growing starts dying. Be creative.

Chapter Eight

The 6th Step– Problem Solving When the Heat's On

"The person with no more problems to solve is out of the game." —ELBERT HUBBARD

A Short, True-Life Problem-Solving Adventure to Set the Tone

My radar observer and I were tumbling out of 56,000 feet, wing over wing and out of control, when I remembered that three out of eight F-101 Voodoo crews before us had survived a "pitch-up" similar to this. But this wasn't a standard pitch-up. No one had pitched up at this high an altitude before. We had entered a nonstandard pitch-up called "inertia roll coupling." We had a chance. I was aware I had a problem requiring immediate attention and a creative, life-saving solution. The heat was on! If ever I needed to be unorthodox and creative, this was the moment.

The manufacturer had supposedly built safety systems into the Voodoo to keep this from ever happening. As this 70-foot-long, 45,000-pound mass of metal tumbled towards the earth like an enormous rock, I had news for the manufacturer. A thought flashed through my mind. The Air Force had told me, "Don't worry. The safety systems will never let you enter a *pitch-up!*" I was worried.

The negative "G" forces were so great the blood vessels in my eyes were starting to rupture. I was on the verge of a "red out." Nevertheless, I was the pilot-in-command and the fate of my aircraft and my radar observer was my responsibility. My radar observer was suitably concerned, as you might well

165

imagine. Since there were no flight controls in his cockpit, he gladly appointed me to the "leadership" role in this crisis.

He might have thought I was incredibly brave to stay with the aircraft and attempt to save several million taxpayer dollars, or just plain stupid with an obsession to play the heroic "jet jockey." The truth was that the "G" forces had me about two inches out of my seat despite my seat straps and shoulder harness. The explosive charge that propels the seat clear of the aircraft during ejection would have crushed my spine since the seat would have already been moving when it hit me. I'm short enough as it is. So I attempted to keep my radar observer calm while I figured out how to get us out of this mess.

Here's the lesson for the leader in any field: *Don't fight your problems with brute force.* As we tumbled out of the sky, I first attempted to fight the roll by forcing the controls to do the opposite of what the aircraft was doing in order to neutralize the forces acting upon us. No good. In desperation, I figured out that the aircraft was designed to fly. Therefore, I needed to get air flowing over the control surfaces of the aircraft. I stopped fighting the controls and neutralized them.

I said the pilot's prayer very quickly as I reached for the "T" handle to release my drag chute. It worked. As we passed through 30,000 feet, about five miles below where the tumble had started, the added drag helped to get the air flowing over the aircraft and I was able to pull out and successfully return to base. As it turned out, the only damage to the aircraft was a bent drag chute door and a battered canopy. Both had to be replaced. The drag chute had caught with such force when I deployed it the lines had actually bent the metal back. As for the canopy, my helmet had battered the inside of the plastic so badly it was no longer usable. Not bad for a short guy. However, my head had been *inside* the helmet as it repeatedly and violently banged off of the canopy, resulting in slightly more than a two-aspirin headache.

Lesson 1: Allowing Something to Work as Designed Usually Gets Better Results Than Pressure

Thankfully, my ability to learn quickly had helped me to become an effective problem solver under pressure. If I had continued to fight the controls, I would have still been fighting them as we impacted the earth. Only when I backed off and helped the aircraft to do what it was designed to do did we succeed in solving the problem. The same thing applies to the people in your organization. They want to do a good job and propel the company toward its goals. When the heat's on and you're tempted to start forcing your imperial will upon them, it's time to back off and remain mindful of what you and your people do best. Perhaps that's why I went to the beach when my boss came to tell me he was looking for my replacement. Forcing the controls had not worked. Forcing them harder would be counter-productive. Give the people in your organization room to solve problems. Use supervision, not surveillance. Surveillance builds an unhealthy dependence and, therefore, the manager ends up solving the problems.

Managers are often the number one source of problems in the organization. The problem-solving leader must remember that, when the heat's on, for whatever reason, it's usually a result of unresolved or unanticipated problems. Make sure the people in your organization can come to you with problems before they get out of control. When they do come to you, listen. A great thought I read in *Cosmopolitan* magazine basically says that, if you come to your boss early with a problem, you gain a partner. If you come late with a disaster, you get a judge.

I've talked about problem solving as a beneficiary of creativity. However, problem solving is such a major priority for the leader it's important to devote an entire chapter just to that process. Someone once asked, "Why can't we be exposed to all of life's problems when we're 19 years old and know all the answers?" Unfortunately, problems are with us from the cradle to the grave. What marks a truly great leader is the acquired skill to solve problems effectively. Like so many other things in life, we get better at problem solving with practice. The healthiest organizations are those that are best at creatively solving and/or anticipating their problems.

Lesson 2: Keeping a Humorous Perspective Can Literally Be a Life-Saver

A Case in Point: Saved by the Worms_____

John Burgess, manager of the Briggs Cunningham Museum, tells the story about "Rusty" Roth and Chuck Yeager and how spontaneous humor brought Rusty back from the edge of disaster. It seems that Rusty was flying an XF-91, which was the first afterburner fighter, and Chuck Yeager was flying a chase plane. These two guys were fishing buddies who often scouted for early-thawing mountain lakes during their flights.

Anticipating the great spring fishing, they bought thousands of worms only to discover the thaw was still a few weeks off. Neither Rusty nor Chuck wanted to take care of the worms and they shuttled the bait from one fella's house back to the other's. Chuck prevailed and Rusty became the permanent custodian of the worms, at least until the lakes started to thaw out.

During this time, they continued to fly, Rusty in the XF-91 and Chuck flying wing. One day Rusty was putting the XF-91 through its maneuvers and wound up in a deadly vertical dive known as an "aerodynamic lock." Rusty couldn't pull the jet out of the dive. He literally had his feet on the console in the cockpit and was pulling on the stick with all his might. No use. He was a goner for sure. Knowing full well the gravity of the situation, Chuck spoke to his friend over the radio and said, "Rusty, what am I gonna do with all them damned old fishin' worms?" Rusty pulled out of the dive—laughing!

Although I've had my share of close calls in supersonic fighters, I'm sure glad that happened to Rusty and not to me. My legs are too short to reach the instrument panel in the cockpit, for one thing. I might have been able to run around in front and push the stick backwards. But the important thing was humor and the perspective that comes with it saved Rusty's life. You will be surprised at what it will do for you in the face of your problems.

Problems Do Have Their Up-Side

Looking at the positive side of problems, it's easy to identify some benefits that rise out of crisis. The Good Book says we should be thankful for problems because *crisis builds character.* I'll go one step further and say that crisis also helps to identify character. As the old saying goes, a good crisis separates the adults from the children. It's important to observe how each of your people responds to crisis. Who stays cool under pressure and who doesn't? Who is best at taking the heat and acting effectively to resolve the crisis? Are different people adept at handling different types of pressure situations? Know who is who in your organization as well as your own problem-solving strengths and weaknesses.

Meeting problems head-on develops your organization's ability to resolve problems over time. *The more you do it, the better you become.* This doesn't mean you should arbitrarily allow or encourage problems to develop. Every time a problem is confronted and licked, it should be a character-building education for you and your entire organization. Part of getting better at problem solving is getting faster at it. An organization which has been learning from its mistakes and problem-solving experiences will have a capacity for accelerated corrective action.

A problem that remains unresolved long enough will become a crisis. A smoldering issue won't get as much attention as a house on fire. If leaders and team members, for whatever reason, are unaware of the smoldering issues, there will eventually be a fire to put out. I realize this is quite a stretch to see a positive side to unresolved problems. However, one good thing about a crisis is that *formerly unresolved problems will finally get handled.*

People who solve problems develop *increased self-confidence.* There is a certain amount of empowerment that comes with the experience of solving problems. The problem itself has an initial amount of power that's proportionate to the amount of disruption the problem is causing in the organization. To resolve the issue so there is no longer any disruption implies that those who attack the problem and defeat it have greater power than the problem. Holding dominion over problems is the substance of self-confidence.

The very existence of a problem or, worse yet, a crisis, indicates existing methods and techniques are somehow lacking and *new methods and techniques are called for.* Depending upon the severity of the problem, minor adjustments might be enough to provide lasting resolution. If the crisis is sufficiently threatening, an entirely new agenda might be in order. Crisis calls for something that doesn't presently exist or, at the very least, a different dosage of existing policy.

Addressing problems large or small should alert us to the possibility that other problems might be brewing. *Increased awareness of other problems* is a major benefit of encountering problems and working through crisis. Out of adversity comes new competitive strategies. I'll carry this thought further shortly. For now, I want to point out that once creative thoughts start cooking, the positive results usually go far beyond what's necessary to solve the problem at hand. The quest for a simple solution can easily be the foundation for development of broader and more beneficial thinking.

Some Inspirational Words on Rising to the Occasion

As Abraham Lincoln said, "The occasion is piled high with difficulty and we must rise high with the occasion." John Ray said, "Despair doubles our strength." It's true a smooth sea never develops a skillful sailor. Solving problems sharpens us. Problems often herald the arrival of good things. When you're up against a seemingly insurmountable problem, chances are you're on the brink of a great discovery. If you're not making mistakes (what author Richard Bach calls "unexpected learning experiences"), you're not making discoveries. Henry Ford said, "Failure is the opportunity to begin again more intelligently." "Defeat is nothing but the first step toward something higher," according to Wendell Phillips.

Look for problems. Become what Connecticut entrepreneur Stew Leonard calls a "problem finder." Problems are darkness and solutions are light.

It's important we don't become overwhelmed with the difficulties we face. We must become larger than the situations in which we're involved. We need to be constantly open to change. Flexibility is the other side of rigid indecision and indecision never solved anything. We can't change the past. We can only change the future which begins *now.* We mustn't feel remorse about our problems; we must feel resolve. It is our sacred duty to keep ourselves in condition to accomplish the biggest things possible in the moment. There is a great sign on Roy Acuff's door that says, "There ain't nothing come up today that me and the Lord can't handle." Amen.

Mental Preparation for Problem Solving

To mentally prepare for problem solving, you must first commit yourself fully to solving the problem. This means making an iron-clad contract with yourself and your organization that the problem you're presently facing will not return again for lack of a sound resolution. Second, clear your desktop of all distractions. This is difficult. However, it's important to rid yourself of anything other than what's required to solve the problem at hand. The reason for this is the top of your desk looks like the inside of your mind. At my seminars I usually have one or two people faint on me when I compare the condition of a desk to the condition of the mind. Yet, it's true. Don't believe those little signs that say "A neat and tidy desk is the sign of a sick mind." I tend to be as unorganized as the next person, so don't feel as if I'm being condescending with this. Experience has simply taught me the truth and I've now learned to be far better organized.

Lastly, work logically, step-by-step, from start to finish or from finish to start. Whether you work deductively or inductively, working systematically helps you to avoid retracing your own steps. It helps to establish goals that act as way points so you can pause in your process and pick up next time from a familiar and clearly defined point without losing ground. When goals are reached, appropriate rewards help to mark progress emotionally and launch the next stage of the process. Even if a goal represents a half day's effort or a full day's effort, a week-long effort or month's work, the commensurate reward is an important component of a problem-solving mind-set.

To recap the three steps toward mental preparedness for problem solving:

1. Make a total commitment to solving the problem.

2. Clear your desk of all distractions.

3. Work on the problem systematically.

The Problem-Solving Process

A Case in Point: Go Fly a Kite

The Niagara river gorge is 800 feet wide with a 400-foot-wide river channel. Water rushes through the channel at 24 miles per hour. Engineers in the middle of the nineteenth century faced a real challenge when assigned the task of building a railroad suspension bridge to span the chasm. No boat could withstand the current and drag a cable across the rushing waters. There was no helicopter in those days to "chopper" a cable across.

So creativity came to the rescue. A contest was held in which the first young person who could fly a kite across and secure the kite string to a tree on the opposite cliff would receive a prize of ten dollars. Homan Walsh, flying his kite from the American side, was the first to have a companion secure the kite string on the other side.

In 1915, Edwin Markham told the rest of the story like this:

> The builder who first bridged Niagara's gorge,
> Before he swung his cable, shore to shore,
> Sent out across the gulf his venturing kite
> Bearing a slender cord for unseen hands
> To grasp upon the further cliff and draw
> A greater cord, and then a greater yet;
> 'Till at the last across the chasm swung
> The cable—then the mighty bridge in the air!

By 1855, trains were crossing the 1160-foot-long bridge, 230 feet above the river, and it all started with a kite string. Can the difficulties we face be as insurmountable? Don't we have infinitely more resources available to us now? Nevertheless, now, as then, long journeys begin with small steps. More than anything else, we must not lose our perspective or, more importantly, our sense of humor in the face of problems.

Step 1. Identify and isolate the problem. What exactly is inhibiting progress toward predetermined goals? Not everything is a problem. Learn to distinguish between a problem and an annoyance. Develop a perspective on the problem from all angles. Leaders will view a problem in one way, while staff members and customers probably see things quite differently. Who has the best angle? The view from the top is not always the most accurate.

Further clarify the problem by writing it down in clear-cut terms. Illustrate the problem on paper or explain it to someone else who knows nothing of the problem to help insure you have a complete picture and are not assuming too much. Going through these exercises helps to highlight the important information about the problem and dispense with the irrelevant.

Step 2. Gather all information relevant to the problem that might prove helpful in finding a solution. Anything that exists might somehow be helpful, including all relevant printed and audio/visual information. Talking to people who have addressed similar problems can shed a broader perspective on whatever it is you're facing. Consult your problem-solving journal that I'll describe after Step 6.

Step 3. Make a list of all possible solutions to the problem. Using storyboards and imaginars, allow your mind to "free-wheel" at this point. Don't eliminate any potential solution out of hand. Remember you're looking through a kaleidoscope and the picture will become clearer the longer you let the pieces tumble.

A great deal of mental energy will be expended in this step. Anticipate some frustration, disappointment and depression. The good news to keep reminding yourself and your organization of is that, when the problem seems the most impossible, you're usually nearing a breakthrough discovery.

Step 4.   After you've listed the possible solutions to the problem, ask these questions:

1. How well will this particular solution work?
2. Is this solution affordable?
3. Can we implement this solution?
4. What new problems will this solution create and can we handle the new problems?

Step 5.   Select what you and your team feel is the best solution to the problem. This step can be marked by a dry throat and sweaty palms, depending on the size of the problem you're facing. This anxiety might be brought about by the fact that the best solution you've been able to come up with seems bizarre to yourself and outsiders in addition to being risky. The greater the innovation and creativity, the fewer the guarantees of success.

Don't let the risks at this stage frighten you into an endless cycle of procrastination. As Dr. Norman Vincent Peale says, you (and your organization) are only as big as the problem that stops you. Enthusiasm, mixed with a good measure of the unorthodox, is a reliable antidote for procrastination.

Step 6.   Put the solution into action. This means applying as much of the solution to the problem as possible. Don't allow your idea to fail out of timidity and excessive caution. If the dosage is too diluted, the solution might appear ineffective when a more appropriate concentration of solution would have worked. I'm not suggesting you "throw out the baby with the bath water." However, it isn't much help when the cure is worse than the illness. The key word in Step 6 is "action."

At a glance, then, here is the six-step problem-solving process:

Step 1—Identify the problem.

Step 2—Gather all relative information.

Step 3—List all possible solutions.

Step 4—Test possible solutions.

Step 5—Select the best solution.

Step 6—Put the solution into action.

A Problem-Solving Journal— for Future Reference

After a problem has been solved, it's important to study the experience for the lessons it contains. Write a dated description of the problem and the solution in a journal or a notebook using the answers to these questions:

1. How will I improve the solution if the problem emerges again?
2. What can be done to prevent this problem from reemerging?
3. Does the solution have broader application to other problems?

The initial solution to a problem might be the gateway to even better methods and techniques in the future. Peter Drucker summed up the true nature of solutions when he said, "Most (solutions) fall between *almost all right* and *probably wrong.* As much as we would like the heavens to part and a clap of thunder to confirm that the solution we've selected is the right one, it's usually more a cautious optimism at best."

We are often tempted to view the first workable solution to a problem as the end of the story when the first workable solution might only be the first step in prevention of similar problems. New methods and techniques, developed for the solution of one particular problem, can frequently be successfully applied to other problems just as the Disney Rain Parade in Florida led to the Electrical Parade in California and, later, in Florida.

Problem solving is part and parcel of the leadership challenge, and all of the creative issues and characteristics of an effective leader come into play. An effective leader is an effective person. You don't find people who run a terrific organization and corrupt their family or vise versa. Somewhere, somehow, given enough time, who a person is privately emerges in the public person. Someone who is good under pressure privately, will be good under pressure publicly. Someone who appears to have a split personality, appearing strong under pressure at times and fragile at other times, is likely to be good at disguising fear. The effective leader doesn't cover up fear. He or she faces fear, acknowledges it, respects it, and then moves ahead anyway. As I mentioned earlier, problem-solving skills and confidence can be developed over time. Crisis exposes character.

What To Do When People Are the Problem

Any time you have more than one person in an organization there is a potential for conflict. How you manage disputes is extremely important to the health and welfare of your team. Don't expect to win any popularity contests as a fair and unbiased umpire. If you have successfully mediated a conflict, both sides will feel both vindication and disappointment. When nobody is completely elated at the outcome, you can be assured you maintained your objectivity. Even Solomon didn't make everybody happy. Don't expect to be more effective than Solomon. Just be as effective as you can. John D. Rockefeller said, "I will pay more for the ability to deal with people than any other quality in a manager."

A 6-Step Approach to Personnel Problem Solving

Here are some steps I have found helpful when dealing with people of all ages who are engaged in various forms of interpersonal conflict:

Step 1.   At the very first sign of a dispute, isolate the principal parties and meet with them, in person, together and face-to-face. Do not simply suggest they go work out their differences by themselves. This will result in the parties going back into the general population of the organization and recruiting sympathetic people to their particular side of the conflict. The divisiveness this creates will damage productivity and morale.

Step 2.   Don't allow yourself to be pulled aside to hear one party's version of the conflict. Insist that all parties be present before they plead their cases. Listen with empathy to all sides of the problem. Don't get caught up in one account versus another. Showing favoritism will discredit you as a fair and impartial leader, resulting in a loss of respect from some of your team members. Let everyone know your primary concern is the best interests of the organization.

Step 3.   After you've listened to both sides of the story, have the conflicting parties repeat their *opponent's* version to the satisfaction of the opponent. This exercise tends to rid the process of any highly charged emotions. When people go through the motions of understanding the other person's point of view, it's virtually impossible to keep the animosity pumped up. Anger feeds on ignorance. Reciting the facts as the other party sees them has a tremendous calming effect and, more importantly, brings any misunderstandings to the surface. This doesn't mean the leader provides the interpretations. The parties involved in the dispute must recite each other's perspective in order for this to be effective.

Step 4.   Without making a decision, schedule a follow-up meeting later that same day if at all possible so the dispute will not fester overnight. This will also help to eliminate phone calls to your house at night. However, the second session informs the conflicting parties that the leader is not going to be rushed into a decision. Neither party can fault the leader for being methodical.

Step 5. Independently gather any further facts, if necessary, and reconstruct the situation step by step. Make your decision and test its validity by leaving out personalities. The easiest way to eliminate the influence of personalities and test for validity of your decision is to reverse the roles in the new scenario. This is your high standard of personal ethics at work.

Step 6. At the follow-up meeting, both conflicting parties must be present. State your reasoning and then your decision. Reasoning always comes before the decision so both people are following your logic toward the decision. If you start with the decision, the party who feels as if he or she has lost will tune out and won't hear why you decided the way you did. Furthermore, the party who feels as if he or she has won won't really care how you came to your decision either. If you don't do an effective job in selling the logic behind your decision, the party that feels a loss will appeal to a higher court, namely the rest of your organization. Handle any questions or objections honestly and with diplomacy. Be straightforward.

The Third-Person Compliment

Sometimes people simply have personality incompatibilities that don't result in any major conflicts, just constant irritation. This is when it's particularly important for the leader to have that individual knowledge of his or her people I've talked about. Know what each person's strengths are so you can give each person a compliment on that strength and say, "I'm not the only person here who feels that way." The person receiving the compliment will want to know who else feels that way.

That's your cue to identify the individual with whom that person has a personality conflict as the secret admirer. The fires of resentment will go out overnight because it's impossible to say bad things about someone who you *think* is saying good things about you. I can hear the accusations of management manipulation already. However, I believe that bringing people together for the best interests of the organization and their own personal growth is no vice. Besides, the idea of the third-person compliment I've just described originated with Dr. Norman Vincent Peale, who is undisputedly a man with a high standard of personal ethics.

The Personal Problem

Another reason why an effective leader must have an individual knowledge of the people in his or her organization is so he or she can detect when a person's personal problems are beginning to affect his or her production. Edward Everett Hale once said, "Some people have three kinds of troubles:

all they ever had, all they have now and all they expect to have." Obviously, a good sense of what an individual's production has been historically is necessary to make such a determination. If a leader senses a personal problem has infiltrated the workplace and it hasn't affected an individual's performance, approaching that person about the problem is risky. The first question you're likely to be asked is, "Have my problems affected my production or the quality of my work?" If your answer is no, you're likely to hear, "Then my problems are none of your business." When the individual's performance is suffering and, consequently, other people are being affected, only then is it time to intervene.

Conclusion: Ruminations on the Problem Solver's Art

In case you or anyone in your organization falls into that very human habit of feeling like nobody else could ever know the troubles you've known, included here are some others with troubles to keep you company. Remember Elbert Hubbard's maxim, "When life gives you a lemon, open up a lemonade stand"? People who reflect the truth of reality back to us in wonderful sayings are people who obviously are not without problems themselves.

I have never heard of any better summation of life's paradoxical nature than the words Charles Dickens chose to begin *A Tale of Two Cities*.

> "It was the best of times,
>   it was the worst of times.
> It was the age of wisdom,
>   it was the age of foolishness.
> It was the season of light,
>   it was the season of darkness.
> It was the spring of hope,
>   it was the winter of despair.
> We had everything before us,
>   we had nothing before us."

The best and the worst are never far apart. They kind of go together like darkness and light or problems and solutions. Turmoil often gives us not only strength, but new direction as well.

Problems are not to be feared or avoided, but rather should be sought out and confronted with all the creativity we can muster. The Chinese word for "crisis" is composed of two picture-characters. One means "danger" and the other means "opportunity." Problems and opportunities will always be with us. Take care of the problems before they take care of you. If you're planning to build your dreams of tomorrow, you've got to be honest with the reality of today. When a little boy was asked how he learned to skate, he innocently replied, "By getting up every time I fell down." Falling down is reality. Don't ignore it. What is your "bounce back ability" or BBA? Luxury and comfort are rarely the crucibles for great victories.

Some great thoughts from some great people:

"Many (people) owe the grandeur of their lives to their tremendous difficulties."
—CHARLES SPURGEON

"I'd rather change my mind and succeed than have my own way and fail."
—ROBERT H. SCHULLER

"Nature, when she adds difficulties, adds brains."
—EMERSON

"You shouldn't be robbed of your right to make mistakes."
—BERYL MARKHAM

"Any apology that doesn't accompany change is an insult."
—TESSIE ROSE

"The Spartans did not inquire how many the enemy are but *where* they are."
—AGIS II

"Circumstances have rarely favored famous (people)."
—MILTON*

(*) Blind and wrote his first epic after he was 50 years old.

"The gods look at no grander sight than an honest (person) struggling with adversity."
—ORISON SWETT MARDEN

"Often defeated in battle, always successful in war."
—MACAULAY'S description of Alexander the Great

"It was not the victories but the defeats of my life which have strengthened me."
—SIDNEY POYNTZ

"You can tell the character of the (person) by the choice made under pressure."
—WINSTON CHURCHILL

"Progress is what we have left over after we meet a seemingly impossible problem."
—NORMAN COUSINS

"Failure means mental surrender."
—ORISON SWETT MARDEN

"What I need is someone who will make me do what I can."
—EMERSON

"(People are) not the creatures of circumstances. Circumstances are the creatures of (people)."
—DISRAELI

"Both adversity and prosperity can make fools out of (people). Prosperity makes more fools than adversity."   —HUBBARD

"Adversity unlocks virtue; defeat is the threshold of victory."
—ORISON SWETT MARDEN

"Many of life's failures are (people) who did not realize how close they were to success when they gave up."   —THOMAS EDISON

"We can only appreciate the miracle of a sunrise after we have waited through the darkness."   —ANONYMOUS

"What counts is not necessarily the size of the dog in the fight—it's the size of the fight in the dog."   —DWIGHT D. EISENHOWER

"The nose of the bulldog has been slanted back so he can breathe without letting go."   —WINSTON CHURCHILL

"When one door closes, another one opens. But we look so long and regretfully upon the closed door that we do not see the one that has opened for us."   —ALEXANDER GRAHAM BELL

"A word of encouragement during a failure is worth more than a whole book of praise after a success."   —ANONYMOUS

"There comes a time in the affairs of (people) when you must take the bull by the tail and face the situation."   —W.C. FIELDS

"When I was young I observed that nine out of every ten things I did were failures, so I did ten times more work."
—GEORGE BERNARD SHAW

"The absence of alternatives clears the mind marvelously."
—HENRY KISSINGER

"Most people don't know how brave they really are."
—R.E. CHAMBERS

"I have learned to use the word *impossible* with the greatest caution."
—WERNER VON BRAUN

"The only thing more desirable than talent is perseverance."
—ANONYMOUS

"It is not good enough that we do our best, sometimes we have to do what's required."   —WINSTON CHURCHILL

"Although the world is full of suffering, it is also full of the overcoming of it."   —HELEN KELLER

"Success is partial to the persistent person."   —DR. FRANK CRANE

"I laugh when I can and live with the rest."   —WILLIE NELSON

"You're never beaten unless you give up. You may have a fresh start at any moment you choose."   —MARY PICKFORD

"Experience is not what happens to you; it is what you do with what happens to you."   —ALDOUS HUXLEY

Chapter Nine

The 7th Step– Managing Change When the Heat's On

"To improve is to change, to be perfect is to have changed often." —WINSTON CHURCHILL

Change—the Only Constant

Crisis cries out for change. Unmanaged change will create a crisis. When the heat's on, nothing is more obvious to everyone involved than the fact something different needs to be done. A change needs to be made. If everything were constant, predictable, acceptable, and pleasurable, there would be no need for change. You wouldn't be reading this book. As we all know, that's never the case, at least not for long. The secret to successfully preparing for change is not to make your policies and procedures timely, but to make them time*less.*

An old saying teaches us nothing is as constant as change. That thought is as true today as it ever was. So is the maxim that says some things never change. By combining these apparently contradictory thoughts, we can conclude that the reality of constant change never changes. The only thing never changing is change itself. This means good news and bad news to the leader.

The Choice: To Forge Ahead or Do the Denial Dance

The good news is there is always a better way to do things. There is always a loftier goal to attain. People and potential can always be elevated. There are always lessons to be learned. We can never know it all. When old Ticky burned his hand on that horseshoe, he didn't unlock the secrets of the universe. But he did learn something new. A horseshoe doesn't have to be glowing red in order to be hot. Can that fact change the way a leader experiences the world? You bet.

Part of the problem presented by change is change itself has a confused identity. We have traditionally been taught that change is bad. Back where I grew up some of the older folks would say, "Don't worry, everything will turn out all right if you just *stick to your knitting.*" When you translate that theory into corporate terms, it begins to explain a great deal of corporate behavior.

If you think you're missing something when corporate heads and managers appear to give lip service to the importance of change and then do everything in their power to resist change, you can relax. You're not missing anything. The fact is you're seeing the dance of denial related to a shortage of confidence and courage to change. It takes courage and confidence to live on the edge. Yet that's where all growth and progress occur: at the edge. The confidence to channel change into productive and rewarding opportunities comes from the application of leadership techniques. Change has become a buzz word. As a result, businesspeople everywhere feel compelled to talk about change in positive terms, as they should, while they continue to secretly harbor negative connotations about it in their minds. Making sure that we, as leaders, are comfortable with change is the first step to helping others in the organization to do the same. As always, and especially with change, the leader leads.

Why You May Encounter Resistance to Change

It's natural to be all charged up with new ideas and enthusiasm when you first enter a new position. I remember when I was first promoted to the level of corporate vice president. I couldn't wait to implement all sorts of new ideas and projects. Much to my surprise, the people at my level and above were not happy to hear about all of my terrific new ideas. Their advice was to back off and leave things pretty much the way they were. The fact that the particular district I managed desperately needed revitalization was no secret and yet nobody wanted to change anything. I was confused.

Even after I pointed out how desperately my district needed new ideas, I couldn't find any upper-management support for my new ideas. It seemed to me as if they didn't want to know what it was really like out there and purposely shielded themselves from reality. As time passed and I learned to more diplomatically, and sometimes secretly, pursue change, some of the reasons change is resisted became clearer to me.

1. Some people believe accepting someone else's ideas is to admit a personal inadequacy. This is similar to the old "It wasn't invented here" way of thinking or "I didn't think of it so it can't be a good idea."

2. Some people fear new projects will bring about unmanageable new problems. At least with the status quo, we know what to expect from day to day. Anything new must be harder than what we're currently doing.

3. Finally, the obvious but seldom understood preservationist position in top management believes that, no matter how poorly the company is doing, avoiding new and potentially helpful ideas will at least protect their positions. This is why many up-and-coming executives are told not to rock the boat.

Cultivating a Healthy Perspective on Change

The effective leader understands, at the deepest level, change is continuous and is not seduced into thinking the organization has reached utopia just because things are going well. This doesn't mean success should not be celebrated. However, the house doesn't have to be engulfed by a three-alarm fire to be in danger. The fact it's built over an old mine shaft that has a methane gas leak will keep the vigilant leader on his or her toes.

Pumping ground water from deep underneath Florida cities seemed like an innocent activity until the earth began to cave in. Some Floridians learned the hard way that the removal of ground water wasn't the only change going on. An effective leader is aware that change begets change. The universe we live in is a system. When something happens somewhere in the system, it causes other things to happen. I don't profess to understand the universe, except to say that, although hot horseshoes will always burn bare hands, attitudes about horseshoes will continue to change every time one is picked up.

The Leader as a Manager of Change

If something has been done in a certain way for two years, there is an 80 percent chance there is a better way of doing it. I'm not saying it should automatically or arbitrarily be changed. My point is that expanding knowledge and resources will invariably create new and better opportunities. One way to test this contention is to look at an existing method or procedure which has been in place for two or more years and ask yourself how it would be done, given contemporary resources, if today was the first day the need arose.

You might find out the existing methods and procedures do not need to be continued at all. A necessary effort one day might soon become a non-productive tradition or habit. What makes the difference? Change makes the difference. Knowledge seems to expand at a faster rate than understanding. New technologies arise before we know what to do with them. Efforts to solve a particular problem often produce a greater amount of valuable information than is required to resolve the original problem. As long as there are problems, people will seek solutions. As long as people seek solutions, knowledge will expand. The most comforting news for those who desire progress is that there will always be problems to solve!

A couple of other indicators that change is called for in the organization include managers who refuse to delegate responsibilities and a general attitude that nothing can be learned from competitors or other outside sources. The effective leader notices when the principles of effective leadership are not being acknowledged and practiced throughout the organization. If someone refuses to delegate, chances are he or she believes nobody can do the job as well as he or she can. This dangerous thinking calls for change. In a broader sense, when people in an organization begin to believe there is no other way of thinking than their own, change is called for. Continued belief in personal infallibility or the sacredness of an organization's way of doing things will ultimately lead to disaster.

The Foundation for Successful Change

Change is by nature a frightening thing for many people. Change means something new and different is going to happen, and the unfamiliar scares many otherwise stout-hearted individuals. Laying the proper groundwork for successful change is tremendously important. There are two basic steps to laying the necessary foundation upon which new ideas can be sustained.

No Surprises

First, the people in your organization need to feel as if they will receive sufficient notice before any significant change is made. In other words, their experience with your organization should have taught them new ideas are discussed and well-thought-out before being initiated. People don't develop a sense of confidence when they get blindsided with something they weren't expecting. Even if the new idea is a good one, to spring it on unsuspecting people will ultimately produce an atmosphere of uncertainty. In an atmosphere of uncertainty, people tend to proceed cautiously and tentatively. What you want is a group comprised of spontaneous people who have acquired a strong sense of confidence through their experience in your organization.

Think It Through Thoroughly

The second step is much like the first. Time and energy must be focused upon the real challenges of a new idea or project in advance. This will help create the atmosphere in which the new idea can grow and develop. Just like people who always expect the worst will distance themselves from new ideas, people who haven't been prepared for the real ups and downs of implementing a new idea will do the same if they keep getting sold on the great possibilities of a new idea and delivered the real nuts-and-bolts challenges. I've heard it said we should plan for the best, but prepare for the worst. That sounds like reality therapy to me.

Work to make sure your leadership is consistent and dependable. Put a "no surprises" rule into effect. Respect the feelings of the people in your organization. Avoid cooking up schemes in private and then springing them on unsuspecting people who will be expected to carry them out. When a new idea is to be launched, prepare your people for the real experience in their future. Don't set them up for disappointments by simply preaching the expected benefits of the new idea. Nothing is ever accomplished without some effort and investment by somebody. When the real challenge is set forth, your people will rejoice all the more in the success of the idea. Storyboards are excellent for helping to visualize both the benefits and the potential problems in launching a new idea. Look at the up side *and* the down side. Your people will be honest in predicting the down-side consequences of any brilliant new idea you want to promote. Listen to them.

Seeing Change Management as a Sequence of Events

There are six fundamental phases required for successful change management. In a busy organization, you are very possibly involved in several new projects at one time. These phases of change management will help you understand which phases you're in, on each project, as you work through the ten steps.

First of all, there is an *education phase,* when you inform employees ahead of time change is on the way. This sort of warning helps to develop the sense of confidence in your organization I talked about. Next, the *participation phase* encourages input from employees on planning and implementation and is the time for further bolstering confidence and enthusiasm toward the organization and the project. The *communication phase* is when the launching of the project is implemented. This is when strategy and tactics are discussed and put into practice.

The *facilitation phase* is the period in implementation when the leader's "hands on" participation pays the greatest benefits. Communicating and coaching can only go so far. The leader must get personally involved to fully express his or her own investment in the project and the organization. The *information phase* is the period when the leader truly keeps his or her ear to the ground to determine what's working and what's not working. Informal, nonthreatening encounters with your people will give you most of this critical feedback. This is when you might learn that proper delegation is not occurring or thinking is too narrow. Finally, *rededication* is an important phase when the progress of the new project is evaluated and necessary tune-ups and adjustments are made to improve on the improvement.

Dealing with the Three Factions of Change

When the need for change is presented, three factions will typically emerge among your people. The first is the *support faction,* who agree with you the idea is a good one and the change is necessary. The second faction is the *dissenters or detractors,* who disagree strongly with what you're proposing or feel that change would be somehow harmful. The third faction is comprised of those people who are *indifferent* to the idea or need for change. It's important to get as many people on your side of the fence as possible. Your best bet is to work on the indifferent bunch first. They will take less effort to win over than the dissenters and you will have more favorable numbers on your side as you progress through implementation of the new project. The greater the show of support for the change, the easier it is for the detractors to join up.

Selling Change— A Political Necessity

It's up to the effective leader to sell the very concept of change. The concept of change has to be sold in all directions, laterally to peers, down toward subordinates, and upward to top management or stockholders. One way to make change less threatening is to take the focus off of the organization and sell a new idea as a way to meet the challenge of the competition. This shifts the focus from "us" to "them" and also places people who want to resist change in a paradoxical bind. To say no to change is to encourage victory for your competitors. The need to sell the concept of change is part of the evil but necessary politics of people or, if you prefer, office politics.

The Launch

There are 10 basic steps you need to complete in successfully launching a new idea. Getting most of them right isn't good enough. It's important that all ten steps receive your attention. These steps are like building blocks. The blocks on top depend upon the blocks on the bottom.

1. Let your enthusiasm for the new idea show.   Your people get their cues from you. No individual in your organization will be any more excited about the idea you've endorsed than you. Your level of enthusiasm is infectious.

2. Presell key people.   When you're storyboarding a new project in your imaginar, one of the important considerations is always, "Who needs to get behind this to make it fly?" You don't want somebody influential grimacing when you announce your new idea to the organization. It's much wiser and more expedient to consult with influential people in advance and get their input so they will endorse the plan when it's announced. Be up front with each individual you wish to consult with; invite them into your office for a cup of coffee and tell them you want their input. Close the door and let them blow up at the aspects of your new ideas you anticipate they will have the most trouble with. In this manner, their dissension will be private and you will have a chance to work through it before the plan goes public.

3. Explain all the reasons for changing.   It's important to be extremely thorough when presenting a new idea. For the reasons I've already explained, you don't want to dwell on the positive benefits of the new idea to the exclusion of the real facts about what it's going to require to get the job done. Many people might not fully understand the need for the change. Don't leave them in the dark. Make sure everyone understands the who, what, where, and why of the new project.

4. Discuss the risks.   Anticipate that your people are going to have reservations about venturing into the unknown. It's your job to present valid reasons for assuming the risks involved. Good people will listen and respond. Don't expect anyone to follow blindly.

5. Show anticipated results.   Nobody likes to be sold a bill of goods that will never be delivered. There are good benefits to be realized for both the organization and the individuals involved or else you wouldn't be promoting this new concept. The key here is to be realistic. Demonstrate how the new idea will help the organization meet its goals as well as promote personal growth for the people involved with achievable methods.

6. Promote what the project is, not what people might think it is.
Sometimes people get carried away with bands playing and flags waving. As realistic and accurate as you try to be, it's possible at least some of your

people are going to selectively hear what they want to hear about the new project and potentially disregard the rest. Have them explain it back to you. By getting your people to teach you back, you will be able to determine how thoroughly they understand what you've tried to communicate. There's no more reliable way to measure someone's understanding of a new idea.

7. Encourage disagreement. You can always expect some people will disagree with the new idea. However, it will strengthen the project if you encourage intelligent and healthy scrutiny of the new idea. This also gives the doubters their say and keeps them from feeling that nobody listens to them. At the same time, you establish an atmosphere of openness. People won't feel something is being arbitrarily thrust upon them.

8. Establish short-range goals for each individual. If the task seems too large and unattainable, people lose interest quickly. When big jobs are individualized, the tasks seem more attainable and each person involved has an increased sense of personal involvement.

9. Keep influential people on board. It's not enough to only get the initial endorsement of influential people in the organization. As the project progresses, these people will continue to have an impact upon the ongoing morale of the group. By influential people I don't just mean those people who are in powerful, executive positions. I'm referring also to those people who tend to be informal leaders in the rank and file.

10. Stay on top of problems. Be hyper-vigilant for problems that arise as the new project progresses. An unresolved problem that festers overnight or over a weekend can dampen the spirits of your team members. The effective leader needs to spot problems quickly and jump on them with lightning speed. This lets your people know you are with them and available to help wherever and whenever needed. The result is a strong sense of cohesiveness and confidence.

Some Change-Related Milestones to Anticipate

All the hard work you've invested to sell a new idea to the organization can be lost if you haven't adequately prepared everyone or you are not prepared yourself. If you truly understand how a new idea typically develops, you will be in a much stronger position to manage the change as it occurs.

First of all, as a new idea evolves in implementation, positive benefits will begin to appear accompanied by some real problems. Anticipate the struggle to accommodate new methods and techniques won't be as much fun as discussion of the benefits was at the kick-off meeting.

Second, since benefits are difficult to measure early, focus on the new problems and their effect on morale. At this point the threat to the organization's morale is the most critical challenge. People will begin to doubt and become discouraged as the process drags on. As the leader, you must be on top of these feelings and coach your people through them. Let your people know you're as invested as you want them to be.

Third, increased productivity and renewed morale will only be present after the leader has demonstrated patience and perseverance through the long process of continually selling the new project. With the people in the organization taking their cues from you, it's important that the leader go beyond verbalizing the work ethic and qualities of self-discipline required to get the job done. You need to demonstrate the qualities you expect. In other words, practice what you preach. If you start to sweat and look like you're going to jump off the top of the building, your people are going to lack confidence in you and the new project.

The "Other Shoe" Syndrome

If sweeping changes are needed, lay out a plan that covers the scope of the necessary changes. If you present the need for change after change in piece-meal fashion, tension will mount in your organization and morale will suffer. If too many changes are made too frequently, your people will develop the "waiting for the other shoe to drop syndrome" and won't become interested or enthusiastic about any change. As a leader, you need to avoid crying wolf too often lest you deafen your people to the sound of the real need for change.

Conclusion: Embracing Change as a Welcome Force

It's important that your attitude about change go beyond merely tolerating it. If you continue to perceive change as a threat or as an enemy, you will be doomed to a lifetime struggle. The terms used to define change are positive and replete with opportunity. "To make different or to alter" sounds to me like an opportunity to spice things up and keep them interesting. "To substitute one thing for another" makes me think change requires a flow of new energies, new people, and new ideas.

Change, in perspective and in context, is to be welcomed. For us to see change as a friendly force, we must remain, above all else, adaptable. We need to go beyond *timely* with our attitudes, policies, and procedures and truly become *timeless*. Timelessness is adaptability and vice versa. By definition, adaptability is the ability to make something fit for a new or more suitable use. The ability to adjust to a new situation or environment means we're not bound by time and circumstances.

A leader in a world of constant change must be adaptable. If such flexibility doesn't come naturally, it must be learned. The future has no healthy place for those who insist on remaining rigid and inflexible. Adapting doesn't mean forcing change. Rather, it implies vigilance and open, informed acceptance of new and, possibly, unfamiliar people and ideas. Adaptability has graduated from an option to an absolute necessity if we expect to become and remain effective in leadership and competitive in the global marketplace. Change guarantees we will never lack the opportunity to do either.

Chapter Ten

Meeting Tomorrow's Leadership Challenges Today

"Even if you're on the right track, you'll get run over if you just sit there." ". . . 'cause the times they are a'changin'."
—WILL ROGERS *and* BOB DYLAN *(in that order)*

Leadership Is Modeling

Everything you work so hard at won't contribute a thing to the past. All of us are working for the future. Tomorrow, next week, next year, or retirement, the payday for today's labor is somewhere in the near or far future, or both. I'm excited by the changing world in which we live because the future is rich with possibilities we haven't even dreamt of yet. Someone once said we don't grow old, we become old by not growing. The ultimate threat to our future is stagnation. Continued personal and professional growth is essential to a tomorrow that will be better than today. The managerial moment of truth comes when you realize that, as the leader, you are the impetus of change in and for the organization. The people in the organization will pay the price in time, energy, and money to grow and develop in their jobs as they see you do the same as their leader.

Walls

In Chap. 1, I introduced you to the world of self-imposed barriers. I bring them up again now because there is no greater threat to future growth and

190

development as individuals and leaders. The timelessness I mentioned in Chap. 9 can never be accomplished if we are restrained by self-imposed barriers of any kind.

The eternal adaptability that will prepare us for tomorrow's leadership challenge can't be contained by anything beyond our personal standard of ethics and the other leadership qualities that we aspire to. The leadership qualities I outlined for you in Chap. 1 are timeless virtues, as good tomorrow as they are today. Such qualities might well be infinitely *more critical* to leading in the future than they have been in the past. The challenges of tomorrow are ever more complex and varied.

A Very Special Birthday Lesson about Walls

A few years ago, I took my wife to prison for her birthday. When I bring this up in my live seminars, I usually get a few quizzical looks until I explain why. She told me it was a birthday she wasn't looking forward to and she really felt like getting out of town and doing something different. I couldn't think of anything more out of town or different than for her to spend six hours of her birthday locked up with the prisoners in San Quentin.

A friend of mine ran a course for the inmates called "The People Builders" and I called him up to see if we could attend. He very graciously said he would make all of the arrangements and closed our phone conversation by telling me not to wear Levi's when we visited the prison. "What's the matter with Levi's?" I asked. "The inmates wear Levi's," he said, "and, in the event of a riot or breakout, the guards shoot at Levi's." Quick learner that I am, I left my Levi's at home.

When we arrived at the prison and the huge steel gate slammed shut behind us, I sensed my terrific idea might not have been so terrific after all. The sound of the second gate slamming shut must have been amplified. The enormous clang echoed between the concrete walls and I felt a chill creep up my spine as my wife and I stood facing the "yard." I said, "Happy birthday, Honey." As moved as I was, she replied, "I hope so." We were standing next to the "adjustment" center where I understand that, before they're through with you, either your attitude or your body will be adjusted, so to speak. Above the adjustment center is "death row" where men wait to die. We began to cautiously make our way across the yard. When I think back on it, I don't know why we were being so cautious. If one of those guys in the crowd of inmates all around us had wanted to become part of our lives, there wasn't anywhere we could have run to.

As we walked, a fellow in a brightly colored sports shirt approached us with a broad smile and extended his hand. He introduced himself as Julian, a poet, and I introduced myself and my wife. Julian handed us a printed card containing a poem he had written about giving a child a smile. It wasn't good poetry as the masters go, but it was charged with emotion. After reading the poem, I commented on the deep feeling in the closing line. Julian said if he had been given more smiles as a kid, he wouldn't have been there. I looked down and saw that Julian was wearing Levi's.

My wife and I made it across the yard and entered the classroom just as it was time to start the six-hour session. The decor was contemporary prison. I'm talking stark. Among the rules of the "People Builders" program was that you sat in your steel folding chair for six hours without so much as a restroom break. Try running a corporate training session like that sometime! My wife and I were heading for the back corner when we were instructed to come to the front where we would be seated. They didn't allow visitors to sit together, so we were separated. There were no guards in the room and no weapons except those the prisoners carry. Realizing this was to be no ordinary stroll in the park, I was a bit on the nervous side.

The two guys who sat on either side of my wife whispered in her ears all evening about what was going on and what had happened in previous classes and she whispered back to them. Only at the end of the class did she learn that one of them was a child molester and the other was a rapist. There's a lesson in that about preconceived notions. I was seated between two interesting gentlemen. The man on my left was the heavyweight boxing champion of San Quentin and looked just like the heavyweight boxing champion of San Quentin should look. I have never seen such a face on a human being before or since. His face looked like he folded it up at night, stuffed it in his mouth and slept with it that way.

The fellow on the other side of me had mastered a clever trick. He had somehow managed to stick his thigh out of the arm hole in his sleeveless sweat shirt. I figured anything that big could not possibly be a human arm. The funny thing was he had another one just like it on the other side. When I learned this man graduated to the "Big Q" after he killed a guard at another prison with his bare hands, I wasn't surprised. Scared, yes. But not surprised. He was certainly strong enough to strangle someone in each hand if he had a mind to. If either one of those guys had leaned over and said, "We're going out of here tonight," I would have said, "Right on. Anything you say. I've got the car keys right here."

Throughout the six-hour session, the point that was hammered and hammered and hammered again was we must forget the past and not worry about the future. That left us with the "now." Our focus should always be on the fullest "present" we can live. Energy spent regretting the past or anticipating the future is energy drained away from the now. Along with our focus on the now, they also hammered home the concept of accepting full responsibility for ourselves in the present.

There is no greater challenge to leaders, old and new. There is no greater promise we can make to ourselves and to our organizations than to live as effectively as possible in the present. There is no better way to prepare for change than to live effectively in the now. Living responsibly today lays the most solid foundation for tomorrow. This all became clear for me toward the end of the San Quentin seminar. It was sort of like flying out of a cloud into crystal clear air. When the group leader looked out over the assembled prisoners and said, "You guys have an advantage over other people on the outside," I thought he was making a joke and hoped against hope that my book-end human wrecking machines had a sense of humor.

It wasn't a joke. Even though we were sitting in the closest thing to Hell on earth and staring out the window and across the yard at death row, the advantage the leader was talking about became clear. He said someone in prison can see his or her walls. There's no question where the boundaries are and how high and thick they are. People on the outside, like you and me, can't see our walls. We all have walls that are just as effective at holding us in as the walls of San Quentin, perhaps even more so. We just can't see them. But they're there just the same.

The leadership challenge is clear. As leaders, we are engaged in the effort to help our people climb over their walls. I say again, personal and professional growth can't occur in confinement. But our first order of business must be to climb over our own self-imposed barriers. We never get rid of our self-imposed barriers. We simply keep pushing them back further and further. Changing economic and social pressures help to push the walls back in on us and the challenge becomes greater. Our effectiveness has to increase constantly in order to insure positive progress into the future. The walls close in constantly and we respond by pushing them back. *The heat is always on.*

The Four All-Important Words

Dream

Dream the great dreams. Unplug. Pull out the stops. Go for the top. Dream. In both the context of images and thoughts passing through your mind and in a cherished hope, it's important to dream. Dreams give us places to go and things to do. They are the good things in our lives that have yet to occur. Dreaming when we are asleep is involuntary. The conscious act of dreaming I'm referring to is a time of ingenuity and creativity. To see the future as it *can* be is the imagination put to productive use. The more we dream, the clearer our vision becomes.

Study

Study everything you can get your hands on to help make your dream come true. Study books, journals, and other published information. Listen to tapes and watch educational videos. Spend time with people from whom you can learn, either at lunch or by enrolling in classes and/or seminars. To study is to apply your mind to the task of acquiring new information. Examine and scrutinize the world around you. Give thought and attention to those things that are most important to your personal growth.

Plan

Plan your time and *time your plan*. Give your time some structure and turn up the heat on yourself when you need to move along. As I mentioned earlier, it's O.K. to have a tiger by the tail if you know what to do *next*. Without a plan, plunging head-long into the future is a risky and potentially unproductive proposition. The bad news for nonplanners is they're going to plunge head-long into the future whether they plan or not. People who know the importance of planning understand how vital it is to design the future. Sure, lots of things will spontaneously happen to us along the way. However, a plan gives us a course to follow. If a ship leaves harbor without a destination, its future is uncertain at best.

Act

All the dreaming, studying, and planning in the world won't move us one inch closer to our goals. Only when we take the initiative and *act* upon our desires will we accomplish the things we've committed to doing. Action is the horse everything else rides upon. Action is a cause, not an effect. The dictionary adds that action requires the exertion of mental or physical power. If you're like most people, the action phase of your life is the most difficult. That in itself is a pretty good indicator of where you need to invest your greatest energy.

The Source of Your Strength

John D. Rockefeller's comment about paying a premium for the ability to deal with people sums up the real expectation of anyone who employs you or me as a manager and, hopefully, a leader. According to David Krajanowski, one of the most significant contributors to business failure is the inability to get things done through other people.

Another major factor that Krajanowski sights in business failure is the neglect of what he terms "succession planning." Training and developing others to be as good and capable as we are is not an optional or ancillary activity. People on the team should be getting better and more well-rounded with each passing month on the job. The team's talents and abilities should be better each month than they were the month before.

I say again it's not new blood that keeps the organization moving forward as much as the personal and professional growth of the existing people.

Constantly striving to build up everyone in the organization is a leader's *primary* job. Too often we fall into the trap of thinking people in the organization are similar somehow to the products we manufacture or different somehow from the customers we serve.

A key to meeting tomorrow's leadership challenge is to understand people are *not* products and they never will be. Furthermore, the people we serve inside of the organization are no less important as human beings than our all important customers and deserve no less respect and courtesy.

Some managers who cling to old schooling might fear that, if they spend time developing the talents and abilities of their people, they will be neglecting their duty to plan for the future. The liberating news for these managers is that developing people on the team *is* planning for the future. Working on ways to help make people more effective always keeps your head up and the future on your mind.

It Is Your Business to Make the Future

Hal Leavitt, speaking as professor of organizational behavior at Stanford's Graduate School of Business, said, "There has been more emphasis on *predicting* the future than on *making* the future." How true. Financial analysts, business gurus, and academics alike stare into crystal balls, computer programs, and other gismos attempting to predict the future, all the while neglecting to consider the effect that people will have on the future. As leaders, our business is to *make the future,* as Leavitt suggests, by building and developing people. Leavitt appropriately points out that pondering what the future *will* be is a passive attitude. As leaders, we need to take a more active position which begins by asking what the future *should* be.

John D. Rockefeller also said, "Good management consists of showing *average* people how to do the work of *superior* people." Many things which are not possible today *will be* possible tomorrow. Accomplishments just out of reach today will be attainable tomorrow, *by the same people.* Effective leaders understand for themselves as well as for people on the team that present behavior is more a result of past experiences than what is happening in the moment. Knowing this, the leader constantly attempts to learn new and more effective responses.

A Profile of Tomorrow's Leader

The leader endeavors to blaze a trail for others to follow. In doing so, there will be markers along the way. Knowing the organization's future rests in the successes of the people on the team, the leader seeks qualities that will lift him or her above the timely and into the timeless, thus inviting everyone in the organization to do the same. Here are 10 qualities I believe will be an important part of the profile of tomorrow's leader:

1. Tomorrow's leader will be organized and know how to establish and work priorities.

2. Tomorrow's leader will establish a never-ceasing pattern of growth.

3. Tomorrow's leader will possess a great understanding of people.

4. Tomorrow's leader will welcome new ideas and fresh perspectives, different from his or her own.

5. Tomorrow's leader will have a keen awareness of team spirit and self-less, organized effort.

6. Tomorrow's leader will be fair and respectful of others, not afraid to question or be questioned, challenge or be challenged.

7. Tomorrow's leader will possess an inner confidence and a thirst for knowledge.

8. Tomorrow's leader will be in shape, physically and mentally.

9. Tomorrow's leader will value creativity and not be afraid to take risks.

10. Tomorrow's leader will be willing to admit mistakes and to change when necessary.

You might wish to scramble these qualities in order of priority, depending upon your unique situation. However, the manager who demonstrates these qualities, along with the others outlined in Chap. 2, *is* a leader for the future. Greatness is timeless. These qualities describe *great* leaders. Let me close by returning full circle to the most prominent characteristics of great leaders from Chap. 2:

1. A High Standard of Personal Ethics

2. High Energy

3. Good at *Working* Priorities

4. Courageous

5. A Committed and Dedicated Hard Worker

6. Unconventional and Creative

7. Goal Oriented

8. Inspired and Contagious Enthusiasm

9. Realistic

10. A Desire to Help Others Grow and Succeed

The Ultimate Challenge

Never be less than your dreams. Someday you've got to look back and ask, "Did I really build my dream or is it too late?" You'll probably wish you had the opportunity to take another shot at that dream. In business, we realize our dreams by building up people—internal customers and external customers. An organization is alive and vital when the leader helps people to grow and climb over their walls.

The ultimate *reward* is not the promotions, perks, and larger paychecks. As nice as those things are, the ultimate reward is the ability to go home at the end of a day and say to yourself, "I saw someone grow *again* today and I helped." That is what it's all about as a leader. Seeing people grow is the only experience in business which brings your heart up into your throat. Leadership is about people. It's as simple as that. The better we are as people, the better we are as leaders. And the better we are as leaders, the better will be the people whom we lead.

For further information on Danny Cox's
speaking programs and recorded training
courses, contact:

Danny Cox
Acceleration Unlimited
17381 Bonner Drive
Tustin, CA 92680

(714) 838-3030
(800) 366-3101

Index

About the Authors

DANNY COX describes himself as an accelerationist, "one who causes faster movement and higher efficiency, and increases productivity." This former supersonic test pilot is one of North America's most sought-after trainers and keynote speakers with almost 2000 presentations to his credit. He holds the National Speakers Association's highest award, the Council of Peers Award of Excellence, a distinction that puts him in the company of such speakers as Dr. Norman Vincent Peale and Zig Ziglar. He is also a member of the highly esteemed Speakers Roundtable.

JOHN HOOVER, formerly a manager with The Walt Disney Company and McGraw-Hill, Inc., lives in Southern California where he writes, produces, and directs entertainment, educational, and corporate training, development, and sales programs for a wide range of clients.